CONFLICT AND COMPROMISE: THERAPEUTIC IMPLICATIONS

CONFLICT AND COMPROMISE: THERAPEUTIC IMPLICATIONS

Workshop Series of the
American Psychoanalytic Association

Editor
Scott Dowling, M.D.

Associate Editors
Judith Fingert Chused, M.D.
Shelley Orgel, M.D.

Workshop Series of the
American Psychoanalytic Association

Monograph 7

CONFLICT AND COMPROMISE: THERAPEUTIC IMPLICATIONS

Edited by

SCOTT DOWLING, M.D.

INTERNATIONAL UNIVERSITIES PRESS, INC.
Madison   Connecticut

Library of Congress Cataloging-in-Publication Data

Conflict and compromise : therapeutic implications / edited by Scott
　Dowling.
　　　　p.　　cm. — (Workshop series of the American Psychoanalytic
　Association ; monograph 7)
　　　Contains papers from two conferences, one held in New York City in
　1989 and the other in San Diego in 1990.
　　　Includes bibliographical references and index.
　　　ISBN 0-8236-1038-1
　　　1. Conflict (Psychology)—Congresses.　2. Compromise formation—
　—Congresses.　3. Psychotherapy—Congresses.　I. Dowling, Scott.
　II. Series.
　　　[DNLM: 1. Conflict (Psychology)—congresses.　2. Psychoanalytic
　Interpretation—congresses.　W1 WO848H monograph 7 / WM 460.5.M6
　C748　1990]
　RC455.4.C65C66　　　1991
　616.89′17—dc20
　DNLM/DLC　　　　　　　　　　　　　　　　　　　　　　91-30989
　for Library of Congress　　　　　　　　　　　　　　　　　CIP

Manufactured in the United States of America

Contents

Section II. The Discussions

Section III. The Authors Respond

Contributors

Jacob Arlow, M.D., Past President, American Psychoanalytic Association; Past Editor-in-Chief, *Psychoanalytic Quarterly*; Clinical Professor of Psychiatry, New York University College of Medicine

Dale Boesky, M.D., Training and Supervising Analyst, Michigan Psychoanalytic Institute; Past Editor-in-Chief, *Psychoanalytic Quarterly*

Charles Brenner, M.D., Training and Supervising Analyst, New York Psychoanalytic Institute; Past President, American Psychoanalytic Association; Clinical Professor of Psychiatry, S.U.N.Y.

Milton H. Bronstein, M.D., Training and Supervising Analyst, Los Angeles Psychoanalytic Institute; Clinical Professor, Department of Psychiatry, University of California at Irvine

Ernest Kafka, M.D., Training and Supervising Analyst, New York Psychoanalytic Institute

Elizabeth Lloyd Mayer, Ph.D., Training and Supervising Analyst, San Francisco Psychoanalytic Institute; Associate Clinical Professor, Department of Clinical Psychology, U.C. Berkeley and Department of Psychiatry, U.C.S.F.

Paul H. Ornstein, M.D., Professor of Psychiatry, University of Cincinnati College of Medicine; Training and Supervising Analyst, Cincinnati Psychoanalytic Institute; Co-Director, International Center for the Study of Self Psychology in the Department of Psychiatry

Robert L. Tyson, M.D., Clinical Professor of Psychiatry, University of California, San Diego; Training and Supervising Analyst (Adult and Child), San Diego Psychoanalytic Society and Institute

Frederick Vaquer, M.D., Associate Clinical Professor of Psychiatry, UCLA; Training and Supervising Psychoanalyst at the Los Angeles Psychoanalytic Society and Institute and at the Psychoanalytic Center of California

Martin S. Willick, M.D., Training and Supervising Analyst, New York Psychoanalytic Institute; Lecturer in Psychiatry, College of Physicians and Surgeons, Columbia University

Introduction

This volume, the seventh in the Workshop Series of the American Psychoanalytic Association, explores the concepts of conflict and compromise formation with unusual candor. Conflict is a topic from the bedrock of psychoanalysis. First discussed by Freud in *Studies on Hysteria* (Breuer and Freud, 1895), it soon became a signature of the psychoanalytic understanding of psychological disorder. It was later recognized, within psychoanalysis, as centrally important to the developmental process as well. Compromise formation was originally discussed by Freud in connection with symptom formation. The term has found a wider use in recent years. In particular, Charles Brenner has presented a widely respected view of psychoanalytic conflict and compromise formation that forms the conceptual background of the present discussion (Brenner, 1982).

The authors of the first six papers in this volume all utilize the concepts of conflict and compromise formation in their clinical work. Thus, these papers, the nucleus of the book, provide a concise presentation of the place of these concepts in psychoanalysis today.

The first three papers are predominantly theoretical in content: Dr. Arlow discusses the concept of conflict in relation to the complementary concepts of trauma and deficit; Dr. Boesky provides a challenging discussion of recent thinking about compromise formation; and Dr. Tyson gives a developmental perspective, outlining the developmental progression from the infant's early conflicts with his caretakers to the complexities of internalized conflict in the adult.

The next three papers by Drs. Mayer, Kafka, and Willick provide clinical material from analytic work with neurotic, characterological, and borderline patients that reflect both the common-alities and differences in the ways in which practicing analysts utilize these concepts in their daily work.

The next section of the book consists of four discussions of the papers. Drs. Brenner and Bronstein speak from the same vantage point as the six authors; Dr. Vaquer adheres to a Bionian, object relations approach to psychoanalysis and critiques the papers from that position; Dr. Ornstein's contribution is a much longer discussion which brings the self psychological perspective to both the clinical and theoretical material of the first six papers.

The two discussions by Drs. Vaquer and Ornstein establish a challenge to the authors which they answer in the final section of the book. The focus in this section is predominantly on the differing viewpoints of the six authors with that of self psychology as enunciated by Dr. Ornstein, with a lesser emphasis on a discussion of the Bionian approach.

It is the intent of the editor that this volume assist the reader in understanding the modern conceptualization of conflict and compromise formation and enable him or her both to recognize and be in a position to evaluate the clinical implications of that position as compared to self psychology and to the Bionian object relations approach. Neither the self psychological nor the Bionian position is presented in detail; rather, an effort has been made to present variations and clinical applications of conflict theory in some detail and then allow the reader to participate in an intense dialogue between well-known, authoritative proponents of differing viewpoints. There is ample clinical material to give substance to the discussion.

Scott Dowling, M.D.

SECTION I
THE WORKSHOP PAPERS

Chapter 1

Conflict, Trauma, and Deficit

Jacob A. Arlow, M.D.

The concepts conflict, trauma, and deficit raise issues fundamental to both psychoanalytic theory and practice. In recent years, as a consequence of the influence of studies in child development and the widened application of psychoanalysis to borderline and narcissistic patients, the relative role that each of these concepts plays in the process of neurosogenesis and therapy seems to call for reassessment and clarification. The purpose of this communication is to make some effort in that direction.

Psychoanalysis is first and foremost a psychology of conflict. Kris (1950) defined psychoanalysis as human nature seen from the vantage point of conflict and, more recently, Richards and Willick (1986) designated psychoanalysis as the science of mental conflict. Throughout his writings, Freud regarded the functioning of the mind in terms of an interplay of forces that stimulated the psychic apparatus into action. This is the essence of psychoanalysis as a dynamic psychology.

After proposing several models for the functioning of the mind, Freud (1923) finally sketched the outlines of a theory of mental functioning that could serve as a framework within which the relations among the various mental elements in conflict could be defined and their function analyzed. In this theory every item of mental life achieves structural status in keeping with the role it plays in intrapsychic conflict. Mediation among the strictly intrapsychic forces and between them and the external world Freud assigned to a hypothetical construct designated the ego. The ego is the final arbiter over the conflicting claims of derivative expressions of the instinctual drives, collectively designated as the id, and moral imperatives and ideal aspirations collectively designated as the superego. In its role as mediator, the ego integrates the realistic concerns of the individual for survival, adaptation, and inner harmony. This mode of conceptualizing mental functioning has come to be known as the structural theory. It represents the conceptual realization of the notion of intrapsychic conflict. Adequate, adaptive ego functioning means that the ego is able to effect a harmonious integration of the various conflicting demands made upon it. This is effected through the formation of compromises, in which the pressures emanating from the different psychic structures find expression without giving rise to pain, unpleasure, inhibition, or dangerous interpersonal or social conflict.

The psychoanalytic situation, which is the investigative and therapeutic instrument of psychoanalysis, is organized in keeping with the principles of dynamic mental functioning just outlined. Under the standard conditions of the treatment situation, what the patient reports as his conscious experience constitutes derivative representations of persistent mental stimuli. The contribution of every component of the psychic structure finds some representation in these expressions. Some of the forces in conflict are quite strident, while others are relatively muted. The analyst is privy to a day-to-day, moment-to-moment record of the vicissitudes of the patient's conflicts, of the relative contribution each agency of the mind makes in the interplay of mental forces.

Through what he says and does the analyst becomes a participant, influencing the vicissitudes of this inner process. By his interventions, the analyst tends to destabilize the equilibrium among the inner forces which the mind has managed to achieve. An analytic intervention may serve to highlight some derivative of the patient's instinctual wish or the manner in which he fends off such expressions and fears of punishment and moral condemnation. The analyst observes the effects his interventions produce on the stream of the patient's associations and the specific ways in which the analysand responds to the ideas and connections of which the analyst has made him aware. In effect, the history of the patient's neurotic conflicts is reenacted in this relationship. The patient responds to the unwelcome ideas the analyst brings to his attention in the same way as, in his early years, he responded on his own to the same unwelcome ideas and wishes when they came to his attention. What seems like a conflict with the analyst is only a reflection of the patient's earlier and persistent internal conflicts. This may be described as the defense transference to the analyst, the counterpart of the wish transference with which we are much more familiar.

In certain respects, what we observe in this interaction is the process of neurosogenesis *in statu nascendi* (Arlow, 1987). Essentially, what I have been trying to demonstrate is how the notion of conflict underlies our technical procedures and is the essential feature of any theory of psychoanalytic technique.

If psychoanalysis is a dynamic psychology, it is also a developmental psychology. The mind develops from the interplay between maturation of inherent, biologically determined capacities and the vicissitudes of experience. Every stage of development provides the individual with a specific set of problems, with fresh goals to be achieved, as well as the threat of potential dangers and calamities. Clinical investigation has made it abundantly clear that the process of neurosogenesis begins in early childhood.

The process derives from the failure of the ego to arrange adequate compromise formations to the inevitable and inexorable instinctual conflicts that are part of the fate of every human being. Because the child's wishes are urgent, imperious, uncompromising, and self-centered, disappointment, frustration, and rage are inevitable. Since the distinction between objective perception and inner wishful thinking is not firmly established, fantasies of the magical power of thought, of omnipotence and destructiveness are taken very seriously. The child's wishes and his fear of the attendant consequences become the basis for the powerful intrapsychic conflicts which the ego must resolve through the process of compromise formation. The successful institution of appropriate compromise formation is represented by progressive development and the enhancement of the individual's capacity. Failure on the part of the ego to effect adequate compromise formations forms the basis for the process of pathogenesis. Usually organized in the form of unconscious fantasies, derivatives of the instinctual conflicts of childhood persist as an active force in the mind of the individual and, under appropriate circumstances, become manifest as symptoms, inhibitions, character deformations, or perversions.

The question that arises is what makes it difficult or impossible for the ego to effect adequate compromise formations of childhood instinctual conflicts. The issue is crucial insofar as treatment is concerned because every therapeutic approach must at some point interdigitate with a theory of pathogenesis (Arlow, 1981). It is at this point that the concepts of trauma and deficit begin to play significant roles in the controversy.

Trauma is the older of the two concepts. It has its origins in the early understanding of the genesis of hysteria. Despite the voluminous literature on this subject, there remains considerable misunderstanding as to what constitutes trauma. In psychoanalysis, trauma is a retrospective concept. Looking backwards, when the analytic evidence indicates that a particular event, situation, happening, or relationship had an adverse or noxious effect upon the individual's development, only then do we invoke the concept of trauma. What is traumatic is not inherent in the nature of the experience, except perhaps in the most extreme forms of abuse. This is a point that Anna Ornstein (1986) has argued most cogently. Esman (1973), Arlow (1980), and Blum (1979) have demonstrated that the primal scene, one of the most frequently invoked examples of a traumatic situation, does not always cause psychic damage or derailment of development. Much depends upon what the potentially traumatized individual brings to the situation, on the nature of the individual's preexisting psychic conflicts (Fenichel, 1945). This is especially true in the case of young children, whose apprehension of what they observe is a rich mixture of external perception and internal fantasy (Arlow, 1969b). Brenner (1986) notes that:

> [T]rauma to the psyche can come about from the outside (i.e., from

external events). It can come about from the action of intrapsychic forces or it can come about from a combination of the two. The last of these is much the most frequent case. With respect to external events, it is the meaning which such events have for the individual that decides whether they are traumatic [p. 200].

As I have demonstrated elsewhere, it is the evocative power that such events have upon repressed, unconscious fantasies that proves to be so unsettling (Arlow, 1969a). To summarize, trauma is a special vicissitude of development, seen in the context of continuing intrapsychic conflict.

I believe it is misleading to concentrate exclusively on the quantitative element in trauma, on the strength of the overwhelming stimulation. Even as we grant that the effect of such experience may be aggravated by the contribution of conflictual wishes and fantasies, what has to be considered as well is the relative strength of the ego, of its ability to contain and control powerful stimuli. Clinical and developmental experience demonstrate that no two individuals necessarily respond in the same way to identical stimuli. In fact, sometimes what is overwhelming to one individual may serve as a spur toward mastery and achievement in another.

Two related concepts are pertinent to this area of discussion: the first is cumulative trauma; the second is deficit. Kris (1956) introduced the concept of cumulative trauma when considering the problem of neurosogenesis. The search for one dramatic incident of a painful nature of the type that Freud sought in his *Studies on Hysteria* (Breuer and Freud, 1895) as the source of his patient's illness usually proves to be a fruitless one. Instead of one powerfully traumatic incident arousing the danger of unpleasure which the ego cannot master, one must be satisfied with uncovering repetitive experiences of an untoward nature whose cumulative effect would serve as the equivalent of the massive trauma one had been taught to look for. This approach, however, again emphasizes the quantitative role of the id impulse in pathogenesis, rather than other factors leading to impaired capacity of the ego to cope.

It is at this juncture that the concept of deficit becomes important, especially in discussion of pathogenesis. It is not clear just who introduced this concept into the psychoanalytic discussion, but Anna Freud does refer to Balint (1958) and the concept of basic faults. In her own assessment of developmental psychology, she states that:

> It is possible to differentiate between two types of infantile psychopathology. The one based on conflict is responsible for anxiety states and the phobic, hysterical and obsessional manifestations, i.e., the infantile neuroses; the one based on developmental defects, for the psychosomatic symptomatology, the backwardness, the atypical and borderline states [1974, p. 70].

She states further:

> Where deprivation and frustration are excessive, this leads not to symptom formation, but to developmental setbacks. It is only in the later course of differentiation and structuralization that the resultant deviations from normal growth become involved in phase-adequate, internal conflicts as they are known to us [p. 71].

In a sense, however, in a subsequent paragraph in the same paper, Anna Freud retracts the sharp dichotomy between conflict and developmental psychopathology by indicating that there is a mutual interaction between the effects of deprivation and the consequences of conflict, an intermingling of elements that are, in fact, inextricably interwoven.

Despite this last caveat, many analysts have used the deficit concept as a model for explaining pathological formations and symptomatology in the adult, especially in regard to those more severely disturbed patients who are classified as borderline or narcissistic personality disorders. Boesky (1988a) has called attention to some of the ways in which the deficit concept has been applied. Some analysts, he notes, claim that, in certain instances, there is a developmental failure to establish clear boundaries between the self and the object. This, they say, is the result of a failure to achieve differentiation between id, ego, and superego. For the most part, proponents of this approach impute the origin of deficits to inadequate or unempathic mothering and tend to trace the traumatic factors to the preverbal period of life.

They feel that, unless certain developmental hurdles are negotiated at the appropriate time, there will be lasting damage to some of the most fundamental capacities of the individual, including the capacity for empathy, for object relations, and even the appreciation of language and logic.

Strange to say, a cursory review of the indices of several of the leading professional journals of our field fails to find a listing of the term *deficit*. Few articles have been devoted exclusively to an in-depth examination of the concept. More often, the term appears in considerations of clinical phenomena, where deficit is involved as an explanatory concept of pathology. As Boesky states, "This series of assumptions is often supported less by data gathered in the psychoanalytic situation than by extrapolations from the direct observation of infants and children, or by analogies based on those observations" (1988a, p. 129).

Extensive use of the deficit concept was made by Bene (1977) in her study, "The Influence of Deaf and Dumb Parents on a Child's Development." In this paper she states that in our technical work we are so concerned with conflict that we sometimes overlook the contribution of deviational development to our patients' pathology. After considerable analytic work, she said, there appear to be areas where interpretation fails to achieve its purpose. Such difficulties, she feels, can be traced to two sources: first, that the resolution of conflicts leaves untouched whole areas of the individual's ego functions, which were affected by developmental delays, arrests, and deviations; and second, that these very arrests or deviations may in themselves result in the individual's failure to have acquired certain ego capacities that are essential if the patient is to take part fully in the treatment process.

Bene's patient was a twelve-year-old boy who was brought to treatment at the Hampstead Clinic because of his solitariness and nightmares. He was the older of two boys, both of whom had normal hearing. Their parents were deaf-mutes. The father was born deaf; the mother became deaf after an illness that occurred when she was two years old. Both parents came from a lower-middle-class background and, as far as the record seems to indicate, the father earned enough to keep the family intact. According to the case report, the parents both had strikingly immature and restricted personalities. The only person in the household when the patient, John, was a child was an elderly great-aunt. She was a withdrawn and seriously depressed person who, according to the case report, afforded little affective contact with the patient, but from whom he had probably learned to talk. We learn little from the case report concerning the father's occupation or either parent's level of education. Nonetheless, they were able to read and write and to communicate with the patient and with his therapists through writing. Both parents had learned to sign, and the patient had apparently learned some signing too, but he did not use it much as a mode of communication with his parents. Only a few examples are given of the mother's lack of responsiveness to the child. When he was troublesome, on occasions he was placed in a room and the door was shut. It is presumed the he cried and no one came to his assistance. On other occasions, when the mother was unresponsive, John tried to establish communication with her by kicking her. Whether or not the great-aunt intervened in any way in John's upbringing is not mentioned. The record does indicate, however, that during the first year of John's life his mother reacted responsively and attentively. The patient remained in treatment for seven-and-a-half years.

The two brothers did not establish close emotional contact with each other, as one might have expected under the circumstances where presumably the parents were unavailable. The younger brother had been an outgoing boy without serious learning difficulties. He seems to have developed some psychopathic traits, but so far as could be judged, his ego development was otherwise normal. The assumption was made that the brother benefited from the fact that John could hear him and respond to him, while John had no such advantage in his first two years.

John had serious problems with arithmetical knowledge and with abstract thinking. He had a tenuous concept of numbers and of time. According to the author's assessment, the patient's capacity for secondary process thinking was impaired. He seemed to lack both the words and the understanding of anything that was not experienced in a concrete way. He was incapable of understanding how one could anticipate an event as a result of one's action if the result was not concrete. Time was measured by the urgency of his wishes and not in conformity with realistic concepts of time.

Bene concluded that, because of the parents' deafness, these important primary love objects were not available when needed, with the result that emotional development was impaired. The patient lived in an environment that did not satisfy his instinctual cravings. A lack of verbal and cognitive stimulation, together with restriction of motility at developmentally crucial times, was responsible for the lag in the development of secondary process functioning. Furthermore, the personality of the parents and their limited availability affected his sense of self and self-esteem, impairing those psychic structures which regulated the patient's tension, anxiety, and well-being.

Almost all of these conclusions, it should be noted, were based upon presumptions of *what might have taken place.* For the most part, precise developmental information is lacking. It is presumed that John developed speech later than usual, although he was admitted to nursery school at the age of four, something which the author admits could not have happened if there had been any serious impairment or developmental lag in his speech.

I have presented this material in considerable detail in order to contrast this experience with the findings in my analysis of a patient whose parents were also deaf-mutes. He was a twin and had an older brother and sister. The parents were foreign born, members of a poverty-stricken family. They had never received any training to overcome the difficulties secondary to their hearing defects; neither had received any education. The parents could neither read nor write, nor had they been taught any sign language. Nonetheless, an idiosyncratic type of sign language was developed within the family and, while it undoubtedly could not convey the subleties of abstract conceptualizations, it served as a most reliable vehicle for the communication of feelings. (An aunt would come into the household from time to time to help.)

The patient came for treatment because of neurotic symptoms secondary to the death of his twin brother at the age of eighteen. I have described his conflicts in earlier clinical communications (1960, 1976) and I will not summarize them at this point. Nevertheless, I will stress those aspects of the patient's personality development which touch upon the issues of defect.

In many respects, his parents' defect served as a spur for development. The patient learned early on that he had to answer the door when someone knocked because he knew his parents would not respond. He became not only a spokesman for his parents but many times assumed a parental role toward them. He became richly attuned to the nuances of speech and the pleasurable aesthetic qualities that language could convey. To be sure, the exercise of eloquent language filled him with guilt when he thought of his parents, but the appreciation for the role of speech led to an interest in the theater. The patient learned early to be self-reliant and to assume responsibility. As he grew up, he was appalled to observe how his friends, who had parents who could speak and who had been educated, were timid, insecure, and afraid to assume responsibility. In fact, when he became a very successful businessman, he employed many of his boyhood friends in his company.

Deaf-mutism in the primary love objects does not of necessity drastically impair their availability in periods of need. To be sure, the timing and the quality of the relationship will be altered significantly by the absence of verbal communication, but there are many forms of nonverbal communication that can be and are richly accentuated under such trying circumstances. It does not necessarily follow that mutism in the parents necessarily results in developmental defects in the child. In my patient, there were many psychological consequences, favorable and unfavorable, that grew out of the experience of having deaf-mute parents, but none of these consequences showed up in the course of the adult analysis in the form of persistent defects. The process of pathogenesis is most complex and multidetermined.

> For the present time, it would appear that it is most difficult to formulate a specific circumscribed theory of pathogenesis. Given the complexity of human nature, we have to conclude that Freud's broad developmental view of pathogenesis as a product of conflict, with all phases of development contributing to the process, still remains our most comprehensive approach to the problem [Arlow, 1981, p. 512].

There is a problem of methodology involved in this issue that was alluded to earlier in this presentation and that I have referred to in two previous communications concerning theories of pathogenesis (1981) and the relation of theories of pathogenesis to therapy (1986). In these contributions, I remarked on the tendency of many analysts today to emphasize the role of traumatic experiences or relationships during the first and second years of life as the source of psychopathology and I noted the trend to indict the mother of the preoedipal phase as the villain.

It is an appealing scenario. Where precise genetic material is difficult to obtain, a putative model situation can be involved, which is then foisted upon later manifest symptomatology. This is very appealing to patients, since it takes the origin of their difficulties back to a period in their lives when they had only needs and no responsibilities. Hence, there could be no blame and no need to feel guilty. I also noted how such theories could play into the fantasy wish of the analyst to act as a "rescuer" by taking on the role of the good new object, the helpful mother who puts the patient back on the proper developmental track from which he had been derailed early in life by his unempathic, unavailable primary object. The invitation to play roles in treatment, thus, is greatly enhanced and has been enshrined, in a certain sense, in the views of analysts who feel that the mutative factor in psychoanalysis is not interpretation, but something in the relived, benign, helpful, reformative atmosphere supplied by the experience with the psychoanalyst (Loewald, 1960; Modell, 1976; Winnicott, 1963).

When deficit comes to represent a form of developmental trauma, the effects of which are distinct from those of intrapsychic conflict, then its manifestations have to be dealt with, not by interpretation, but by other methods. Many of the technical innovations proposed by Kohut represent derivatives of this approach. For others, the treatment setting becomes a "holding environment," which compensates for a very early experience of gratifying, secure physical contact with the mother that was assumed to have been inadequate or missing.

Deficit theorists make extensive use of the concept of the "good new object." Originally, this concept was introduced by Strachey (1934), who saw the therapeutic process as resulting primarily from mutative transference interpretations, which had the effect of ousting the bad introject of the mother and replacing it with the good, benign introject of the analyst. In more recent expressions of this approach, the analyst becomes the good new object who presumably supplies a type of experience the individual needed but had never experienced previously in relation to the primary objects. It is a fact, however, that many, if not most, patients have in the course of their lives met "good" people, understanding, would-be helpful individuals, but did not seem to profit from the experience with these good new objects. They continued to repeat their unconsciously determined modes of behavior. It is not until the meaning of their behavior is interpreted in terms of their underlying conflicts that change begins to take place.

Many issues remain to be sorted out as a result of this ongoing controversy. The overriding consideration, of course, is the question of evidence. The data of adult analyses are unconvincing regarding the isolated persistence of the effects of developmental deficits that are not part of conflict. The type of object relationships that purportedly lead to the genesis of deficits cannot escape involvement in the inexorable process of conflict. No doubt there are developmental lags and failures during childhood, but whether these findings can serve as a basis for excluding certain forms of adult psychopathology from the overall influence of conflict remains in my mind a dubious proposition.

Chapter 2

Conflict, Compromise Formation, and Structural Theory

Dale Boesky, M.D.

The principal importance of compromise formation as an aspect of psychopathology lies in its ability to account for symptom formation. The principal importance of compromise formation in our theory of technique lies in its ability to account for the formation and therapeutic resolution of resistance and therefore its ability to explain therapeutic change. This paper is therefore predicated on the view that the terms *conflict, compromise formation,* and *resistance* are conceptually inseparable. This is in sharp contrast to the ideas of those who view psychopathology and conflict as issues which can be separated.

Definitions: Conflict and Compromise Formation

Intrapsychic conflict connotes not just any opposition between two tendencies in the mind, but an opposition between two or more wishes, tendencies, attitudes, or ideas of which at least one is excluded from conscious awareness. Both sides of the conflict may be unconscious, but at least one *must* be or we are speaking of "conflict" in other than a psychoanalytic frame of reference.

A compromise formation is the polyphonic interaction (Waelder, 1936) of the components of a given conflict that achieves the maximum possible gratification with the least possible psychic pain. The components of a conflict may be described at a highly abstract level. For example, we might speak of conflict between the id, the ego, and the superego, and as we shall see later, this has caused some confusion. These were the terms which Freud used in 1923 when he first introduced what we have come to call his tripartite model or structural theory. Later I will discuss some of the numerous modifications of structural theory which have led to the modern view of compromise formation. Each of the components of intrapsychic conflict has a complex developmental interaction with all of the other components of conflict. Thus, in order to understand the concept of compromise formation one must have prior knowledge about the developmental and dynamic interaction of each component both alone and in concert with all the other components. It is thus necessary to view both the developmental–longitudinal as well as the cross-sectional, dynamic integration of each component. At the present time, modern structural theory states that the four components of conflict include drive derivatives, unpleasant affects such as anxiety or depressive affect, defenses, and superego aspects. Futhermore it is necessary to link one's understanding of these components to the cardinal danger situations of childhood as these are revived in pathogenesis and during treatment in the transference.

For those not yet familiar with the pioneering contributions to this topic by Charles Brenner (1982) I would recommend his book entitled *The Mind In Conflict*. Much of what I say in this paper alludes to his ideas and assumes some prior acquaintance with his work.

Definitions of Components of Conflict

The drives are the wellsprings of human motivation; they include two categories, libidinal and aggressive. By aggressive we mean to connote the drive derived aspect of destructive human behavior.

Although there is no inherent antagonism between the ego and the drives, derivatives of the drives may give rise to unpleasure and therefore to conflict. The key idea here is that psychic pain is the prime cause of human conflict. It is only when a wish threatens to cause psychic pain that conflict ensues. We speak of drive derivatives to distinguish between drives as an abstract generalization connoting the drives of all mankind versus drive derivatives which connote the concrete manifestation of the influence of drive activity in a specific person at a specific time. Thus those who adhere to these views speak of the id as an aspect of mankind and the drive derivatives as an aspect of the individual person.

Affects are complex psychic phenomena that include sensations of pleasure, unpleasure, or both but always together with ideas. The development and differentiation of affects is only incompletely understood at this time. Brenner contributed the important idea that we should elevate the group of depressive affects to full equivalence with anxiety as a source of unpleasure in evoking conflict during the course of human development. Psychic conflict ensues whenever gratification of a drive derivative is associated with an unpleasurable affect.

It was not until his 1926 monograph, entitled *Inhibitions, Symptoms, and Anxiety,* that Freud described the origin of these affects as lying in the unspeakable horrors which haunt the childhood of mankind. These are the cardinal dangers of object loss, loss of the object's love, castration, and punishment by the superego motivated by guilt. Thus in one stroke in this remarkable book written in his seventieth year, Freud radically altered his view of anxiety as the cause rather than the effect of repression. At the same time with his description of the cardinal dangers of childhood he welded structural theory to object relations. It is still not appreciated that modern psychoanalysis begins with this book, and furthermore, that since that time structural theory has been an object relations theory.

Defense constitutes any psychic activity whose function and purpose is to reduce unpleasure. Defenses don't disappear after analysis, nor do they become normal as a result of analysis. It is the pathological compromise formations which change. Defenses are not accomplished by any particular mechanisms but by any mental activity which is most useful for the integrative functioning of the ego. The list of defense mechanisms which we all have memorized constitute the result of the defensive achievement rather than the method by which the achievement occurred. There can never be a complete catalogue of these defensive methods because the entire range of human mental functioning is the potential reservoir for defensive activity. Anything a person is capable of doing or thinking can also be done in the service of defense. Thus the drive derivatives themselves, viewed from the angle of compromise formation, can serve a defensive purpose while simultaneously achieving partial gratification. This is of course the essence of the compromise viewed politically: no one is left completely gratified or completely unhappy. The drive derivative might afford pleasure or require defense, or itself become a defense in accordance with the dynamic balance between defense and drive gratification which is normally shifting and mobile rather than static.

The superego includes those aspects of psychic functioning that have to do with morality, and is itself a large group of diverse compromise formations resulting from the conflicts of antecedent, especially oedipal, developmental phases.

There is far more than identification involved in the formation of the superego. In the past there has been a tendency to emphasize only the aggressive drives in the development of the superego. From the side of the drives, libidinal aspects are also an important aspect of the normal masochism which is part of superego formation.

Many compromise formations may be normal rather than pathological because intrapsychic conflict per se is a normal and universal feature of the functioning of the human mind. Then we want to ask exactly what is it that determines whether a specific compromise formation is pathological or not. Basically it is a quantitative difference which proves decisive.

A compromise formation is pathological when it is characterized by any combination of the following features: too much restriction of gratification of drive derivatives, too much inhibition of functional capacity, too great a tendency to injure or destroy oneself, or too great conflict with one's environment [Brenner, 1982, p. 161].

Examples of Compromise Formation

I will now give examples of the diverse forms which compromise formation can assume since some readers may be wondering how they can tell whether or not something is a compromise formation. Once again there can be no all-purpose, global definition of the appearance of all compromise formations, anymore than there could ever be a definitive catalogue of human pleasure and pain. But there is another reason that we will never achieve a descriptive definition encompassing all compromise formations. That is because the notion of compromise formation is a theoretic construct which is intended to give a lawful explanation of human behavior. Thus we should distinguish observable clinical phenomena from the term *compromise formation* as a theoretic term introduced to organize our understanding of these observable data. One will only be able to "see" a compromise formation by thinking in these terms and then deciding for oneself on the basis of experience if this has been a useful way to think about the patient. I will now give clinical examples of sublimation, of acting out, and of identification to show the usefulness of compromise formation as a method by which to better understand patients.

A Sublimation

A man in analysis for conflicts that impaired his ability to work had learned to play the clarinet as an adolescent. During one particular summer, he would take his clarinet with him when he worked away from home, and on lonely walks he would stop and play where no one could hear him. During the analysis the patient recalled that one of the boys he had lived with that summer distressed him by masturbating at night in such a way that he could be heard. Revolted by this the patient had taken his clarinet and again gone off by himself to play. Later in life he collected recordings by clarinet virtuosos and took great interest in his son's clarinet lessons. When he was a child he was awed by the appearance in his home town of a famous jazz clarinetist and he treasured this musician's autograph. He loved many kinds of music rather indiscriminately and was especially fond of sentimental songs and would often cry over them.

This man was terribly frightened by violent fantasies about competition with male rivals. His clarinet playing proved to offer him a disguised opportunity to express an unconscious masturbation fantasy in which he won the admiration of adoring crowds without risking direct competition with male rivals. In his sexual fantasies he feminized himself so as to avoid danger from his rivals. This was expressed also in a fantasy of stealing his rival's strength by sucking on and then biting off the man's penis, swallowing it, and using it for himself. His mouthing of the clarinet thus allowed him to gratify libidinal and sadistic drive derivatives; it defended him against the danger of retaliation by other men; it allowed him considerable gratification in the sphere of reality as well as the fulfillment of important forbidden competitive sexual wishes related to his father and his son; yet when he played his instrument he felt that he was only a poor imitator of the real man who could really play well, and so he was punished by his failure. This attitude paralleled his chronic self-belittling attitude about his work performance compared to that of other men.

On one occasion the patient had a dream about the clarinet. He was at a dance. The clarinets were all in the front row of the band. One of the musicians was a little black boy who removed the clarinet from his mouth and imitated the sound of the clarinet with his voice. Then a former male teacher appeared in the company of two intimidating women and the teacher waltzed off leaving him alone with one of the scary women.

The dream exactly paralleled his childhood and adolescent experience in which his father repeatedly left him alone to deal with the overwhelming conflicts induced by his mother's seductive and controlling behavior with him. As a consequence he could never feel pleasure in his penis if he touched it. He could only masturbate by rubbing his penis against the bed sheets and then he felt pleasure not in the shaft of his penis but in his perineal area. So in the dream he could only be the little black boy pretending to be a real musician but never allowed to use the forbidden instrument. Both his sublimation and his dream were compromise formations utilizing his musical interest. But there are substantial differences in the comparative structure of these two compromise formations as well as in their duration. The sublimation endured throughout his life and the dream occupied but a moment of his sleeping thoughts.

Acting Out as a Compromise Formation

A woman in analysis was embarrassed to describe her wish to have her husband "do a certain sexual thing to her." All efforts by me to help her were to no avail. Gradually she became increasingly angry and demanded that I should say something more. She was tired of doing all of the talking and hearing nothing more from me to show whether what she said had any meaning or importance. When I asked her if she might be embarrassed about telling me about this sexual matter she felt that I was patronizing her and tried to embroil me in an argument. When I asked if she might be annoyed with me because telling me about this sexual matter seemed to be distressing her, she denied this and insisted that my interest in why she wished me to speak expressed my needs rather than hers. All that she wanted was that I should just talk to her. Obviously she did not mean that literally since I was indeed speaking to her.

At about this time she blurted out that she wanted her husband to perform cunnilingus on her. It was then possible to help her to see that her acting out or her enactment with me expressed the defensively altered forbidden wish to make me also use my tongue on her by forcing me to talk. This wish was forbidden because it had specific incestuous and sadistic meaning for her in the transference. Notice also that it is merely the frame of reference which governs whether or not to describe her enactment as an acting out or as a transference resistance. In this instance both terms are relevant and accurate. Her acting out in the transference in this manner allowed her to achieve several purposes simultaneously. In the service of the prevailing drive derivatives she gratified forbidden sexual and sadistic fantasies. In the service of defense she avoided painful feelings of guilt by projecting the onus of causing pain onto me and by covering her guilty fear of punishment with concerns about embarrassment.

She had dealt with similar matters in the past without embarrassment as a factor. Furthermore her superego interests were gratified because she invited punishment by trying to provoke me into becoming angry with her or inviting me to be unkind to her. Considerations of reality were highly important as well in that it was her actual task as a patient in analysis to communicate to me as best she could just what it was that was distressing her. It is typical that when we view resistance as a compromise formation we can then see that the patient who thinks he is being uncooperative is consciously unaware that the imputed misbehavior is highly communicative and valuable.

An Identification

A man in analysis for a severe depression revealed in various ways during a lengthy analysis that, for a variety of reasons, he unconsciously wished to be like his mother. One of the most important problems had to do with his father's severe emotional problems, which required lengthy psychiatric hospitalization when the patient was thirteen. The subsequent failures of the patient's older brother in his adult life rekindled the traumatic conflicts about defeating his male rivals, which were evoked originally by his father's collapse and subsequent failures. His mother had a highly ambivalent attitude toward her husband and sons and expressed this by encouraging all of them to rely on her for everything possible. She was the one who cleaned up everyone's mess; his father was a bitter man who blamed everyone else for his unhappiness. Gradually the patient's mother took over the family business altogether. She kept two sets of books, one for the IRS and the other for her actual needs. She did not have to raise her voice to get her way. She was very skillful at manipulating people in contrast to his antagonistic, abrasive father.

In the analysis the patient also kept two sets of books, just as his mother had done. He consciously withheld reporting details of his sex life and delayed reporting other important matters for lengthy periods of time.

When I would ask him about his often telling me only months or years later about important experiences and events, he mockingly dismissed the significance of his behavior. He treated his business partner in the same manner as he treated me in that he was quietly hostile and controlling but outwardly cordial. Thus he controlled his business partner and his analyst exactly as his mother had controlled her family. All the employees knew that if they needed an answer they should come to him rather than to his bombastic partner.

He also had a deeper motive for assuming the mantle of strength with which his fantasy endowed his mother. He was unconsciously convinced that he was merely a phallic extension of his mother and that he could not exist independently without her. For this reason when she died he was unable to shed a tear and his identification with her was enhanced so that he could keep her alive within himself. His entire sense of adequacy depended on the approval of his mother or her later symbolic replacements. His identification with his mother intertwined with his profound dependence upon her gradually became one of the most important resistances in the analysis. By imagining that he was just like her, he fulfilled a group of complex wishes. He achieved sexual and hostile gratification by defeating me when I represented his father and older brother. If he could have the analysis on his terms, just as his mother controlled his father, he could defeat me. For many years he had smoldered about all the doctors he knew whom he felt were so smugly superior to him. By withholding information from me he defensively avoided frightening and depressing issues linked to his dangerous fantasies. By floating forever in the timeless illusion that all his needs would be gratified by me with no effort on his part he also fulfilled the wish to have his mother restored to him in the treatment.

At the same time that his feminine identification spared him the wrath of male rivals, he was always vulnerable to depressive affect because he felt like a fake man, and this was his punishment for having outdone his father and his brother. We can thus discern the diverse achievements of his compromise formation in which he lived out the fantasy that he was his mother.

Discussion of Vignettes

These vignettes are reported to illustrate issues I wish to discuss
rather than as descriptions of the actual work with these patients.
As such they are like crudely drawn stick figures in comparison to
full portraits, but they will serve to illustrate that in three clinically diverse phenomena we can observe the same interactional
influence of the components of conflict in the visible form of a
compromise formation. I wish now to place this fact in the his-
toric context of the evolution of the concept of compromise formation in the ongoing development of psychoanalytic theory.

I have deliberately selected an example of sublimation, acting out, and identification in order to illustrate the differences
between earlier and modern views of compromise formation.
Prior to the advent of modern structural theory, sublimation was
still viewed merely as a drive vicissitude, acting out as a defense,
and identification as the consequence of oral incorporation. For
many years sublimation was considered essentially an alteration
in the aim of certain drives and often it was viewed as the ideal of
mental health in that presumably sublimation represented the
culturally valuable antithesis of repression. As I have shown elsewhere (Boesky, 1986), this is not the case. We would now say that
even though many artistic, scientific, or other culturally valued
pursuits are important to mankind, the sublimations which led
to their fruition were developed in the matrix of intrapsychic conflict entailing complex compromise formations. In addition to
drive derivatives, every sublimation entails defensive aspects,
object relations, fantasy, affective components, reality considerations, and at least some form of superego activity.

The same state of affairs existed with the concept of acting
out. During the topographic phase of analytic theory from
approximately 1905 to 1926, the only theoretic alternatives
which Freud could provide for repression were acting out and
remembering. If the patient continued to repress his traumatic
memories he remained ill. If he could be helped by analytic treatment to remember he would recover, but in the course of the
therapeutic struggle and as a resistance to remembering as the
repression barrier was lifted the patient might act out. Acting out
was merely an elaborately altered form of remembering and

communicating. In the view of modern structural theory, acting out is considered a compromise formation with a complex structure (Boesky, 1982). Finally, identification also was viewed in much simpler terms in the first stages of the tripartite model of 1923 (Abend and Porder, 1986). There are important advantages to viewing identification also as the final outcome of the functioning of the entire human mind, which is another way of saying that it should be viewed as a compromise formation. To account for identification we can now replace introjection, which is itself a piece of jargon to describe a fantasy, with the view that identification expresses a wish to be like someone else and that the wish itself is a compromise formation. The prior views that sublimation was only a drive derivative, acting out was only a defense, and that identification was the principal if not the exclusive mode for building up the superego was the theoretic equivalent of trying to play a string quartet on just one violin.

History of Our Views of Conflict Components

To describe the historical evolution of the components of conflict in psychoanalytic theory would really require a full description of the entire history of psychoanalysis itself. Psychoanalysis is in fact still defined by many analysts as the science of human behavior viewed from the angle of unconscious conflict. That is why it was originally called a depth psychology and why it still deserves that name. The word *dynamic* has from the dawn of psychoanalysis connoted the opposition, interaction, and compromise of opposing forces and tendencies in the human mind. What has changed and what has been gradually improved throughout the history of psychoanalysis is our view of the nature of the components of conflict and our conceptualization of where and how the components of conflict are dynamically engaged in opposition as well as in cooperation.

The magnitude and scope of these changes in our theory can only be schematically outlined here. Beginning with the sexual and self preservative instincts we have moved to the sexual and aggressive drives; from the original equation of defense and repression to the recognition that any mental function can be

used in the service of defense; from the view of repression causing anxiety to exactly the reverse; from postulating only anxiety
as the affect associated with conflict to an awareness of the equal
importance of other affects, especially depressive affect; and
from the view of the superego formed primarily by introjection
and identification to the superego as itself consisting of a complex group of compromise formations.

The shift from Freud's original topographic model to his
tripartite model of id, ego, and superego represented the correction of theory by clinical experience. It will be recalled that it
made no sense to postulate the opposition of the systems Ucs.
and Pcs. when in reality the defenses themselves were just as
unconscious as the drives. The classic monograph by Arlow and
Brenner (1964) described the numerous advantages of the structural theory compared to the topographic theory. The critical
alteration introduced by the structural theory was therefore not
only a different view of the components of conflict but of the location of the conflict as well. All of these changes are by now
familiar. What remains still unappreciated is this. In the sixty-five
years since the appearance of the tripartite model there have
been substantial alterations in our understanding of psychological development, object relations, defense processes, affects,
transference and countertransference, unconscious fantasy, drive
derivatives, and, finally, in our methodology of validation.

All of these changes have had the cumulative effect of substantially altering the structural model of 1923, even though we
continue to use the same terms: id, ego, and superego. Parenthetically, the term *ego psychology*, which was so popular a
few decades ago, was a misnomer in that it metanymically substituted a part, the ego, for the whole, which was the tripartite model.

Numerous psychoanalytic contributors have carefully built
up this new knowledge during the past fifty years without much
fanfare or polemic insistence on forming new schools. As a consequence we can speak not only of change in our theory of the
components and location of conflicts, but also in the progressively increasing tendency to decrease the level of abstraction in
many of our reformulations of structural theory. When we speak
now of compromise formations we are less prone to say that there

was an id–ego conflict and more likely to describe the specific drive derivatives and defensive processes. We are closer to the terra firma of individual persons who are suffering than to the thin stratospheric abstractions of the id, ego, and superego.

Levels of Abstraction

There has been an increased prevalence of an antitheoretic bias among mental health practitioners for some time now. Some of those who deprecate theory pride themselves on their clinical skill as though theory and practice could be easily separated. Others are haunted by the specter of inhuman, cold, dessicated theoreticians. The fact is that we simply cannot do without theory, and there are no clinical observations made by anyone, even those who consider themselves atheoretic, that are not determined by preconceptions.

There is also nothing inherently negative about highly abstract theoretic formulations such as the id, ego, and superego. Confusion about levels of abstraction and the value of theory has been an important cause of these misunderstandings. The issue is not that any theory is too abstract or too concrete but whether it is optimally integrated with the data it purports to explain lawfully. An example of the defensive misapplication of abstract theory is the patient who explains in the first hour that he has an unresolved Oedipus complex. In a similar manner, the author who explains that his patient, who has a perversion, suffers from a conflict between his id and his ego is telling us very little. Many have criticized structural theory because the terms *id, ego,* and *superego* depersonified human beings and failed to account for object relationships. This criticism reflects confusion about frames of reference. Object relationships are usefully viewed as complex groups of compromise formations. Transference is an example of this. An object relationship cannot and should not be tacked on to *id, ego,* and *superego* as a fourth dimension of compromise formation, because the terms represent very different frames of reference. Nor have those who advocate the use of structural theory ever forgotten about the critical importance of object relations. Instead it has been understood that any human relationship expresses a variety of complex compromise formations mediated by all of the conflicts evoked in the relationship. Thus the object relationship is never a separate component of a compromise formation; it is part of every single one of the components of conflict which comprise the compromise formation.

In a similar manner we do not speak of narcissism as only a part of the ego but we understand that it is part of each of the three agencies of the mind. Our behavior and feelings about those we love and hate express a compromise between drives, unpleasure, defenses, superego considerations, and reality. This is equally true of normal as well as pathologic object relations. There is an object related aspect to each component of each compromise formation; but we deal not only with individual compromise formations.

I wish here to introduce the idea that in our daily clinical work we deal not only with single compromise formations but also with groups of compromise formations which may themselves be in conflict with each other. Symptoms are rarely caused by only one compromise formation. Enduring, major symptoms are not the consequence of a solitary id–ego–superego conflict but instead are the result of the interaction of complex groups of compromise formations. Each separate compromise formation has its own id, ego, and superego components. Compromise formations are like political compromise in that each new solution creates new problems.

Example

A man who had a symptomatic need to perform intercourse exclusively on his back did this in part to avoid the fantasy danger of castration, but he then felt depressed because he wasn't manly. Then to ward off this depressed feeling of lowered self-esteem he blamed his wife for his sexual problem. If only he had a more responsive wife, he could be more virile. His antagonistic behavior led periodically to arguments and to her withdrawal from him, which he both wished and feared. And so it went.

So we can see that in our clinical work we deal with a dynamic, unstable equilibrium of groups or aggregates of mutually incompatible compromise formations, not with static or linear id, ego, or superego configurations. Yet in the heterogeneous complexity of our diverse theoretic notions we also benefit at certain points by utilizing highly abstract levels of description. The ordinary clinical phenomena we observe cannot often be reduced to the tripartite division of three agencies of the human mind any more than the painter's palette and canvas could be reduced to the three primary colors. In our clinical work we deal with a rainbow of hues and shades of color nuance. In this context I now refer back to the patient whose sublimation and dream both utilized the playing of his musical instrument. Each of these two compromise formations, the dream as well as the sublimation, represented at the highest level of abstraction a conflict between id, ego, and superego. Yet we would understand little more if we stopped our comparison of these two compromise formations at that level of abstraction than if we announced that a man and a fish are both vertebrates.

Modern structural theory like any scientific hypothesis is imperfect, evolving, and incomplete. For all of that the theory of compromise formation is not only our best explanation for pathogenesis, it is also our most advantageous theory to account for clinical improvement. The basis for this strong claim is this: the mobilization and resolution of resistance is the primary vehicle for therapeutic change during psychoanalytic treatment. Resistance itself is a compromise formation.

But is everything a compromise formation? Is there anything which is not a compromise formation? Shall we abandon compromise formation as a useful concept because it is applied to too many phenomena—to both insight as well as resistance; to symptom as well as dream; to transference as well as sublimation? Obviously not. We use this valuable notion of compromise formation extensively because it is advantageous to us in organizing our understanding of the complexity of the data gathered in the psychoanalytic situation. We again confront a problem of confusion in frames of reference. The concept of compromise formation is intended to describe the dynamic interaction of the components of conflict. Viewed at that level of abstraction, a sublimation and a symptom seem hard to distinguish from a dream. All are compromise formations, as are character traits. The value of compromise formation as a concept is to organize our understanding of data and not to homogenize or reductively simplify the mind. In the domain of chemistry all matter in the universe is viewed as the visible form of the unseen interaction of atoms and molecules. Analogously, psychoanalysis is the science of the conflicted human mind and so in the domain of psychoanalysis all human behavior is viewed as the compromise formations which ensue from the interaction of the components of intrapsychic conflict.

One important dividend afforded by the use of compromise formation as an organizing concept is to provide a better distinction between parts and wholes in the dynamic flux of the psychoanalytic process. For example, to this very day it is still not sufficiently appreciated that resistance and defense are not synonymous. Defense is only one component of resistance. Resistance is a compromise formation and therefore it includes defense as well as drive derivatives, unpleasure, and punishment. The essential changes by which treatment can be effectively gauged can be most usefully viewed as an alteration in resistances as well as alterations of pathologic compromise formations, even though we can also speak more abstractly of a structural change in the relations between id, ego, and superego.

The evolution and improvement of modern structural theory has come about by a progressive refinement in our understanding of the nature of the components of intrapsychic conflict. Compromise formation is the concept which at this time affords the best clinical view of the manner in which the human mind copes with conflict. For many years our literature has resonated with controversy about whether to equate therapeutic change with structural change in the relations between id, ego, and superego. It was argued that the tripartite model was too abstract and that what we required was a theory which was closer to the level of observation and which could better account for the person and his object relationships. With the refinement of our views of compromise formation we are well on our way toward these goals.

Chapter 3

Psychological Conflict in Childhood

Robert L. Tyson, M.D.

Every psychoanalyst agrees that conflict exists in all of us. Most analysts accept Freud's findings that mental health or illness is based, not on the content of particular conflicts, but on the degree of success or failure in coping with the conflicts to which everyone is subject. Thus, it is not conflict itself that is pathological, but difficulties and inadequacies in the means and resources available to the individual for conflict resolution.

However, this remarkable degree of agreement does not extend to how to define conflict, to what its origins are, to what it is that is in conflict, or, as clinicians, to what to do about it. The study of normal or expectable conflict in children can, I believe, illuminate these questions and inform our work with patients of any age.

A knowledge of how conflict begins, develops, and elaborates gives the therapist a perspective from which to understand the clinical problems of behavior and symptoms with which he or she is asked to help. But when and how does conflict begin? I will give an example from early in life, and then discuss what we currently know from the developmental timetable about when the elements necessary for the person to experience conflict appear.

31

The Beginnings of Conflict

Joey, a one-month-old infant, was born into an "average expectable environment" (Hartmann, 1939) that included his mother, a caregiver with her own unique psychological and physical capacities. I will use the term *mother* throughout in order to emphasize that the caregiver's subjective experience of the infant over time is important to the child's development and in particular to the child's experience of conflict. An "average expectable infant," such as Joey, comes well equipped with preadapted means for fitting in with what is there, and for beginning interactions with various aspects of the environment, including people.

In this example of infant–caregiver interaction, the visiting observer and Joey's mother were seated in a room next to Joey's bedroom where the baby was napping. The observer heard one-month-old Joey beginning to whimper, listened to his sucking noises, imagined him mouthing and sucking whatever came close to his lips, and heard his increasing distress as manifested by progressively louder vocalizations and sounds of thrashing of arms and legs. Eventually, the baby cried. Meanwhile Joey's mother ignored her son and carried on her conversation with the observer. When finally the observer asked, "Isn't that your baby crying?" the mother replied, in utter contradiction of the facts, "Oh no, that's the baby next door."

Unsurprisingly, in this instance it was not the mother but the observer who was feeling conflict. Indeed, infants are born into environments that are filled with conflict, and in contrast to Hartmann's postulated "conflict-free sphere" of ego development, there is no such thing as a "conflict-free environment." Conflicts in a particular environment are a part of it for that particular infant and have effects on his development. The example also demonstrates how tempting it is for a responsive observer or mother to read meaning into the infant's reactions, an adultomorphic tendency that may well be necessary for optimal growth and development, but which is not necessarily scientifically accurate (Tyson, 1986).

Let us look at how the observer, the mother, and the infant are involved in this conflict situation. To begin with, the observer was in conflict: one impulse was to go to the baby to comfort him, another was to speak to the mother but do nothing, and a third was to say nothing in accord with a common standard of observer behavior. In fact, the observer reports the subjective experiences associated with these impulses, their differing demands, and the attempted resolution.

Next, we may infer the mother to have been in conflict, though she may not have been aware of it at the time. Her behavior was clearly different from what we would expect from most mothers in similar situations. We can best explain it by the hypothesis that the usual impulse to go to the baby was countered by another impulse, just as occurred with the observer, and that her solution to the conflict was to keep herself unaware of her different impulses and of her baby's distress until the observer drew attention to the crying. At that point her next line of defense was to attribute the sounds to the baby next door.

For purposes of this discussion I will paraphrase Brenner's (1979) definition of conflict: psychic conflict exists if there is a sustained existence in the mind of a wish for gratification, the pursuit of which arouses unpleasure such that the person is motivated to take steps to avoid it, that is, to mobilize defense mechanisms to reduce or avoid the unpleasure. In addition to Brenner's definition, we can say that the experience of conflict refers to the unpleasure that is aroused as a consequence of the search for gratification, and the duration of conflict refers to the length of time this unpleasure is felt or defense mechanisms are employed. In the case of the crying infant just described, the observer's experience of conflict is immediately clear to us and to the observer. However, the mother's experience of conflict is inferred by us and probably not conscious to her, most likely highly defended against to avoid the unpleasure involved. What about the one-month-old baby?

There is no evidence that sufficient mental structure exists at birth, and for some time afterwards, to permit the presence in the infant's mind of the elements of conflict as we have defined them. The appearance of psychic conflict is something of a developmental achievement when the necessary components have become available.

To experience conflict according to this definition the

infant must have four abilities: the capacity to anticipate, to make means–ends connections, to use recall memory, and to utilize resources in the service of defense; that is, to find a solution to the conflict. These are all essentially cognitive functions which ordinarily appear as the ego matures (Tyson and Tyson, 1990).

Sometime in the first three months, the infant begins to act in ways suggesting the acquisition of the first ability, the capacity to anticipate; indications of an early form of anticipatory behavior can be seen in neonatal feeding interactions (Call, 1964), and it becomes obvious especially after the smiling response is well established. By four to six months, the infant makes simple means–ends connections and demonstrates both that he understands that his actions influence external objects and that he is now a creature of intentionality. By seven to nine months, fear, surprise, and anger appear as discrete expressions of emotion, the infant scrutinizes his mother's face and begins to respond to her affective expressions, and the unstable beginnings of rudimentary evocative or recall memory are present (evocative memory has been usually thought to appear definitely with the use of language at about eighteen months).

Behavior that serves a defensive purpose has been reported to emerge as early as three to five months in infants living in highly pathological environments (Fraiberg, 1982). However, the usual landmark is the gesture and spoken "no" which appears between fifteen to eighteen months of age. Spitz (1957) believed this heralded a significant new level of psychic organization in which speech as communication replaces action, and in which negativism appears as a result of a true defense mechanism, identification with the aggressor.

To summarize briefly, the infant is born into an average expectable environment which includes people in conflict. However, the infant him- or herself is not capable of beginning to experience conflict until early in the second year of life; only then have the necessary mental structures evolved sufficiently to make this beginning possible. This takes us to the point where we can sort out the kinds of conflict that the child experiences.

Categories of Conflict in Childhood and Their Origins

I will give examples of conflicts that can be inferred by observation of children and that can be divided into the following categories: internal conflict, developmental conflict, and internalized conflict. These three forms of conflict become manifest differently and have different origins.

Internal Conflict

Anna Freud pointed out (1965) that internal conflict results whenever complex personality structure comes into being; there are inevitable inner discords and clashes because each mental structure "has its specific derivation, its specific aims and allegiances, and its specific mode of functioning" (p. 8). Thus the opposing wishes that give rise to internal conflict originate within the mind; they do not have an external source from which they were derived as will be described for internalized conflicts. These incompatible strivings are usually categorized within the areas of ambivalence, activity versus passivity, and masculinity versus femininity. Early in development, they give rise to a kind of background level of conflict to which is added conflict from other sources as development proceeds. The background level of conflict cannot readily be separated out, identified, and quantified in regard to a specific conflict. However, its contributions can be inferred.

For example, the developing ego can be viewed as a psychic structure comprised of an increasing number of functions; these ego functions have in common the aim of mediating among a variety of demands for gratification, the limitations imposed by reality, and the emerging requirements of the superego, as well as to ensure the individual's survival. In this sense the ego may seek to obtain drive gratification, but in accord with various conflicting constraints originating within the ego even before the superego comes to have significant influence. Within the nascent tripartite mental structure of id, ego, and superego, therefore, inner conflict may be (1) intrasystemic or within one structure as just described in the ego, or (2) intersystemic or between structures, as when ego-based efforts to temporize lead to conflict with a wish for gratification derived from an id impulse.

In seeking gratification, a very young child's conflict between the wish for immediate gratification and the need to temporize may surface, and signs of it become manifest in a number of ways, such as in the appearance of symptoms like eating and sleeping disturbances, phobias, and separation problems. However, the observer may not always be able to decide what the origins of conflict are on the basis of the symptoms alone. This is because, according to the psychoanalytic point of view, symptoms themselves only indicate that an effort has been made to resolve a conflict; they are not certain evidence of where the conflict originated, nor is any one particular symptom pathognomonic of the underlying dynamic structure which gives rise to the symptom. The typical clinical problem in childhood contains a mixture of sources of conflict, and part of the clinician's task of evaluation is to sort them out. Those children whose difficulties embody a large contribution from internal conflicts are likely to require longer periods of treatment (A. Freud, 1965, pp. 133–134).

As already mentioned, an example of the mixture of sources of conflict occurs with bisexuality, a common problem area for clinicians who work with children. Physiological and cultural factors interact with the internal conflict associated with bisexuality, a conflict based on the discordance between wishes derived from feminine strivings and those derived from more masculine ones.

At age three-and-a-half, Johnny was a concern to his new stepmother because of his wish to be in bed with his father, his clinging to him, and his frequent attempts to nuzzle and fondle his father's body. He didn't like his stepmother, preferred the company of girls to boys, and expressed the wish to be a girl. His mother had died of a brain tumor one year before, after being progressively less able to take care of him. Here the background balance of Johnny's ordinary bisexual tendencies, which are part of the inborn constitution, was influenced by his fear of object loss, occasioned by the gradual disappearance of his mother and the substitution of the father for her as the primary caregiver. This was complicated by his experiences with a series of nannies of widely varying abilities. The ordinary, expectable developmental conflicts and those of the Oedipus complex were influenced, colored, and in some respects exaggerated by the early emphasis he placed on his feminine strivings. Johnny was referred for psychoanalytic treatment at the age of four-and-a-half because his efforts at solving his conflicts had clearly impaired his development in many areas and were not accessible to influence by any form of environmental manipulation such as limits, changes in schedules, or parental guidance.

Developmental Conflict

The term *developmental conflict* is applied when the infant's wishes for gratification are in opposition to the mother's wishes. No other ingredients are required than a wish that originates in the child's mind, an opposing wish in the mother's mind, and an interaction between them in which these incompatible wishes clash. Thus developmental conflict emerges as an interpersonal and not a psychic conflict, but it is a crucial precursor to the formation of internalized conflicts, defined below. Steps toward conflict internalization, and consequently also toward the pain and discomfort of psychic conflict, begin when and to the extent that the infant abstains from acting on his wish. The abstention comes about either on the child's initiative, for example in efforts to win the mother's love and approval, or because he is prevented by the mother from acting on his wish, or both.

This definition assumes that the infant's wish derives from a phase-appropriate urge that has provided the child with some pleasurable gratification. A necessary qualification of the mother's wish in a developmental conflict is that it be expressed in developmentally appropriate demands or restrictions imposed on the child. If these demands are out of phase developmentally, or if they are not appropriate to the circumstances, for example by being either excessive or insufficient, a developmental conflict becomes instead a developmental interference with pathological consequences.

In this situation, the mother's demands have a meaning and importance to the child in terms of his developmental level at the time. Since mothering requires a series of such demands, developmental conflicts and challenges are an inevitable part of progressive development. Any such conflict may become a developmental interference should it progress to the point at which the expectable unfolding of development is disrupted.

This example illustrates a transient discord in the mother–infant relationship from the age of one month, prior to the time when a developmental conflict can begin. It started when Sara's pediatrician advised supplementing breast-feeding with formula. Her clearly aversive—one might say, distasteful—reaction to the introduction of a new food and a new method of feeding persisted with decreasing intensity for a few days, when it disappeared and she was able to consume from both sources without hesitation. Sara's wishes and those of her mother—if Sara could be said to have wishes—were in conflict, and the elements necessary for Sara herself to experience psychic conflict were not present. At this early age, the infant's aversive reflexes and pleasurable experiences are only just beginning to link up with primitive islands of memory; the capacity to anticipate on the basis of means–ends connections is not present to any useful or lasting degree, and the ability to utilize resources in the service of defense is not yet established.

For several reasons, toilet training is the traditional area to use for examples of developmental conflict. One is that children are often begun with toilet training about the time they are able to walk; now the toddler has available to him many more avenues of response than previously, including representational intelligence, language, and a blossoming fantasy life. Another is that separation–individuation has progressed to the point of the rapprochement phase and the child perceives for himself that his wishes and those of his mother are often different. His ambivalence begins to confront him with complicated choices to make: should he indulge in what has always been pleasurable in spite of his mother's demands to the contrary? Should he give it up because he derives significant pleasure from his mother's response? Should he give it up because he fears his mother's response? Or should he refuse her request because to agree means to give up something valuable of himself either symbolically or in the sense of his feelings of autonomy or of omnipotence?

Carl was a boy of three not yet toilet trained. His permissive, understanding, and articulate parents discussed it with him, suggested training pants, pointed out the advantages of not wearing diapers, and discussed with him his concerns over not being allowed to return to his beloved nursery school if he weren't toilet trained soon. He still wanted to wear diapers. Each of the parents then made clear to Carl that if he wanted to be a big boy, he had to get along without diapers; Carl agreed that he wanted to be a big boy, though I'm not sure what that meant to him. He still wanted to wear diapers. It became clear that neither parent had said that they wanted him to give up diapers. The father responded to this insight first and told his son, "That's enough, now I want you to leave the diapers and wear big boy pants starting tomorrow." Within an hour, the father heard his son asking the mother about wearing diapers. She replied with the same degree of certainty and clarity as did the father. Carl said, "Okay." Carl did not return to the diapers, and he had only a few accidents in the next three months since which time his toilet training has been securely established.

What I have presented is, of course, an oversimplified description of a complicated situation. Usually parents are described as being intrusive in their demands that their child be clean, and as being intolerant of the child's lapses or rebellion. It is easy to see how such insistent and poorly attuned parental intrusion can escalate conflict, disrupt development, act as a developmental interference, and provoke rebellion which is compounded by punishment. It is less easy to see how the lack of demands from the parents can act as a developmental interference and impede developmental progress. I believe the example of Carl shows clearly how the child needs what Settlage, Curtis, Lozoff, Silberschatz, and Simburg (1988) call a developmental challenge, what others might call consistency, firmness, or discipline. These last three terms refer to parental behavior without regard to the developmental needs of the child. The concept and term *developmental challenge* has the advantage of including the child's experience and the requisites for optimal development.

The content of developmental conflicts follows the typical

sequence of oral, anal, and phallic psychosexual phases. I have already referred to feeding difficulties and conflicts over toilet training. Masturbation is another area of activity in which developmental conflicts occur. Spitz showed that genital play in infancy, and masturbation with accompanying fantasies that develops from it, are expectable aspects of normal development only absent in highly pathological circumstances. Since children typically indulge in genital play and masturbation prior to the Oedipus conflict, they are likely to elicit constraints on these activities from their caregivers that are understood and well remembered at the level of their cognitive development at the time. Later in life such restraining remarks are reacted to on the basis of a new and more threatening meaning which looms all the larger in the context of oedipal conflicts. Before the transformations brought about in the course of these conflicts, the child is confronted with complicated choices about whether to masturbate or not, like those relevant to toilet training, but with the additional possibility that masturbation can be carried on in secret. It is much easier to keep masturbation a secret than defecation, and secret masturbation is typical of oedipal and postoedipal childhood sexuality.

The concept of developmental conflict helps make clear that conflicts in the mother and other caregivers can influence their "patterns of mothering" (Brody, 1956) and thus impinge on the child's development, affect the intensity of the conflicts the child has to cope with, and become a factor in what resources are available to the child's defensive efforts.

At the level of the developmental conflict, which is a precursor to the internalized conflict, the child experiences no great amount of shame or guilt, and no inner struggle. The child's impulse toward a pleasurable activity is primarily unrestrained and is acted on unless checked by a caregiver. Only gradually does the infant and child begin to anticipate the adult's disapproval; with this anticipation, the child shows signs of beginning to refrain from the forbidden acts in the adult's presence, and then also gradually to refrain from them in the adult's absence as the process of internalization takes place, and shame and guilt gradually make their appearance. Thus the internalized conflict comes into existence, signs of which can be seen sometimes beginning in the second half of the second year of life (Mahler, 1975); this can be seen easily in instances when the child shows his awareness of his ambivalence, that is, that he has different wishes which are mutually exclusive, as to playing, defecating, pleasing his mother, leaving the room, or hugging his mother.

Internalized Conflict

Internalized conflict comes about through the process of internalization, by which means the ingredients necessary for psychic conflict end up all being present in the child's mind and do not require the presence of another person. Of course there are interpersonal conflicts which are not directly concerned with issues of developmental relevance at that moment, and these are subject to internalization as well.

Some characteristics of internalized conflicts are important for the clinician to keep in mind. First, like internal conflicts, they are inaccessible and cannot be affected in any significant way by environmental manipulation. However, conflict resolutions or compromises which have been arrived at can be altered by treatment which permits the interpersonal "revival" and effective interpretation of the original conflicts in a "new edition" in the transference.

Second, the internalized version of the conflict is not exactly the same as the original conflict between the mother and the child. What gets internalized is profoundly affected and distorted in the process of internalization by the intensity of the child's wishes, defenses, and earlier experiences, and the level of cognitive functioning at the time.

Third, a child's first defensive response to the pain of conflict is to externalize the conflict to the extent that resources allow. It is this externalization which draws the environment into battle with the child who accepts the struggle in exchange for the relief from the pain of unresolved internalized conflict. The parents and the clinician, confronted with what appears to be a difficulty in social adaptation or a behavior problem, may miss its origins in internalized conflict unless a careful developmental assessment is done, as suggested by Anna Freud with her developmental profile (A. Freud, 1962, 1963, 1965; Nagera, 1963; Meers, 1966; W. E. Freud, 1968).

The Process of Internalization

I want to return to what happens at the start of extrauterine life and to the complex process of internalization, because it plays such a crucial role in establishing internalized conflict. I will briefly review the internalization process, the mental mechanisms of identification and introjection which are a part of that process, and the internalization of the signal function and its importance to psychic conflict.

Beginning at or very soon after birth, the infant is an active participant in and interacts in progressively more complex ways with the world and people around him—broadly called "the environment." These interactions are crucial for the development of his mind and they make it possible for internalizations to be made in the form of mental representations. By a mental representation I mean:

> A more or less stable and enduring image formed in the mind of an object or thing existing in the external world. A mental representation combines and is built from a variety of multidetermined perceptions and impressions about the object or thing. A child's mental representation of his mother, for example, is built from a wide range of images and impressions about the mother, as well as from images of the child himself in interaction with the mother [Tyson and Tyson, 1990, p. 331].

As the term is used here, a mental representation includes affects and experiences associated with the mother, and these may be either of pleasurable or unpleasurable qualities (such as those inherent in conflict), or both. Thus the developmental or other conflicts associated with the mother become part of the child's internal world as constituents of mental representations.

As the memory function and other ego capacities come into operation and mature, the infant's inner world is constructed from mental representations of the important people in his life and of his interactions with them, including the conflicts already described. These mental representations become the nexus of emerging psychic structures, the id, ego, and superego—structures or systems of mental functions grouped according to their similarities.

Said another way, internalization is that ongoing process by which "regulations that have taken place in interaction with the outside world are replaced by inner regulations" (Hartmann and Loewenstein [1962, p. 48]; see also Hartmann [1939]; Jacobson [1964]). This means that, as the infant's ego matures and his capacities increase, he becomes progressively more able to perform for himself those caregiving, comforting, and regulating functions (or "regulations") that the mother performed for him. In the course of this development he becomes more autonomous. That does not at all mean that he becomes more distant from his mother; it does mean that his relationship to her matures, which is to say that he needs to rely progressively less on the auxiliary ego and auxiliary superego functions available from the environment as he becomes progressively though slowly better able to perform these functions himself.

Internalization is a process ongoing for years, one in which mental representations are formed, differentiated, and elaborated. As time goes on, these representations embody both the functions previously in the mother's hands and the conflicts and disagreements that arise between mother and child. At the same time, self–object differentiation is taking place; that is, self representations are gradually distinguished from object representations. These processes take place in the mind and refer to distinctions between mental representations of self and object, and not simply to the ability to make distinctions between the existence of oneself and that of another person.

The conflicts that are internalized by the formation of self and object representations can be influenced in several ways. Two important influences come about through identification and by the formation of introjects.

The term *identification* refers, among other things, to changing a part of one's self representation to become more like an aspect of an object representation. The motivation may vary; for example, in one instance a child's identification with the aggressor may be made in a defensive effort to protect himself; in another instance an identification may help the child to feel closer to what he perceives as an admirable or lovable part of a loved person. In general, an identification tends to lessen psychic conflict with the source of the identification, though it may result in greater conflict with someone else. For example, a child's identification with an aspect of the mother may increase his experience of conflict in regard to his father's wishes.

In terms of the child's relationship with his mother, the term *maternal introject* refers to those representations of the mother which embody the authority previously invested only in the person of the mother herself. It is the presence of this introject which continues aspects of the developmental or other external, interpersonal conflicts in the form of internalized conflicts (Tyson and Tyson, 1984).

One party to the conflict, that part of the representation which contains the mother's demands, eventually ends up taking part in superego functioning, along with a number of other such representations and demands. Observations of children well under the age of five show many examples. After a recent earthquake, for example, a girl of two years, ten months was heard to answer the phone by saying, "Hello! We just had an earthquake. I didn't do it, mommy didn't do it, daddy didn't do it, and my sister didn't do it. It just did itself!" (Christine Lapides, personal communication).

This child clearly has a highly developed sense of responsibility and had puzzled out for herself from the family's conversation that neither she nor the others were guilty of having caused the damage. We could say that she was responding to her maternal introject when she answered the phone the way she did.

The last point to be considered is the signal function of affect. The origin of signal affect exemplifies that functions as well as conflict can be internalized. In brief, the capacity to utilize signal affect is a developmental achievement brought about through the child's identification with the mother's responding to his tension states with her own signal affect. Then the child eventually signals danger for himself as the mother did to begin with. The signal function of affect is necessary for the child to experience and to tolerate the experience of conflict in a developmentally appropriate way and not to be overwhelmed or traumatized by it or by the associated affects. The exercise of this function makes it possible for the infant and child to anticipate by experiencing a sample or signal of the consequences of an action. Without this function, either the consequences are not anticipated, or the affect is experienced in full, traumatic force rather than as a signal. Anxiety is the most studied affect and so one hears often of the signal anxiety function. Jones (1929), Rapaport (1953), Jacobson (1953), and Brenner (1974b, 1975, 1982) have made clear that other affects may also be used as signals.

The capacity to exercise the signal function of affect has developmental origins in the mother–infant relationship; the nature of this relationship determines whether or not the subsequent utilization of the signal function will be adequate and appropriate. The process by which this capacity is internalized begins in the first year, so that by seven months the majority of infants can be observed to scan the mother's face and react to her expression, especially when there is something strange in the environment. In a number of developmental studies (Sorce, Emde, and Klinnert, 1981; Emde and Sorce, 1983) in which this phenomenon is called "social referencing," infants of fifteen months are shown to rely regularly on the mother's affective responses to decide whether to proceed in a strange situation. The mother's affective responses that are utilized by the infant in this way can be described as an auxiliary ego signal affect function. The baby relies on this function progressively less as development, that is, internalization, proceeds and he is able to rely on his own internal perceptions and signal affects to evaluate his circumstances and decide on his responses.

One can imagine in some detail, as Tolpin (1971) did, the importance for the establishment of the signal affect function of the mother consistently and appropriately "rescuing" the infant at times of heightened tension. However, I would disagree with Tolpin's position that such responses from the mother are sufficient for the establishment or structuralization of the child's signal function. As Ritvo (1981) pointed out, in order for the infant to give the signal of distress or anxiety consistently at the appropriate time, and for the subsequent internalization of the signal function, the mother's previous responses must have been consistently in response to the child's actual signals of distress. The reason for stating this so carefully is because there are mothers who "rescue" their infants but not in response to the infant's signals, but for example on the basis of what the mother perceives, imagines, or fears might be the case. Only if the mother's helping responses are to the child's distress signals will the child develop and internalize a signal affect function.

Ritvo details other reasons why the effective operation of the signal function may be interfered with. These reasons include strain trauma (Kris, 1956) or cumulative trauma (Khan, 1963) operating over a relatively long period of time. A common consequence of such forms of trauma is a distortion or intensification of aspects of the infant's developmental experience, and consequently a disruption of the normal internalization process, rendering the signal function vulnerable.

Discussion and Summary

The capacity to be in conflict is a developmental achievement that requires certain mental abilities not present at birth—the capacity to anticipate, to make means–ends connections, to use recall memory, and to utilize defenses in finding a resolution.

I have focused on the earliest categories of conflict based on the sources of the conflicting wishes or impulses. These categories are the internal conflict, the developmental conflict, and the internalized conflict.

After discussing internal conflict, examples were given of developmental conflicts from different developmental levels and of how the process of internalization transforms interpersonal conflicts into internalized conflicts. This results in certain characteristics of internalized conflicts—their relative inaccessibility to change, their distortion as compared with the original conflicts, and the typical defensive reaction of externalization.

The process of internalization can be viewed in terms of the parallel processes of self–object differentiation and of the formation of mental representations that embody experiences of interpersonal interactions. These mental representations may be affected by identifications and by introjections and thus change over time to play an important role in superego functioning.

Finally, the importance of the internalization of the signal affect function can be seen in the child's ability to tolerate conflict and not be overwhelmed and traumatized by it.

The possibilities for conflicts increase markedly with entry into the oedipal phase, as the child's triadic fantasies embody his wishes to play the role of one parent with the other and to exclude or get rid of the competing parent. This is a difference from the preoedipal, dyadic relationship when the wish to get rid of one parent is simply to be in exclusive possession of the other rather than to take over their position and role (Tyson and Tyson, 1990). Conflicts of loyalty appear, partly based on internalized injunctions against aggression, partly based on fear of loss of a loved parent, and partly because of fear of retaliation.

A temporary solution to these dilemmas involves externalization or displacement of elements of the conflict to others; for example, other family members, peers, and the school situation, as well as internal accommodations such as repression, identification, and sublimation. The child's capacities and preferences for solutions to these problems are dependent in large measure on what went on before, and indeed his burden may be significantly greater if earlier conflicts persist or were dealt with insufficiently. The clinician is often enough faced with a disturbance which has significant oedipal elements but is also pervaded with earlier conflicts which must be addressed as well. The immediate solution to these conflicts is often temporary because they are reworked in adolescence, providing a second chance for the oedipal conflicts, and a third chance for the preoedipal problems to find solutions.

In response to a study of the developmental sequence of conflict almost twenty-five years ago (Nagera, 1966), Anna Freud said that a delineation of how conflict appears and develops makes it possible to apportion "pathogenic impact to external and internal interferences," to locate "internal influences in any part of the psychic structure or in the interaction between any of the inner agencies" and to build up "step by step . . . an orderly sequence of childhood disorders, of which the infantile neurosis is not the base, but the final, complex apex" (A. Freud, 1966, p. 9).

Anna Freud's metaphor of steps along the way to a complex apex can fruitfully be applied to the emergence and evolution of conflict. It begins with the most basic forms of conflict, which appear simply as a consequence of the appearance of mental structure, and progress to the more complex forms as a consequence of internalization. Next, there are similar steps from the simpler content of early conflicts to the elaborate configurations that differentiate as the child's world widens and the Oedipus complex becomes established. And last, there is a parallel pathway of steps along which defenses mobilized to cope with conflict elaborate from the archaic turning away to sophisticated defenses utilized to cope with progressively more challenging conflicts at each developmental level.

In conclusion, the picture of conflict development with which I want to end is of a double pyramid; the base begins with the early developmental conflicts which may skew or tilt the entire structure. It builds up to an apex or node with the infantile neurosis and oedipal conflicts; but then the apex broadens out so that conflict does not end there but passes through it as a point of transformation. Past that point I suggest that all conflicts cannot be understood simply in the terms of the time of their origin, but must instead be seen as affecting and affected by all conflicts before and after, and by all the solutions and attempts at solutions that have been made along the way.

Chapter 4

Therapeutic Strategies in Dealing with Neurotic Patients' Marital Problems

Elizabeth Lloyd Mayer, Ph.D.

The idea of intrapsychic conflict is at the heart of analytic thinking about psychology. In a way that makes it a hard thing for an analyst to discuss: talk about practically anything from a psychoanalytic point of view, and you find you're talking about conflict. Worse, talk about *neurosis* from the point of view of conflict and it is practically a tautology; the *fact* of intrapsychic conflict and the compromise solutions it invites are precisely what define the thing we call neurosis.

So I realized, in taking on the topic of "conflict in the neuroses," that I needed a way to limit my focus. I began by thinking about instances in my practice where the notion of intrapsychic conflict provided not just the general underpinning to my thinking about a patient, but where it actually made a radical difference in how I approached a patient and the kind of treatment plan the patient and I developed.

Several patients came to mind, and as I thought about what they had in common, I realized that each of them had come to see me expressing a version of the same problem. Each was female, each was married, each had at least one young child, and each had come to see me in significant distress about the state of her marriage since children had been born. And, during my initial consultation with each of them, certain similar questions about the causes for their unhappiness arose: questions about relations between the sexes, questions about how men and women raise children together, and so on, questions which are far from easy to answer in this day and age. Finally, with each of these women, it was at the outset quite unclear that answering these questions by working at understanding individual intrapsychic conflicts would supply the best *kinds* of answers, the ones most likely to alleviate the distress they were feeling. So, during my first meetings with each of them, I thought about recommending a number of different things. I thought about couple's therapy. I thought about support groups for mothers of young children. I thought about feminist educative approaches, focusing on how these women's dilemmas were a function of the cultural bind in which so many women today are shocked to find themselves as, with the birth of children, traditional gender role distinctions suddenly invade the most modern of marriages. And of course I thought about individual psychotherapy or analysis, based on the idea that unconscious inner conflict was at the root of these women's pain.

Unsurprisingly the strategy I settled on for helping these women was not the same in each case. I did refer one for couple's therapy with her husband. I recommended to another that she read Arlie Hochschild's recent critique of the U.S. family, *The Second Shift,* and suggested she call me back if altering child care arrangements didn't solve the problem. But several of these women I took into analysis, and it was for them that the idea of *intrapsychic neurotic conflict* made all the difference in how I decided I would try to be helpful to them. Parenthetically, it was not that these latter women didn't have plenty of communication problems with their husbands—the criterion I generally use for recommending couple's therapy. Nor was it that they weren't caught by the dilemmas of working "the second shift" that Hochschild describes so convincingly for most mothers these days. But, what was more important, as I got to know these women, was my sense that those problems weren't the basic ones. In different ways it emerged that each one had, since becoming a mother, felt *compelled* to see her husband in ways that made her unhappy, far beyond what she recognized to be "realistic." And at some level, more or less conscious, each was aware of this quality of compulsion and aware also that the man who had been lovable before children had somehow lost his lovability. Even in our preliminary explorations of these feelings the sense of internal conflict was palpable.

Now, I will do two things. First, I want to describe a bit about one of these cases. I will try particularly to focus on what I mean when I say that a sense of conflict was palpable and on how my work with this woman was based on working with that conflict.

Second, I want to describe something about how we came to understand the conflict. Specifically, I will describe how this woman's experience of marriage and motherhood was especially influenced by issues of the negative oedipal phase. More broadly, I will suggest that, for certain women, the choice of a husband is powerfully determined by a need to defend against frightening yearnings to be not with a man, but with their mothers. These women pick men who help them feel free of those deeply conflicted wishes; and for awhile, often quite awhile, the solution works. But because the wishes *are* conflicted, it is an uneasy solution. As life proceeds, the forces that fuel the conflict shift. Specifically, as these women become mothers, their unconscious relationships to their own mothers are profoundly reworked. This reworking leads to a change in each woman's underlying defensive requirements, especially in terms of her unconscious relationship to her mother. To the extent that her husband was loved because of how he figured in filling the old defensive requirements, he can no longer be loved in quite the same way. One outcome may be the presenting picture I described earlier: the man who had seemed lovable before children somehow loses his lovability.

Annette was in her midthirties when she came to see me. She and her husband had married ten years earlier—two promising young academics in related fields. For the first seven years all had gone well. They had friends, interests in common, and they loved each other. Then she had become pregnant. During our first session Annette told me that, looking back on it, this was when things had begun to deteriorate, though at the time she had attributed episodes of unhappiness to the immediate stress of pregnancy. They wanted a family, however, and soon she was pregnant again, a year after the birth of the first baby. By the time I met Annette, the older child (a girl) was three, and the younger child, a boy, was one.

In great detail, Annette mapped out all the familiar stresses: two ambitious careers, not enough child care, nights of too little sleep, and days of feeling torn between the demands of work and children. Most of all she talked about her resentment of her husband, Joe. His career came first. He helped at home but not enough. He loved the children but it didn't feel like real love. She couldn't enjoy his lovemaking any more. Tough as being a single parent would be, she wondered if it might be easier. She thought a lot about taking the kids and leaving. She felt angry and disappointed, all the time.

In our initial sessions, one of the things that struck me most was how elusive Annette's complaints were as we tried to explore them. They were elusive in a particular way: her resentment was genuine, but every complaint, as we pursued it, turned into not quite the *real* complaint. So what started as despair about how Joe didn't help get the children up each morning turned rapidly into how he fixed them breakfast but didn't get them dressed. Not getting them dressed turned into how he didn't act like he really wanted to fix breakfast. Not wanting to fix breakfast turned into how he did it differently than she would, and so on. Every once in awhile the barrage of complaints would turn to sadness and Annette would express real fondness for Joe and a longing for the days when they had been able to love each other.

I must tell you that in our first session I heard very little about Annette apart from what her marriage was like. But I did feel I was learning a lot about what I take to be a *sine qua non* for doing any sort of analytic work with a patient, that is, about the fact that exploring how a patient feels about whatever brings them to treatment very quickly leads to an awareness of contradictions and paradoxes, a sense of things not being quite what they seem. When that sense is present, I think it can be one of the first indications that intrapsychic conflict is significantly feeding whatever's being talked about. And when a patient is able to be puzzled and curious about *how* things aren't adding up, there is real promise that analytic work will be helpful.

So in Annette's case, I was encouraged in the direction of analytic exploration by the very elusiveness of her complaints, as well as by her ability to be perplexed about why it seemed so hard to get to what was really upsetting her about Joe. As Annette and I established some consensus between us regarding what was puzzling, she became increasingly convinced that there was a lot she didn't know about what motivated her complaints and about how mixed and how conflicted her feelings were. At that point analysis as a therapeutic mode began to make sense to Annette. Also (and I think this is not uncommon), while she was dismayed by her increasing awareness of internal conflict, she was also reassured by it. It was dismaying to feel that the fault wasn't all Joe's. On the other hand, if her angry perceptions of him weren't entirely realistic, there was hope that the marriage could be salvaged. With this hope, she began to relax into the treatment and tell me things about herself apart from her marriage.

Annette was the youngest of four children, raised on a U.S. Army base. Her parents' marriage she viewed as civil but not terribly happy. When she was five, her mother had been diagnosed with tuberculosis and sent to a sanitarium for a year. During that year Annette had seen her mother rarely and she recalled how sad and lonely the year had felt. As she went on to talk about her mother, she found herself surprised by how readily tears came. Her mother had died five years earlier and she wondered if perhaps she hadn't really mourned.

I began to hear about an ongoing problem which her marital difficulties had temporarily pushed to the background. She had for years been subject to episodes of intense anxiety with women whom she admired or wanted as friends. With an academic advisor this anxiety had been at times paralyzing. In relation to peers she would become painfully preoccupied with gaining the friendship of a particular woman or group of women. Once gained (and she was good at gaining it) it was never satisfying in quite the way she'd envisioned it would be.

I learned too about an affair she had begun a year prior to our meetings and had recently terminated. Her lover was a man she had met through her daughter's play group, the divorced father of another child in the group. She had fallen deeply in love with him, feeling a kind of tenderness and mutual nurturing which she had never experienced with Joe. However, she had felt very guilty about deceiving Joe and had finally been decisive in cutting the relationship off. Striking in her descriptions of her lover were his feminine qualities. She had particularly loved his sensitivity and gentleness, expressed both toward herself and his young daughter.

In this material, something of the intensity that infused Annette's ties to women, is, I think, apparent. It was increasingly to enter Annette's awareness as an organizing issue in her life. Now I shall jump ahead one year into Annette's analysis. I shall describe a session which I hope will give a sense of how her initial complaints about here marriage were still there, but altered in a way that had to do with how we were coming to understand the nature of her conflicts.

She began this particular hour by talking about how much she'd enjoyed the previous afternoon with her children. She was grateful to the analysis, since she thought it had helped her feel less burdened by them. When Joe had come home she'd been glad to see him and had tried to engage him in the game they'd been playing. He'd been pleased and eager. But she'd felt her own interest evaporate. Why? She was back to old familiar suspicion: How much did Joe really want the children? His way of playing was rougher, clumsier than she liked. (I said at that point, "He doesn't *mother* the children.") She began to cry; nor did he mother her. Her lover had. But Joe was a good *father*: why wasn't that enough? She remembered a dream. In it she was pregnant, close to term, and she was with another woman who was also pregnant. Their bellies were huge. They were both tan and naked. They caressed each other and it was blissful. She was shocked by the frank homosexuality of the dream but the feelings had been wonderful. What a contrast to her feelings about Joe. Maybe that was what so chronically disappointed her about him; she would never have those feelings with him, he would never be that woman. She was silent for a moment and her mood shifted: she found herself thinking about how comfortable Joe was in social gatherings and how unlike her mother who had been inhibited at parties. His ease with people had been one of the first things that had drawn her to him. He didn't worry about being included by others the way she did. But back to the dream: she guessed she had missed having her mother around while she was pregnant.

Certainly she missed her now, as a grandmother to her own children. If her mother were still around, would she be less demanding of Joe? She wanted to share the children with a woman; she really wanted that. In the dream she'd had it: two women, no men.

At the level of the obvious, Annette is still married and relatively happy about it. The pressure at home has eased, partly because Annette is struggling more with herself and less with Joe about certain issues. Paradoxically, this has freed her to struggle more openly with him about other issues, with the result that they are in fact sharing the work at home more equally. (This, incidentally, I view as a byproduct of our work together, not the attainment of an objective we had set. I mention this because it bears on the initial decision about how to treat a patient like Annette. My guess at the outset had been that if Annette could become more aware of how her conflicts motivated her, she would find herself able to start making whatever changes were useful in the outside world, and altering the division of labor at home turned out to represent one such change.)

But beyond changes in the marriage, Annette was becoming more conscious of a number of things. I spoke earlier of how my first step toward engaging Annette in analysis had involved our establishing some consensus regarding what was puzzling in Annette's complaints. A year later, that consensus was broadening to include a general framework within which we were starting to understand Annette's fundamental conflicts. Her longing to feel connected with her mother figured centrally. So, in the hour I just described, she kept coming back, more or less explicitly, to the question of how much her dissatisfaction with Joe had to do with how he didn't fulfill those longings. She was starting to explore a fantasy—more apparent in the dream than it had been to date—that men are extraneous and women can be completely fulfilling to each other. In conjunction with this fantasy she finds herself reflecting on the other side, how part of what she likes about Joe involves his being *different* from her mother, and how she does value that difference. She wants what he has to offer too. Then she returns to the dream and links her mother with the woman who was so gratifying. This back and forth, by the way, exemplifies for me the everyday way in which we see derivatives of intrapsychic conflict manifest—the expression of a wish, the expression of a defense against that wish (often in itself representing an opposing wish), then back to the first wish. As Annette becomes increasingly aware of this back and forth she will become more able to see ways in which many of her attitudes and behaviors represent compromises designed to maintain a careful balance of forces between the opposing sides. With such insight, of course, will come greater freedom to alter that balance of forces, to think, feel, and act differently.

But back to the hour I was just describing. Based on hearing the kind of material it included, I was forming some pretty strong hypotheses about the sorts of childhood wishes and anxieties which were impinging on Annette's current experience. In brief, she seemed to me to be struggling especially with conflicts of the negative oedipal phase, conflicts defined (for the girl) by wishes to exclude her father and be a perfectly satisfying partner to her mother. The more I heard about the problems in Annette's marriage and her life in general, the more I was convinced that these negative oedipal issues had a special salience for her. Using them as a kind of template made sense out of her strivings and anxieties in a way that was organizing for both of us.

Still, neither of us was convinced that such a formulation would have lasting mutative potential for Annette, that is, could offer her more than an intellectual framework within which to understand her problems. It was only as we experienced directly, in the room together, how her conflicts enforced particular compromise solutions in her relationship with me, that the formulations we had developed came convincingly to life.

Annette's analysis lasted four years. As I looked over my notes on our work together, I found myself reflecting: why four years? Of course that led to the more general question of why any given analysis lasts as long as it does. To really answer that is another paper, but I do want to mention one thing that struck me as I thought about Annette. I realized that, in a certain sense, the last three years of her analysis added remarkably little to what I had felt able intellectually to formulate about her central conflicts quite early in the analysis after, for example, the session I have summarized here. This observation sounds dismaying, and it is certainly the kind of observation that has fueled plenty of criticism of the analytic method. But ultimately I don't believe it *is* dismaying. I think it simply reflects something about how the analytic process works. Among psychologies, psychoanalysis is distinguished by the brilliantly cohesive formulations about mental functioning and intrapsychic conflict which its concepts permit. However, much of what makes psychoanalysis an effective therapy involves processes which go beyond what is involved with producing those formulations, valuable and orienting though they are. Analysis takes a long time (and four years *is* a long time, even if short by analytic standards) not because compelling and accurate formulations about patients' dynamics are so hard to come up with. It takes a long time because gaining a lively experience of what those formulations really mean in an immediate and day-to-day way happens gradually and, most of the time, not very dramatically. Yet it is that slow, less than dramatic integration which gives conviction to formulations, turns them into genuine insight, and eventually permits meaningful change.

I shall try now to describe how Annette and I worked at that process of integration. I shall focus on an episode during which certain shifts in her transference toward me became evident for the first time.

Early in her analysis, Annette's feelings about me were characterized by slightly nervous idealization punctuated by brief moments of sadness. In a general way this was hardly a surprising transference picture since it recapitulated many of her prior relationships with women, especially women in authority. As time went on we learned more and more about these feelings. The idealizing way she felt about me increasingly led her to recall her mother. Although, during adolescence, Annette had frequently been in overt rebellion against her mother, she now found that she was remembering more about how, as a child, she felt like she had loved her mother utterly. The mother she recalled from those years was beautiful, feminine, fascinating, loving. No wonder, Annette thought, she had missed her mother so terribly while her mother had been at the sanitarium. When she felt sad during our hours, she was reminded of how sad that year had been. She thought it was the same sadness, experienced with me because she was sad about the limits on our relationship, and sad about how those limits would always leave her longing for more.

The problem with this explanation was not that it wasn't true. It just didn't take us very far. Two years later the same episodic sadness would suddenly infuse Annette's mood, little altered by what we had understood to date. Its precipitants were usually unclear, and Annette's attempts at identifying them were unsatisfyingly global and vague.

At that point a parapraxis (that peculiarity of speech so wonderfully labeled a Freudian slip) intervened. To understand the slip, some background will be useful. Soon after starting analysis, Annette had become aware that I was quite active in a local musical organization. A friend of hers was on the Board of Directors and, not knowing that Annette was in analysis with me, the friend occasionally spoke of my involvement. For a long time what I heard from Annette was in keeping with her generally admiring transference to me: it was wonderful that I had time for such activities, and so on. While she told me that she never encouraged her friend to talk about me, she also said that she hadn't been able to discourage it since she didn't want her friend to know that she was in analysis. Certainly I had the impression that Annette enjoyed this extracurricular connection, though she regularly refuted the idea that it meant much to her one way or the other.

But one day she had a falling-out with her friend. She mentioned this only in passing and made no further reference to it over the following weeks. However, her sadness during our hours seemed to me to increase. The explanation she offered—that it was a repetition of how she'd longed for her mother—was by now familiar but seemed increasingly inadequate. Why did the sadness arise only at certain times? Why was it increasing? Why was she so unable to come to terms with it, leave it behind, or transform it in any way?

Then one day she commented that she had encountered the friend whom I knew. She had not felt much: "Only a little angry with _____," and she mentioned the name of another friend. I was puzzled and asked her whom she'd been angry with. She in turn was puzzled: the friend whom I knew, of course. But, I pointed out, she'd said another woman's name. She was surprised but realized I was right; she'd meant to say the first friend's name.

I, of course, was curious about the slip and we tried to analyze it. The second friend, it turned out, was a psychotherapist whose practice was in a building near mine. She reminded Annette of me. I wondered the obvious: could *I* be the one Annette was a little angry with? She became sad. This time the sadness wasn't momentary; she *stayed* sad. She hated the idea of being angry with me; she didn't want to be. However, we both noticed that she didn't say she wasn't.

Her thoughts returned to the first friend, the one I knew. Toward *that* friend she realized that she really was angry, angrier than she'd thought. That friend was smug, selfish, greedy. As we pursued these complaints I was reminded of my earliest meetings with Annette and what had happened with her complaints about her husband. Annette's sense of injury had been powerful but no complaint, once explicit, had quite stood up to scrutiny. Now it was the same, only this time in relation to her friend. Finally, resentfully, Annette commented that I probably didn't get a chance to see any of her friend's ugly traits in my dealings with her. When I saw her we probably just had a good time, working together on our joint projects. Her tone was bitter and for the first time her jealousy became apparent.

Now the interesting thing was, she'd never before expressed jealousy about my dealings with her friend. In fact, she'd always emphasized how she admired our work together, enjoyed hearing about it, and was glad I was doing it. However, one thing had changed. She was no longer hearing from her friend about what I did with the friend. She could no longer entertain the fantasy, conscious now for the first time, that by listening to her friend's accounts, she was part of everything the friend and I did together. In this context I learned something new. For all those months she had not merely listened, she had also made several unobtrusive suggestions to her friend about sources of funding for our organization, some of which the friend had actually pursued. So, in falling out with her friend, she had lost more than an opportunity to passively share in my outside life. She had also lost a form of active participation, a secret way of helping me and feeling needed by me.

As this became explicit, Annette's anger toward me reached

the surface. She was angry because she felt jealous, because she felt thwarted in her secret helpfulness to me, and most of all because she was bitterly disappointed at the disruption of what had been our happy and gratifying relationship. Her idealizations of me began to come under review, and what had seemed admirable about me now became grounds for criticism. My interest in anything outside psychoanalysis was a particular target, as Annette questioned whether I was sufficiently devoted to my profession, thereby to her and to what the two of us were doing together.

To be overly schematic about it, this material describes what in retrospect I would call negative oedipal transference. The relevant issues are obvious: idealization, longing to be specially loved, rivalry, jealousy, fantasies of being my secret partner, fantasies that she would be the one to give me what I needed, fury at feeling excluded, and so on. Certain of the feelings—idealization and longing—Annette readily associated with feelings toward her mother. Others, however, like jealousy and anger, had been pointedly absent from Annette's recollections, despite our having found frequent reason to speculate that such feelings toward her mother had existed. The crucial thing about her experiencing those feelings toward me was that they ceased to be the subject of conjecture. Annette vividly encountered how powerfully those feelings motivated her, as well as how effectively her idealizations functioned to prevent her from being conscious of things like jealousy and anger, things she did not want to feel. In her furious disappointment with me she recognized aspects of the furious disappointment with Joe which had initiated her analysis. Both of us had disappointed her as a certain kind of maternal equivalent. Neither of us was fulfilling the image from her dream: the woman with whom she could be blissfully pregnant. In short, both of us had disappointed her as negative oedipal objects. It was via these sorts of recognitions that Annette became slowly able to develop a meaningful picture of what she had longed for with her mother, how she had felt disappointed, and how that longing and disappointment continued to dominate many aspects of her life.

Finally, now, I want to return to where I started, and make a few general remarks concerning how the ways in which negative oedipal conflicts can affect certain women's experience of marriage and motherhood.

The negative Oedipus complex represents a normal phase of development for girls (boys too, though I won't go into that here). When the particular struggles of the negative oedipal phase are not satisfactorily negotiated, development proceeds but it bears the stamp of unresolved conflict. In particular, aspects of the child's *positive* oedipal wishes, wishes toward the opposite gender parent, may become drawn into attempts at settling what was unresolved in the negative oedipal phase.

This I believe describes what happened with Annette and bears on the question of how motherhood can sometimes affect marriage. Annette did not remain fixated at the negative oedipal level; she moved on to consolidate an interest in her father and a preference for heterosexuality. However, both that interest and that preference were significantly burdened by the extent to which they filled certain defensive functions for her, warding off still-active wishes and disappointments involving her mother.

So, when it came to choosing a husband, Annette's particular constellation of positive oedipal needs were not the only influences. Her choice was equally determined by her need to avoid negative oedipal conflict. She picked a man who, partly by being emphatically different from her mother, suited both sets of needs. And, as I described earlier, this compromise worked well—until she became pregnant.

I do not have the space here to go into the many meanings which becoming a mother had for Annette, but I do want to mention several ways that motherhood contributed to a reworking of her unconscious relationship to her own mother and, in the process, impinged on her relationship with her husband. First, the reality of having a baby triggered a revival of Annette's early fantasies in which her mother was the imagined partner, the one she most desired, and the one with whom she wanted to have that baby. To the extent that Joe had suited her because of how he *didn't* remind her of these fantasies, their revival challenged one of her reasons for choosing him. In fact, he turned into the wrong partner. (This brings up an interesting issue, by the way: the role of external reality in stimulating intrapsychic conflict and compromise formation. It is when reality challenges or conforms to crucial unconscious *fantasies* that it takes on special significance in reorganizing intrapsychic equilibrium. The reality of having a baby did have this special reorganizing significance for Annette, as, perhaps, it has for many women.)

In becoming a mother herself, previously threatening identifications with her own mother became acceptable and actually desirable. For the first time since before Annette's rather stormy adolescence, she found herself *wanting* to be like her mother. She increasingly recalled positive aspects of how she had felt about her mother during childhood. As Annette began to identify not just with the child in those recollections but with the figure of her mother as well, the regressive pull of those memories diminished, making them less dangerous and more accessible to consciousness. Again, traits of Joe's which had once reassuringly reinforced her wish to be different from her mother started to threaten rather than reassure.

Lastly, Annette's entry into motherhood signaled a major shift in her narcissistic valuation of herself. She had turned to her father and later to other men in part to escape from a sense of narcissistic injury which she felt she had experienced at her mother's hands. Her mother had left Annette when she'd gone to the sanitarium but, even more, her mother had ultimately preferred being partner to her husband, Annette's father, than to Annette. Annette was left feeling hurt and lacking in that sense of feminine competence which Sheldon Roth (1988) has described as a crucial outcome of a sufficiently gratifying negative oedipal phase. In having her own child, Annette's sense of narcissistic injury was significantly repaired and, to the extent that her interest in men represented a flight from feeling injured, that interest lost some of its prior function.

In all this, I have emphasized consequences of the fact that Annette's marriage served to defend against unresolved negative oedipal conflicts. I haven't talked at all about many other things; the way in which her marriage represented, for example, a triumph of positive oedipal wishes, nor have I spoken of the relation of preoedipal to negative oedipal strivings in Annette. Instead I have tried to demonstrate how the concept of intrapsychic conflict can be useful in understanding certain kinds of marital difficulties. Because marriage is an institution subject to so many varieties of stress, sociocultural and interpersonal as well as intrapsychic, I believe it is especially important that we engage our psychoanalytic skills in the difficult task of teasing out which of those stresses are primarily rooted in the intrapsychic realm. Conflict and compromise are concepts that can crucially elucidate our efforts in that direction.

Chapter 5

Technical Considerations in Treating Patients with Character Disorders

Ernest Kafka, M.D.

Nonpsychotic, nonorganic psychopathologies have generally been subdivided into symptomatic disorders and character disorders. In symptomatic disorders, the subject makes a self-diagnosis of psychopathology, often based on an estimation that painful affects such as anxiety, guilt, shame, or depressive feelings of low self-esteem are excessive, given the conditions under which they arise, and/or that they cause inhibitions of action. For instance, a person may conclude that the level of anxiety he experiences in anticipating an examination or an airplane trip is more severe than he can explain as proportional to the risk he judges to be associated with the activity that is feared, and that this contributes to a restriction of performance. Such patients wish to be relieved of specific complaints and are consciously motivated to seek help.

In character disorders, certain activities may feel impulsive to the subject. Other activities may fail to produce the conditions they are consciously intended to achieve, or may have unwelcome consequences. Sometimes people with such character structure seek therapy because they conclude they are failing to live up to their capacities, as when careers or social relationships do not advance satisfactorily. Sometimes they are induced to seek help by relatives, friends, teachers, or others, who persuade them that their behavior is getting them into trouble of one kind of another, or that they are not managing to live up to their potential for gratification or success.

Failed romantic attachments, difficulties in adapting to changing circumstances, or repeated, seemingly inexplicable unwanted responses on the part of offspring or authorities may induce such a person to seek consultation. Alternatively, this type of individual may need the advice of others in spite of having little or no understanding that he may be provoking the unwelcome social consequences and/or may be rejecting those he consciously wishes to attract. Often enough, such patients have no specific complaints, are uncertain that anything is wrong with them, or feel pushed into treatment by others. Given their uncertain motivation, introducing such patients to treatment often involves difficulties. The recommendation that the therapist should strive to make their ego syntonic but problematic behavior more ego alien is often difficult to follow.

The therapist knows that the two categories of patients—those with symptom disorders and those with character disorders—are not as dissimilar as they may seem on the surface. The therapist will understand that unconscious conflicts affect all manifestations of behavior, including thoughts and associated feelings and acts, and not only symptomatic expressions. He or she may well anticipate that the symptomatic patient who accepts treatment will soon discover he or she also has character problems, and that the patient who presents with character problems will soon discover symptomatic restrictions or avoidances.

In both types of presenting complaint, the therapist has the advantage of knowing that the symptoms and the behaviors the patient employs are manifestations of unconscious conflicts that might be more successfully resolved if they could be revealed to the patient and better understood. The task is to discover and help the patient understand her or his unconscious conflicts and their unwanted, as well as useful, effects. It behooves the therapist to be attuned to signs of unconscious conflict.

Signs of unconscious conflict are many, though often subtle. They include slips of the tongue, dreams, embarrassments, hesitations and suppressions in talking of certain matters, pressured speech or impulsive acts, signs of the irrational in symptoms, seemingly inexplicable painful affects, transference prejudgments, and other evidences. Demonstrating such signs to the patient may lead the patient to the understanding of how unconscious wishes, fears, and defenses enter into unconscious conflicts and affect everyday behavior.

In people with character disorders, symptomatic evidences are absent or subtle and may be difficult to demonstrate. However, one phenomenon on the border between symptomatic and seemingly reasonable behavior, that is to say, transference distortion, is ubiquitous. Every patient has a variant of the symptomatic in the transference attitude. This may involve, among other possible attitudes, fear, unusual admiration, curiosity, or embarrassment. The patient may regard the therapist as having no emotional life.

Patients' theories and feelings are reflected in their behaviors toward treatment and the therapist, and reveal irrational prejudgments. Often enough, patients can see that their attitudes are irrational. They can accept that the treatment situation is not actually as frightening as they think, or as potentially gratifying as they wish, and this realization can help them accept the fact that they are profoundly influenced by unconscious factors. If parallels between transferences and behaviors in ordinary life can be demonstrated to exist, patients with character disorders are likely to become more motivated to understand their unconscious mentation, and to accept the labor and discomfort this pursuit occasions. Careful attention to and tactful interpretation of transference distortions can go a long way toward helping patients with character disorders become more aware of their fears and avoidances, and helps them recognize the unconscious, often undesirable gratifications their behavior affords them.

Two clinical illustrations follow. In both cases, the material is disguised to preserve confidentiality, and selected and abstracted for the sake of focusing on the point to be illustrated, that is to say, that careful demonstration of the paradoxical and prejudgmental elements revealed through transference manifestations is a particularly valuable tool in the treatment of patients with character problems, whose conscious motivation for treatment is not great.

Clinical Illustration 1

The patient was a professional woman in her early forties. She had been involved for eight years in a relationship with a man ten years her junior. This had begun shortly after her divorce from her husband, whom she married at age twenty-four while in graduate school. The marriage had been amicable but not passionate, although the sexual aspects were described as satisfying. The patient believed she was eager to have a family. However, the husband steadfastly refused to have children. He claimed that his experience as a child of divorced parents had convinced him that having a family would be undesirable for him, and he preferred to devote his energy to his professional life, which required a great deal of travel, and which he found sufficiently gratifying. At thirty-five, the patient reached the decision that her wish to have a family and a closer relationship with a man meant that she would have to look elsewhere, and the couple divorced as a consequence of that conclusion.

The patient soon became involved with her current companion, who was a junior in her office when they met, and who had, in the intervening time, achieved approximately her own level of responsibility. This man had been importuning her to marry him for several years, but the patient seemed unable to make up her mind. She wondered whether he might be too young, or whether she loved him as much as he loved her, or whether having a child with him might be a mistake. She had discussed her inability to make up her mind with the man, and with various friends, and they had persuaded her to try professional help. However, she was unconvinced that anything was wrong with her.

After explaining her situation in the early interviews, the patient went on to complain that one reason why she thought treatment would be unlikely to help, beyond the fact that there was really nothing wrong with her, was that she thought that the conditions of treatment were unfair and degrading. She objected to the idea that she would have to pay for missed sessions even if her absence were to be caused by illnesses or work responsibilities. She could not understand why the therapist had the right to select the time for his vacation, while, if she took time off, she would both miss her appointments and have to pay for them. She objected to the notion that the appointment schedule could not be easily altered.

I responded that, certainly, embarking on treatment meant that she would have to make certain concessions, but that the advantages might be worth the trouble. As to fees, missed appointments would have to be paid for only if the hours could not be filled, and I would try to be as flexible as possible about making up hours or changing them if she could provide reasonable advance notice. Somewhat mollified, the patient agreed to try, and a three-times-a-week schedule began.

The patient then proceeded to describe the history of her development. She was the older of two children, having a brother five years younger. Her parents were both in their midthirties when they married. Her mother, a nurse, gave up work when she became pregnant shortly after her marriage, but often complained about having no career. Both parents were eager to have children and they were delighted when the patient was born, though it turned out that both would have preferred a boy. In the event, repeated attempts at another pregnancy soon followed, but, when the patient reached puberty, and discussions about sexuality and pregnancy came to take place, she learned that conception had been difficult for her mother, and that several miscarriages had occurred before a brother was conceived, and born.

The patient claimed to have no memory of her mother's pregnancy, or of the birth of the eagerly desired son, but a later story was that she was disappointed that the baby was a boy, rather than a girl who would be a better playmate. Her memory of her relationship with her brother in childhood revolved mainly around instances when she felt she had to make concessions to him, such as baby-sitting in her early teens, when she would have preferred more freedom, or tutoring him in

school subjects, or having to attend his performances as a Little
League ballplayer.

I asked whether her feeling of being put-upon and having to
make concessions in relation to therapy resembled her feelings
about having had to be too accommodating in relation to
her brother.

The patient responded that she felt burdened then and now
when she was unfairly restricted, but that any other similarity was
coincidental. She went on to describe her current romantic
relationship as involving similar restrictions about which she also
felt resentful. Her companion had been more cooperative in the
past, but since he had been awarded a series of promotions, he
had demanded more and more concessions from her on the
ground that he had to work late and travel for business; therefore,
he often could not take an equal share of the domestic duties. I
commented that her lover, like her brother and me, seemed to
her to demand excessive concessions. She agreed, and added
that her evaluations at work generally reflected still another arena
in which excessive demands were made on her. She was usually
congratulated on her effectiveness but she was also informed that
her unwillingness to take on responsibility, which she usually
thought of as an unwillingness to be exploited, stood in the way of
her advancement.

She responded to my remark that the work situation was
evidently yet another setting in which she thought excessive
demands were made, by telling me that my comment only proved
her point, inasmuch as I evidently thought her unreasonable,
and wanted to add my critical voice to those of others. She added
that now, having experienced two months of treatment with no
benefit, she was planning to stop coming, especially since a vacation she had planned before starting with me was coming up, and
she had no intention of paying for the time.

I expressed surprise that she had not mentioned this plan
before. The patient said she thought there would have been no
point in doing so. She had had to pay for her trip in advance,
and couldn't change her time off from her job because the
whole thing had been arranged months before. I pointed out
that she seemed to be making an assumption about my attitude.
Did she believe I would demand that she revise an unrevisable

arrangement she had made before starting treatment? Indeed she did, she said. If she had been mistaken, she would continue the treatment.

Other examples of mistaken prejudgments appeared. In one instance, the patient alluded to having received a promotion months after the event, and when I expressed surprise that she had not mentioned this earlier, the patient maintained that I was interested only in problems, not in successes. I replied that her belief that I was only interested in problems might well reflect the fact that she insisted on relating to me according to the view that I am a domineering, demanding person, despite the absence of supporting evidence to that effect.

At another point, she expressed reluctance to discuss a worry about a friend's health, this time on the ground that I expected her to be strong and uncomplaining. I noted that she seemed to believe I wanted to hear neither about success nor about worries, and that this made me wonder what she thought might be my interest in doing my work?

The patient benefited by the demonstration that her theories about therapy, and about what she anticipated about the therapist's attitudes, might be based on preconceptions, and that they seemed somewhat refractory to revision. She realized that her experience of the treatment was incorrect, and also that this discovery seemed not to modify her ideas and feelings about treatment significantly.

However, the conviction that her attitude in treatment was irrational did lead to her accepting that she evinced certain character traits. They included a defensive attitude that seemed to make learning and adaptation difficult, and a naive childlike stance in relation to putative powerful adults, of whom the analyst seemed to be one, who could confer wealth and other power, but who were demanding and depreciating. In many ways, she could see, this combination of defensive, yet childlike character traits represented her experience as the resentful, covertly rebellious older sister who wished to resist her parents' desire that she defer to her younger brother's needs, while, at the same time, she wished to occupy the indulged brother's preferred place.

While these conclusions had little effect on her behavior, they

did influence her in the sense that she became convinced that her
romantic and professional life were both restricted because of
inner factors, and she entered analysis. Analytic work revealed
much about this woman's underlying conflicts. For example, it
became apparent that her reluctance to marry had to do with her
fear and guilt about her competitive wishes, originally relating to
her younger brother, but now directed toward the younger
brother substitute, her lover, and toward the potential infant.
The character trait of being childlike and put-upon served both
as a defense against feared enactment of her incestuous and competitive sibling wishes, and as a punishment for them, and it also
allowed for a certain gratification of her hostile, negativistic,
ultimately murderous desires.

Her selection of her first husband now appeared to have served
her unconscious wishes to avoid the possibility of gratifying her
hostile wishes toward a child, who represented both an envied
boy competitor and a sibling rival. She had used her husband's
attitude as a way of avoiding awareness of her own phobic
attitude. She could blame him and feel morally superior, while
feeling put upon, a degree of discomfort that assuaged her
unconscious guilt over her equally unconscious rivalrous sexual
wishes and hostile inclinations toward male brother representatives. Continuing analysis led to the further understanding of
some of her phobic attitudes, and to a lessening of their influence
on her.

Clinical Illustration 2

The patient was a thirty-two-year-old man who came for consultation because of depression that followed a failed romance.
He was worried that he might never be able to form a permanent
relationship. He had had both homosexual and heterosexual
relations since adolescence. None of these had endured for more
than a few months until a romance developed with a woman
coworker a year earlier. An intermittent sexual relation with this
woman had gone on for six months. Even though he had to fan-
tasize a large penis to maintain his potency, he felt reassured by
this relationship since he hoped he would be able to marry and

have a family. However, the woman broke off with him and began to see another man, a superior at work. This precipitated depressed feelings and led to the consultation.

The patient's manner and his description of himself led to the conclusion that he presented the picture of an apprentice. He acted compliant and respectful in the interview. He presented what seemed to be a coherent and full history. His response to questions was cooperative. He was humorous and even entertaining.

He said he would accept any recommendation I made and was prepared to borrow in order to pay whatever my fee might be. He would try to arrange to adapt to my schedule. He was eager to solve his problem. However, he could say little about what he thought his problem might be. He realized there must be something about him that disappointed people; perhaps it was his lack of sustained sexual interest.

The history he presented over a period of some months was as follows. The patient was the younger, by three years, of two brothers. The elder brother suffered from an impulsive behavior disturbance connected with birth anoxia, and had often attacked and hurt the patient throughout early childhood. The patient's father worked for a corporation which frequently moved him from place to place, so that the patient rarely lived in the same community or attended the same school for more than two years, until he was sent to boarding school when he was fourteen. The mother was a painter who spent most of her days at her studio, where she could not be interrupted, leaving most of the care of the children to maids.

The patient professed to believe that he had had a very fortunate childhood, and was lucky to have a gifted mother, through whom he was exposed to culture, and a successful father, who was able to supply all the necessaries and many of the luxuries of life. Further, the patient thought that the brother's difficulties were well handled by his parents, who seemed to devote much attention and money to him, constantly being involved with tutors, therapists, and daily problems.

The only period of unhappiness he recalled was when he went away to boarding school, where he felt extremely lonely and homesick for his mother, whom he had adored. He developed insomnia and gastrointestinal pains. However, he attached himself to an older boy, who introduced him to mutual masturbation and fellatio, and occasionally performed anal intercourse upon the patient, all of which the patient accepted without great enthusiasm, but gratefully, given the fact that the older boy was protective and seemed to care for him. After this boy left the school, the patient become involved in transitory homosexual relationships, mainly with older boys or men, but occasionally, he took what he called the big brother role.

Analysis was undertaken. As the months passed, it became gradually evident that the patient's attitude in the analysis, while polite, correct, and generally cooperative, was also tepid. The patient seemed emotionally uninvolved. Hints that similar attitudes also manifested themselves at work and in his social relationships appeared. For instance, after a party at which a woman seemed attracted to him, the patient dreamed he was a space explorer, far removed from earth. I suggested the interpretation that he seemed to remove himself from human contact in the dream. This was followed by the patient's picking up a homosexual partner for a sexual fling, which I again interpreted as an effort to present himself as independent in the sense of not needing others. Perhaps, I ventured, he had never surmounted his disappointment and anger at his mother, who, he might well have thought, had betrayed and abandoned him when he reached adolescence.

This line of interpretation seemed to have no effect. The patient continued to deal with me in a polite, but mechanical way. As the evidence mounted that the patient was not simply aloof but regarded me as simply a mechanical person, as a kind of robot who would teach him how to live, I could point out how he dehumanized me, and that this attitude toward me was quite critical and angry. This seemed more meaningful to him, and had the consequence that he became aware that he had other views of his parents, and particularly of his mother, besides the cursory idealizing cliches of which he had been consciously aware. He remembered angry and critical thoughts and sadistic wishes toward women, whom he had wanted to seduce, dominate, and abandon, as he had felt treated by his mother.

The patient began to report feeling tearful at the movies, especially over scenes of reunions between children and parent figures, but the attitude he displayed in the analysis altered very little.

In the second year of the analysis, I pointed out to the patient that he displayed no curiosity about me when I made unusual changes; for example, when I canceled or changed scheduled appointments. I reminded him that, by contrast, comparable events in other relationships invariably gave rise to lengthy suppositions, anger, disappointment, and curiosity. He had expressed concern about his parents' health when both had had rather severe upper respiratory infections, but had made no comment when I had displayed the signs of a cold and subsequently canceled several hours. He failed to inform me about an important matter he was engaged in at work until some time later, and when I called this delay to his attention, he lamely explained that he thought I would not be interested. Gradually, it became possible to show him that he maintained an aloofness that might well invite an aloof response in his social and work circumstances, and that this attitude was covertly critical and rejecting of me.

In the third year of the analysis, the patient seemed to respond to my announcement of a vacation by seductively exposing himself in the men's room on his office floor. This was a rather risky behavior given the attitude about homosexuality he thought was prevalent at his office, but he also clearly wondered what my sexual response to him might be. My suggestion was that this behavior might indicate that he did not wish me to leave and wished both to seduce me and to threaten that he might behave even more dangerously in my absence in order to provoke my guilt. He now revealed past fantasies of being dead, so that his mother would be overcome with grief and guilt over having neglected him.

The patient then had a dream in which his brother had an accident in which he lost a finger, and then, fantasies of forcing anal intercourse on me, which took him by surprise, occasioned when I kept him waiting for a few moments. That he wished to control me, to seduce me, and disappoint me and that both sexual and vengeful wishes had been concealed and at the same time gratified by the compliant, apprentice behavior that was designed to enlist me as his prisoner–helper older brother and mother, became clearer and could be more convincingly demonstrated. As a consequence, the patient's emotionality intensified. He came to experience feelings of love, anger, and fears of punishment. Concurrently, his reports of his work life and of his relationships, including his relationship with his family, revealed that he had come to behave in a much more original, independent, assertive, and generally gratifying way.

Conclusion

Both these patients illustrate a not infrequent presenting picture and evolution during the course of therapy. Both entered treatment with little conscious understanding that character traits they believed to be reasonable and logical gratified unconscious sexual and aggressive wishes, unconscious self-restrictions, and unconscious self-punitive trends. Neither patient consciously experienced behavior that they estimated to be irrational, noticed symptomatic limitations, or felt unexplained painful affects. In both cases, irrational elements in their expectations about treatment, and in their attitudes toward the therapist became evident. These transference attitudes, mixtures of behavioral, affective, and ideational contents, and parallels between transference manifestations and behavior outside the treatment situation could be discussed over the course of time. With diligent effort, the evidence these revelations brought forward led to the appearance of signs of unconscious conflict in symptomatic expressions as well as to a sense of conviction and understanding of the unconscious conflicts the behaviors represented. Gradually, more adaptive resolutions of their unconscious conflicts could then be achieved.

Chapter 6

Working with Conflict and Deficit in Borderline and Narcissistic Patients

Martin S. Willick, M.D.

There is a general consensus among psychoanalytically oriented clinicians that the diagnosis of borderline personality disorder refers to a heterogeneous group of illnesses. According to the psychoanalytic concept, these patients are sicker than patients we classify as neurotic, but are not as disturbed as patients who fit into the various categories of psychosis. This definition of borderline personality disorder in terms of severity is in contrast to the one put forward in DSM-III where the syndrome is defined by its descriptive aspects only (APA, 1980). The framers of that diagnostic manual preferred to remain atheoretical in regard to the pathogenesis of most mental disorders because they felt that by confining themselves to descriptive features they could achieve greater consensual validation regarding diagnoses. The descriptive features listed for borderline personality include impulsive behavior, lack of control of anger and/or intense anger, impaired object relations, volatile mood swings, disturbances in the sense of self and identity, separation anxiety, and feelings of emptiness.

The psychoanalytic definition likewise emphasizes these phenomenological features, but also includes, in contrast to the view put forward in DSM-III, some considerations of the developmental level of the pathology. Although there is not firm agreement among psychoanalysts about the etiology and pathogenesis of the borderline group of disorders, most feel that the roots of borderline pathology lie in impairments in development during the second and third years of life, prior to the consolidation of object constancy.

In regard to the narcissistic character disorders, the DSM-III and the psychoanalytic descriptions of the manifest syndrome are also similar, but once again, most psychoanalysts who are interested in studying these disorders consider that the etiology is rooted in early impairments in the development of the cohesiveness of the self.

In addition to tracing the significant impairments in development in borderline and narcissistic conditions to the first two or three years of life, object relations theorists have contributed significantly to the understanding of borderline patients. Self psychologists have also contributed to this area, and have directed their attention also to the study of the narcissistic disturbances. Both believe that these early impairments lead to ego defects or ego deficits, some of which are conceptualized as occurring independent of conflict involving the sexual and aggressive drives. These ego defects are often thought of as involving impairments in the formation of psychic structure prior to the structuralization of the ego when instinctual conflicts are considered to be exerting their most profound effects.

In discussing the concept of ego defects or deficits, we are faced with an immediate problem; it is not easy to say exactly what we mean by the terms. For instance, it is easy to say that someone who is born blind has an innate defect in visual perception, or that someone with Down's syndrome has a cognitive defect. There are also cognitive ego deficits that are acquired due to organic illnesses such as Alzheimer's or Parkinson's disease. Although the concept of defect or deficit may not be adequate to describe the impairments in schizophrenia and bipolar illness, most thoughtful clinicians recognize that there are profound biological abnormalities that cause ego defects in these conditions as well.

However, when psychoanalysts discuss ego defects in borderline and narcissistic patients, they are usually referring to deficits that arise from impairments in psychological development rather than innate deficiencies or organic illnesses (see Meissner [1978] for a review of the ego defects found in borderline patients). For example, the following statements have been made about borderline and narcissistic patients: that they have not achieved object constancy; or that they have defective or pathological internalized object relations; or that they do not have a stable or cohesive sense of self; or that they cannot adequately soothe or comfort themselves; or that they need constant narcissistic supplies to bolster a defective sense of self-esteem. Some analysts believe that such deficiencies in ego functions are unrelated to the sexual and aggressive conflicts seen in neurotic patients. They claim that the roots of the problem are failures in the capacity of the mother to nurture or empathize with the infant, causing basic defects in crucial internalization processes. Although these analysts also acknowledge that borderline and narcissistic patients have significant intrapsychic conflict as well, they believe that the structural deficits are primary, with conflict superimposed on these primary ego deficits. Other analysts, like myself, believe that it is very difficult when trying to understand the pathogenesis of borderline and narcissistic conditions, to separate ego impairments which are the result of psychic conflict from those that have arisen apart from conflict and have to do with basic structure formation.

Since our understanding of the etiology and pathogenesis of any illness governs our therapeutic endeavors and strategies, these considerations about conflicts and deficits arise in any discussion about the therapeutic technique used in dealing with borderline and narcissistic patients. Those analysts who believe ego defects arise apart from conflict advocate a different psychoanalytic or psychotherapeutic technique in treating pathology involving ego defects in contrast to pathology caused by intrapsychic conflict.

Killingmo (1989), for example, believes, following the self psychologists, that more disturbed patients develop self–object transferences rather than object transferences, and therefore require a different type of therapeutic strategy. He maintains that for the patient dealing with conflict, it is the analyst's task to

unveil or reveal repressed meaning; for the patient with structural deficit, it is the analyst's task to assist the ego in experiencing
meaning, or to establish meaning. This latter task requires the
analyst to offer "correction and separation of distorted or dif-
fused self–object representations . . . and to bring about structuralization of aspects of object relations which has not been
accomplished in previous development" (p. 67). Although
Killingmo acknowledges that conflicts develop after the onset of
deficits and are often a consequence of them, he believes it is
important to try to differentiate the two.

Case Illustration

Rather than addressing this important issue in the abstract, I will
discuss the psychoanalytically oriented treatment of a borderline
case with narcissistic features to demonstrate another way to
work with and conceptualize the problem of ego deficit and psychic conflict.

The patient, whom I will call Carol, was twenty-seven when
she came to see me for a consultation because her parents, who
had had psychotherapy themselves, were distressed that her
treatment with another analyst was not going well. It was difficult
for her to tell me if she thought it was going well, and she reported
that she was very influenced by her parents' opinion.

Despite her inability or reluctance to express her own
opinions, I did manage to learn the following from her in the
initial consultations: she had been in a four times weekly treatment on the couch for about one year. Most of the sessions were
filled with silence, which often lasted forty minutes at a time. She
could not respond to the analyst's questions about what she was
thinking. She was not sure that she had learned anything about
herself, but she had developed a profound attachment to her
analyst, missing him on weekends, often coming early to her
sessions just to be able to sit in his waiting room, and wanting to
drive to his summer vacation home to be near him. Despite the
intensity of her feelings, she could not discuss them with him.

Responding mostly to my questions, Carol told me that she
had entered treatment because she had become depressed upon

returning to her parents' home with her two children after her divorce. She felt that her parents were angry at her and that her mother did not want to take care of the grandchildren while Carol worked. She had originally seen the analyst while in college because she had many doubts about her husband to be. Her treatment at that time was conducted three times a week and lasted for two years until she married.

Her marital choice did prove to be a poor one. Her husband, who overworked and was rarely home, was alternately a tyrant and a clinging child. He dominated her and she responded to him like an obedient slave. After a number of years she left him, returning home with her children, fearing that she was a terrible mother. Her four-year-old son already had significant separation anxiety and was very negativistic, and the two-year-old daughter was excessively shy and lagged behind in development. Carol had no friends and was chronically anxious. She felt that she could not talk to people because she did not have anything to say, and saw herself as having no genuine values in life. It was only during the second session that I learned that she had been adopted. Although her analyst knew this fact, she had never been able to speak to him about it. She had a brother, who was a natural child of her parents, who was three years younger than she.

The reason she returned to her analyst six years later, despite a not very satisfactory previous treatment with him, was that he had not forgotten her. When she called and asked if he remembered her, and he replied that of course he did, she knew that she would return to him. Now, however, she had some doubts about what she was gaining from her treatment and therefore consented to come for the consultation with me.

I felt that she was too attached to her therapist to leave him, and, indeed, she never expressed a wish to do so. It was only later that I realized that, here, as elsewhere, she never expressed her own wishes and always looked to others to tell her what to do. It was also only later that I realized that she wanted me to tell her that I wanted to treat her. This is a theme that was to recur throughout the treatment.

I told Carol that it would be very difficult for her to leave her analyst and that she should try to talk to him about her feelings toward him and what she understood about her treatment. Much to my surprise, she called me later and asked for a third session, during which she told me she had decided to leave her analyst and to see me. She now admitted that she felt she really wasn't getting anywhere but had been afraid to leave him. Since she had never told me why she wanted to be in treatment, I asked her, and this question took her aback. It was as though she just wanted to be with someone to take care of her. Finally she said that she wanted to be a better mother and to overcome her fears of being with and speaking to people.

I believed that she was withholding a great deal. Rather than being devoid of meaningful thoughts and fantasies, there were many things about which she was aware but could not discuss. I also believed that I could not succeed with her by being silent and waiting for her to talk. I was prepared and determined to be actively engaged with her if she could not speak more easily to me.

Two technical issues arose immediately. One was that the patient was unable, or I should say unwilling, to start the session by speaking first. Although I will discuss this important phenomenon later, suffice it to say now that for the first four years of treatment I started each session. Another dilemma was the patient's request to use the couch. I had felt that this was an error on the part of the previous analyst because patients like Carol usually cannot bear the lack of face-to-face contact. She, however, said that she could not talk to me while I was looking at her. It made her too uncomfortable. She could go no further with an explanation. I decided to proceed as she wished. She has been on the couch four, or at times when scheduling problems occurred, three times a week, for six years. I am still not sure about the nature of her difficulties in being looked at, although certainly they have to do with fears that I will be able to see something about her body that she herself is not aware of and that she will then be mortified.

Carol developed an immediate, intense transference attachment to me, which is not unusual for a borderline patient. Within three weeks of starting treatment, she began to experience painful separation feelings on the weekends. During these times she felt that I did not exist. She said, "I cannot picture your face or remember what you are like. You cease to exist for me."

Because of her distress, she would drive past my office (which is in my home) during the weekend to maintain some contact. Although distressed, she was not in a panic as some borderline patients are with separation. She also found it hard to believe that she could not remember me, though she remembered me well enough to know where my office was. Therefore, the expression "you no longer exist for me" represented a complex mental phenomenon.

I would like to use my patient's subjective experience and my handling of it to illustrate the importance of maintaining a dynamic point of view in the face of what might appear to be an ego deficit. Many analysts have written about the phenomenon in which the borderline patient cannot sustain an image of the therapist or any other needed object in the face of separation. It can be considered to be a failure in the development of object constancy or, as Gerald Adler (1985) conceptualizes it, a failure in the capacity to maintain evocative memory. Adler believes that borderline patients have a developmental defect which interferes with their capacity to retain the image of the object when the object is not present. He traces its roots back to the first few years of life, to a failure on the part of the child to develop the necessary soothing introjects which would otherwise sustain it during separation. He believes the child cannot retain the image of the "good" mother because it has an insufficient reservoir of internalized good experiences with her.

This "defect" is usually conceptualized as being unrelated to conflicts involving the drives, but, rather, is thought to be due to a basic insufficiency in the mental representation of the self, caused by various failures on the part of the caretaking person. The clinical description of the phenomenon is generally agreed upon. To variable degrees, these patients cannot sustain the image of the analyst. I do not necessarily quarrel with the idea that this is a developmental defect, as long as it is understood that such "defects" can arise from conflicts and can be altered in therapy by insight and working through. The danger in conceptualizing this impairment as a defect is that it may lead to the therapist's reluctance to make interpretations of conflict or lead them to relate the phenomena entirely to failures on the part of the mother during the first year or two of life.

When my patient began to describe her experiences, I already knew that she defended herself against painful affects as much as possible. She frequently wanted to be by herself when someone disappointed her; at other times, she desperately needed to be with the object of her need. Since I felt that the patient was defending herself against even more painful feelings, I said to her, "One of the reasons that you cannot remember me is that if you could you might feel terrible longing and would feel more bereft that I am not with you on the weekends." Although she did not immediately respond, I learned later that my interpretation made an impression on her. Such interpretations are useful for many borderline patients because they show patients how some forms of their distress or symptoms can be understood in terms of wishes, fears, and defenses.

A few months later the feeling that I did not exist on the weekends took on a somewhat different quality and I said to the patient, "I believe you are angry with me that I do not see you on the weekend and you try to get rid of me and get me out of your life and mind." This interpretation was directed both at her self-protective attempts and her anger.

In the third year of treatment, well after these distressing separation experiences had begun to wane (she now tolerated weekend separations and vacations much better) she was able to articulate more fully what this experience was like for her. She said, "If you're not with me, I feel I never had you. It's like you never existed for me and with me. I then feel like I made you up and that you are really with someone else!" I responded, "It sounds as though your feeling now is like a profound feeling of jealousy." She answered, "It always was!" It was only in the fourth year of treatment that she was able to tell me that she really wanted me to sit in the office twenty-four hours a day, waiting for her only, and that she did not want me to have other patients or family.

What she also was experiencing during these weekends of the first year when I "did not exist" for her, was that she wished that I had never existed. She deeply regretted having allowed me into her life so that she would need me; better that I had never existed. This theme was to come up over and over again as she started to date during the third year of treatment. Every disappointment brought with it the feeling that she had been a fool to hope that someone would really want her.

If you work as a therapist for a long enough time with these patients, experiences which may seem like ego deficits at the beginning of treatment turn out to be quite complicated symptoms partaking of conflicts from many levels of development and not solely those of early infancy. If the failure to sustain an image of the object is seen only as a developmental defect, interpretations of meanings, motivations, and emotions are more likely to be neglected. A therapist is much more likely to say something like this, "You cannot retain me in your mind because your mother never made you feel she was emotionally available to you and you could not gradually build up the idea that she would be there for you even when she left the room or left the house or went away for the weekend." Later on one would add, "Because of this you did not build up inside yourself the capacity to soothe yourself or to calm yourself. You are totally dependent on someone else to soothe you or you try desperately to do it through your acting-out behavior."

These words may well describe some aspect of the truth about the patient's development. But I believe one should be very cautious in ascribing pathology to defects which derive from the very early months of life. First, it may very well be inaccurate, and it is certainly information that we cannot really obtain from our treatment method except by speculative reconstructions. Second, it will lead to an inhibition of the understanding of the role of conflict in causing the particular defect which one is addressing. Most conflicts, as in this patient, are derived not only from preoedipal issues but also from later issues of sibling rivalry and romantic jealousy. What one gradually comes to understand about such symptoms is that they are elaborate compromise formations derived from the instinctual drives or wishes, defense mechanisms, and superego components. Furthermore, all of these aspects of the compromise formations are, in themselves, attempts at solutions to conflict and have a particular personal history involving the patient and his or her parents and siblings.

I will mention another aspect of this patient's difficulty in maintaining a concept of me as a supportive and reliable person. All during the first year or so, she would periodically return to visit her first analyst, always without telling me in advance. She did so at every juncture in our work when she felt that I did not want her, did not accept her as she was, made demands on her for cooperation, and whenever she felt insecure about my commitment to her. At the end of the initial consultation, when I agreed to treat her, I told her that it sounded as though she mainly wanted to be in her analyst's office and did not feel that she had to do any psychological work to understand herself. She acknowledged that this was the case, and said she was prepared to try. After a few months, however, I confronted her with the fact that she hardly volunteered any information or gave any indication of having thought about what I said to her. She did not respond but after the session called her previous analyst and went to see him. She told him nothing of what had transpired to make her call him, but was content to just be with him and to know that he would see her no matter what she did.

Anything which threatened our relationship made her want to run back to her previous analyst, despite her awareness that the therapy had been unsatisfactory. She felt he was totally accepting whereas I required her to think about herself. She really did not want to see him, but wanted to make sure she could always go back home to him after I gave her up. If he answered the phone she had a hard time telling him she just wanted to make sure he was there. He would always tell her to come and see him, and even when she no longer needed to do so, she would go. The reason was that "HE WANTED TO SEE ME."

She often presented herself as a victim needing to comply and incapable of protesting, but it frequently turned out that she was secretly gratified by the person's demands on her. For example, at one point when she and her former husband were arguing about his visiting rights, he insisted on staying in her apartment after the children were put to sleep and, by dint of his persistence and persuasion, forced her to have sex that evening. Her insistence that she couldn't refuse or fight back concealed her not-so-unconscious wish that he still desire her. Actually, it was this feeling that had made her marry him despite her better judgment. She believed that no one would ever want her. Not only did he want to marry her, but his family seemed to like her as well. Although I will return later to the issue of her having been adopted, the many ways in which the meaning of this fact influenced her emotional life are clearly apparent in this narrative.

I would like now to turn to another issue of technique with such disturbed patients that is relevant in any discussion of ego deficits. I have mentioned that the patient never initiated a session but waited for me to do so. Since I have emphasized how important it is to interpret to the patient the conflicts which underlie the behavior, how is it that I permitted myself to be supportive in this way? Isn't this really acknowledging the presence of an ego defect by doing something for the patient that she cannot do for herself? Is it not legitimate to infer that she needed me to provide something which her adoptive mother could not and which led to a defect in her own ego functioning? First, let me say that despite starting each session, I always made the issue of her not being able to speak first a topic for our investigation. What guided me in the conviction that I had to begin each session was not some preconceived idea that I had to provide a "holding" environment, or that my spoken word was to function like a "transitional object" for her, or that she needed to use me as a "self-object." I did so because of my initial experience with her and my awareness of the lack of success of her previous treatment during which her analyst was often silent. She could not or would not speak first. It was our task to find out why this inhibition, or, if you will, this motivated behavior, was part of her personality and her mode of relating to people. I was willing to do what I could to facilitate the treatment process without necessarily understanding what this behavior meant.

I realized early on that this patient could not and would not ask for any help. From the very first, I told her that the reason she could not start the session was that if she started, it would mean that she was requesting something from me—that I would listen, that I would be interested, that she wanted me to help her. She was unwilling to take the risk of asking for those things from me because my answer might be no. She had initially told me a memory of early childhood, without linking it with anything meaningful in her current life. When she was about five years old she cut her chin while playing in the garage. It started to bleed, but she would not go in to ask her mother for her help or comfort. When she finally went into the house, she desperately wanted her mother to notice. She kept leaving her mother "clues," but her mother did not realize what had happened.

I was to use this story as a paradigm of the patient's relationship to me and to others. It did not matter to me how absolutely accurate this memory was. I was careful not to conclude that her mother had failed her in times of need, although from other things she said, we might presume this to be the case. I began to tell her that at the beginning of each session she wanted me to figure out what was bothering her, or how she had reacted to our last session, without having to tell me herself. She left "clues"; if I really cared about her, I would realize what they were.

I continued to initiate each session, sometimes with a question, sometimes with an extended greeting, and sometimes with an attempted interpretation of why she wanted me to begin the session. Gradually, other wishes and fantasies began to emerge, either from my own guesses or from her finally telling me what she was thinking. She wanted to be sure that I remembered her from the day before; she wanted to know that I remembered what we had talked about; she wanted me to ask her what happened on the date she had the night before; she wanted me to tell her what it was that was important to talk about so that she wouldn't start with something that didn't interest me.

For the past two years, she has been more willing to begin the sessions herself. I had spent a great deal of time translating the patient's expression, "I can't start the session," into "I do not want to start the session." We have also been able to start to deal with her withholding and her coerciveness. She knew if she were silent, I would speak first; she wanted to force me to speak so that she could be reassured that I cared about her; it also gave her a feeling of power over me. All of these issues had to be explored in the context of other aspects of her life.

Did Carol's inability to start each session represent a defect which necessitated an alteration in my usual technique? My feeling is that it is not helpful to see it as a defect. An alteration of my usual technique it certainly was, but I do not conclude that I am giving the patient what her mother had been unable to give her. I alter the technique because, for the time being, it is apparent to me that this is necessary in order to conduct the treatment. I hope to be able to learn more about why this was necessary for her. For now, I consider her need to be a manifestation of a number of different wishes, fears, and defenses, which I have enumerated, although I do not presume to know them all. The patient still has some difficulty in beginning a session, and if I try to wait and sit out her silence, it does not, as yet, lead to something productive. Perhaps at some later time that battle will have to be engaged.

One of Carol's most persistent transference feelings went something like this: she was convinced that I was sorry that I had taken her on as a patient. She was a burden: she had frequently caused me to change hours to accommodate her; she was a bad patient who not only could not start the sessions but talked very little, could not be entirely honest, and was really unable to freely tell me her thoughts. She felt that if I had known what she was really like, I never would have taken her on as a patient. As a doctor I was obligated to treat her, but as a person I really would not want to be involved with her.

She slowly realized that these feelings were not much different from those that she had toward her mother. She knew nothing about her natural mother and did not want to know. But she believed she would never have been adopted had her mother known what sort of little girl she was getting and that her mother regretted ever having adopted her. Why did she think this? She felt she had been a shy and unattractive child who hid behind her mother's skirts, and a bother to her mother because she was frequently sick and irritable. She thought later that nothing she did pleased either of her parents.

It is clear what a profound issue her being adopted was for Carol. I have shown how she would do anything in order to be wanted. Although Carol initially never spoke freely about the fantasies surrounding her adoption, as I brought them to her attention in a meaningful way she was able to acknowledge their importance to her. But, as important as such fantasies are in the life of every adopted child, we would place more emphasis on the mother who raised her. A child's fantasies about being adopted are derived primarily from experiences and conflicts which took place with the adoptive parents. What kind of mother left Carol with such uncertainty about her basic security?

As the treatment progressed, I learned, especially through its reliving in the transference, that the patient felt that her mother really did not pay sufficient attention to her. Carol remembered coming home from school and wanting to talk, but her mother was always on the phone and refused to get off. After a while,

Carol stopped asking and began to leave her "clues." She felt that her mother really did not remember important things about her—things that she should remember if she really cared about her. In her adult life, whenever someone showed that they remembered something she said or did, she was enormously grateful, although she could not verbalize her gratitude. She also wanted people to know what was troubling her without her telling them; they should anticipate her needs without her having to ask for them to be gratified or taken into account.

As these modes of relating were consistently played out with me, I would at times inquire, and at other times offer conjectures, as to what had occurred in her relationship to her parents to make it necessary for her to try to coerce people to recognize her needs without her having to reveal them. Among my conjectures, of course, were those that dealt with her mother's responses to her needs. Not long ago, Carol told me of an incident which shed a great deal of light on her behavior. A friend of the family was being cared for by her mother following surgery. She told Carol's mother that she had been instructed to drink a lot of water postoperatively. However, she did not ask Carol's mother to bring her water so she did not do so. In telling Carol about this incident her mother remarked, "I guess I'm the kind of mother who needs to be asked."

It was typical of Carol that she did not ever say that her mother did not respond adequately to her needs. First, she wanted me to know this without having to tell me; and second, she often feared she was too demanding, selfish, and greedy to be entitled to ask for anything. This latter feeling masked a not very deeply repressed resentment that she actually was entitled and should not have to ask. It seems to me to be more useful to understand that Carol's behavior was a result of the solutions she adopted to deal with the many conflicts engendered by her mother's particular inadequacy than a consequence of a defect in her ego functioning derived from the fact that certain of her needs were not adequately met by her mother.

What distressed Carol so much upon returning to her parents' home after she left her husband was her perception, not entirely erroneous, that her mother was not thrilled at the prospect of caring for her grandchildren. Carol felt that her mother was caring for them out of obligation rather than love, just as she had

thought that her mother had taken care of her out of an obligation implied by adopting her. Nevertheless, both parents were
quite concerned about her, were fully supportive of all her treatment, and have been very involved with her children. For her
own part, Carol was not much of a daughter, preferring to be
alone, always feeling easily criticized, and reluctant to enter into
any adult relationship with her parents. Her father, whom she
felt to be more genuinely loving, was experienced as overly rigid,
demanding, and critical. This impression is supported by transference responses in the analysis.

For a long time I heard almost nothing about her brother,
who was pursuing graduate studies in the Midwest, although I
had drawn her attention to the possible effect on her of his birth.
She did not express feelings of rivalry toward him and, indeed,
maintained that the brother did not fare any better at her
mother's or father's hands than she did, even though he was their
natural child. Finally, however, intense feelings of resentment
and rivalry were expressed in relation to the amount of money
her parents were giving to their children.

Recently, while we were dealing with this issue of rivalry and
jealousy, she had a number of sessions during which she was
more silent than usual. I wondered whether her reluctance to
speak had something to do with what we had been talking about.
She now said that she had always been afraid that if she spoke
more freely she "wouldn't produce enough; some other patient
will come along who will do it better and then it will be all over for
me." I would then get rid of her. I told her that this sounded like
something she could have felt after her brother was born. She did
not remember anything about what she had felt then, but she is
aware how much she feels competition with other patients and a
corresponding rejection by me.

I then asked her why she didn't make every effort to try to
"produce well" here; why didn't she try her best to speak freely
and be the best patient if she feared I would get rid of her if she
didn't "produce enough." Why didn't she try to win me over so
that another patient wouldn't be such a threat? She responded by
saying she never was that way even as a child at home. She would
prefer to give up and go off by herself. I said that there probably
was an important reason for her to react that way.

After some period of silence she said, "I think it is a test for you. It is a test to see if you will do what my natural mother did when I was born and maybe what I felt my mother did after my brother was born. I want to see if you will stay with me even if I don't produce enough. If I don't talk much and am not the kind of patient you really want and you still want me to come here, then I feel that you really care about me."

I wish to stress that for years the patient had insisted that she knew that I didn't really care about her, that I wasn't interested in what she had to say, that I was sorry that I had taken her on as a patient, and I would be glad to get rid of her. These profound feelings existed, of course, in all of her relationships. But behind these conscious feelings lay a number of unconscious fantasies and conflicts which had to be uncovered and understood.

Carol was reenacting with me a very powerful and compelling fantasy in order to undo her terror at being sent away for being bad and inadequate. She was determined to be a "bad" patient to see if I would stick with her and not turn my affection to someone who, as she said, "would produce better and then it would be all over for me." This is how she had behaved with her previous analyst who she knew was prepared to see her forever no matter how she behaved. It will be remembered that when, early in the treatment, I had expressed dissatisfaction with her cooperation, she wanted to leave, and called up her previous analyst. She never wanted to be challenged in this way. She should be accepted even though she was not "producing enough."

Actually, the state of affairs was even more complicated. She was making significant progress in her treatment and had made many changes in her life. These positive changes were precisely the things she was most reluctant to tell me. She wanted me to believe that she was the best patient without her having to tell me or without demonstrating this to me. Overtly, she behaved like a bad patient; I should love her nevertheless and see all the clues she was leaving that she really was the best patient. She was afraid of being replaced by someone who did better.

The gradual emergence of her profound jealousy of her brother helped us to understand an incident that occurred during the third year of treatment. The patient's hour on this day came after I saw a woman whose infant had to be changed in the waiting room after spending the hour in a nearby park with the father. Despite the fact that I leave ten minutes between sessions, this caused an overlap and Carol came in and witnessed this scene.

She came in and lay down on the couch without responding to my greeting. I finally said, "I guess you were upset by what you saw in the waiting room." She was silent for a minute, then got up from the couch and walked out! I then received a call from her similar to ones I had received many, many times before. She always left the same message on the tape, "This is Carol So-and-So. I'm not coming back anymore." After a few missed sessions she returned. Over the next few sessions, she told me that what upset her was not that this woman was there in her place, changing a baby, but that I would allow it to happen. "Knowing what you know about me, you should not have allowed this to happen. You should have gone out and told her she could not do that because I was coming. If you really cared about me you would know this without my having to tell you." The patient had seen other people in the waiting room before. It was the specific scene of a baby being changed and my imagined interest in both mother and baby which had infuriated her.

Conclusion

It is not possible, in a brief presentation such as this, to give sufficient clinical material to illustrate all the complex issues involved in working with conflict and deficit in borderline patients. Nevertheless, I have tried to use this case discussion to demonstrate how the usual psychic conflicts elicited by feelings of rivalry, jealousy, and anger and the defenses mobilized to deal with them, must be understood when working with borderline patients. Whether one conceptualizes the patient's difficulties as indicating ego defects or not, it is important to understand that such deficits are intimately related to and intertwined with psychic conflict.

It is extremely difficult to differentiate between conflict and ego deficit in our actual clinical work. While we may very well deviate from our usual position of relative neutrality in patients with severe psychopathology, we should not be too quick to

conclude that a basic deficit is present that is unrelated to conflict and is derived from failures in structure formation early in
life. The danger in doing so is that the therapist may neglect to
help the patient to see how intrapsychic conflicts and the compromise formations developed to deal with them have shaped
his or her life.

SECTION II
THE DISCUSSIONS

Chapter 7

Conflict and Compromise: Therapeutic Strategies for Clinicians

Charles Brenner, M.D.

A therapeutic strategy is a plan for treatment. What the authors of this book have aimed at answering is the question, When I have a patient in psychotherapy or in analysis, how do I go about planning the treatment? What advice can you give me on how to proceed?

In analysis as in every other craft there are lots of rules of thumb. What to do with a patient who is very anxious, or with one who is depressed, or who only talks about everyday things, or who never talks about everyday things, or who is silent, or one who talks with every breath. The list is endless and, I may add, the questions themselves are fruitless because the answer to every one is the same. It depends on the patient. Rules of thumb are of little value as guides for what to do in treatment, because no two patients are alike. What applies to one won't apply to the other. To intelligently carry on any treatment you have to understand your patient and the best way to understand a patient, our six authors tell us, is in terms of the structural theory as we know it today; in terms of conflict and compromise formation. Whatever the pathology a patient may show, it is to be understood as a compromise formation that has arisen from childhood instinctual conflicts. When you understand what those conflicts and compromise formations are, you are in a position to decide on the best thing to do; what to interpret first, and how best to say what it is you want to say. More than that, you can decide what main line of interpretation you want to follow.

In Dr. Kafka's first case, for example, he understood that the patient's inability to decide whether to become a wife and mother, as well as her feeling that she was constantly subjected to unfair treatment and to having excessive demands placed upon her, were compromise formations resulting from conflicts over the libidinal and aggressive wishes associated with her younger brother's birth. When the same pattern of being put upon appeared in the treatment situation, Dr. Kafka's understanding enabled him to deal with her reaction in a useful, analytic way. His understanding also made plain to him what the general line of interpretation was to be for many months of his patient's analysis.

What was clear to Dr. Kafka at the start of his second case was that his patient's emotional uninvolvement, his aloofness, was a compromise formation related in large part to conflicts over childhood wishes to get rid of his brother and win his mother's and father's exclusive love and attention. This was the patient who had a dream about being an explorer traveling far off in space. It was this understanding that enabled Dr. Kafka to interpret first the transference and, subsequently, many aspects of the patient's social and sexual behavior in a meaningful and useful way.

Dr. Mayer's rich and interesting case presentation illustrates once more the value of understanding each patient's symptoms and character pathology as compromise formations resulting from childhood instinctual conflicts. Dr. Mayer was able, very skillfully, to help her patient understand that her dissatisfaction with her husband, with wifehood, and with motherhood arose from sources of which she was truly unaware. These sources Dr. Mayer knew must be childhood instinctual conflicts that were much influenced by and tied up with mother's year-long illness when the patient was five, and Dr. Mayer was able in the course of time to understand those conflicts in considerable detail and to interpret them successfully to her patient.

Dr. Willick's case illustrates yet again the importance of an understanding of conflict and compromise formation in guiding one to a useful plan of treatment—to a correct therapeutic strategy. There are many who consider certain of the symptoms one encounters in patients sick enough to be classified as borderline as being due to developmental abnormalities of the ego unrelated to conflict. Such abnormalities or defects, they tell us, must be understood and treated differently from neurotic symptoms that are compromise formations arising from childhood instinctual conflicts. They require a holding environment, corrective emotional experiences, empathic understanding, and so on. Dr. Willick has shown us that this is simply not the case. What are often thought of as ego defects are, in fact, compromise formations and are best treated in the usual, analytic way. One is guided by one's understanding of the underlying conflicts in determining what to say and when to say it, and what general line of interpretation to follow.

The first three papers, by Drs. Arlow, Boesky, and Tyson, laid the groundwork for the three clinical papers. Each of the former is designed to increase our understanding of the role of conflict in mental life to the end that we can better apply that understanding in clinical work. Dr. Tyson was concerned with the steps in mental development that are necessary in order for intrapsychic conflict and compromise formation to occur at all. He gave us examples of internal conflict, of developmental conflict, and of internalized conflict from the earliest months of extrauterine life. These conflicts peak during the oedipal phase of development, roughly between three and five years of age, and are, as it were, transformed during those years. The result is that after that time preoedipal conflicts, to use Dr. Tyson's words, "cannot be understood simply in the terms of the time of their origin" (p. 48). They have become not just intertwined with the wishes and conflicts of the oedipal period but truly part of them. As a child passes through the oedipal phase, what were once preoedipal conflicts become themselves part of that child's oedipal conflicts. What were once preoedipal wishes and conflicts can never be considered as separate and apart from oedipal ones in later childhood and in adult life. Although the subject of oedipal versus preoedipal conflicts in mental life is somewhat apart from the principal focus of the present work, we are indebted to Dr. Tyson for calling it to our attention. I should add that I am thoroughly in agreement with what I understand this position to be.

Dr. Arlow has given us a concise and masterly discussion of one of the centrally important ideas in structural theory, namely, psychic trauma. He has reminded us that Freud's early emphasis on the importance of recovering memories of traumatic events reflected that era's theory of pathogenesis; that is, a neurosis is the consequence of a forgotten, emotionally disturbing experience. As his analytic experience grew, Freud very much altered his ideas of pathogenesis, as Dr. Arlow has noted, ideas that have been subsequently developed and refined. Today we understand much more clearly the relationship between experience and wishes in childhood. As a result we focus on conflict as a whole, on both its inner and its experiential determinants, not just on what experiences have been forgotten. The memory of a forgotten wish or a forgotten fear or misery is sometimes even more important to recover than the memory of a forgotten, so-called traumatic event.

Dr. Arlow also emphasized and illustrated what Dr. Willick took as his central theme, the inadequacy of the concept of ego deficit as something determined simply by improper nurture rather than by the complex interaction of the components of psychic conflict.

Dr. Boesky's paper was exceptionally rich. He began with an excellent survey of the present status of the structural theory, with its emphasis on conflict and compromise formation, and went on to discuss, with the help of illustrative case material, some subjects that have been of special interest to him in recent years: sublimation, acting out, and identification. Incidentally, he wrote a paper on acting out that was published in the *International Journal of Psycho-Analysis* in 1982 and one on sublimation that appeared in a volume called *Psychoanalysis: the Science of Mental Conflict*, in 1986, both of which I recommend most highly. I would like also to underline Dr. Boesky's final remarks on resistance. He emphasized that resistance is not to be equated with defense. Just as a neurotic symptom is never simply a defense, but always a compromise formation that includes wish, unpleasure, defense, and superego manifestations, so a resistance attitude or behavior is never simply defensive. It too is a compromise formation that results from the interaction of all the elements of mental conflict. It includes them all among its determinants, not just defense. At a given time, with a given patient, it may be appropriate to interpret only the defensive aspect of some resistance behavior, but the therapist must always understand that defense is only one of the determinants of resistance. At another time, with the same patient, what may be the thing to interpret is the aspect of drive gratification, or of self-punishment, or of anxiety or depressive affect.

When I had finished reading the six papers, it seemed to me that I could best fulfill my duty as discussant by summarizing and expanding on the many fruitful ideas they contain. My own views coincide with theirs, as is clear from what I have already said. I have no objections to raise, no emendations to suggest. What I shall do is add some thoughts of my own that are relevant to our general topic, thoughts on the subject of transference.

It goes without saying that transference is of central importance in any psychoanalytically oriented psychotherapy. More has been written on the subject of transference in the psychoanalytic literature than on any other aspect of technique. I think that our present understanding of the role of compromise formation in mental functioning permits a new and better understanding of the subject of transference, an understanding that is of great value in one's practical work with patients.

I shall start by correcting a common misconception. The fact that transference is so important in psychoanalytic technique and that it was first described in that context has led to the idea that transference is unique to the therapeutic situation. It is not. Freud (1912) introduced the term *transference* (in German, *Uebertragung*, literally, carrying over) to refer to a relationship between patient and therapist in which the patient transferred to the person of the analyst wishes from the patient's childhood. There is no doubt about the correctness of Freud's observations. Patients do relate to their therapists in ways that are determined by the patient's childhood instinctual wishes and the conflicts associated with those wishes. Transference brings into the treatment situation conflicts and compromise formations from the patient's childhood. That is why the analysis of transference is so valuable a part of psychoanalytic therapy. It is *not* true, however, that there is anything unique or even unusual about the development of transference in a therapeutic situation. Quite the contrary. Everyone, patient or not, relates to other persons in ways that are determined by childhood instinctual conflicts. Every object relationship is a compromise formation resulting from instinctual conflicts originating in childhood and carried over (= transferred) into later life. Transference is an inevitable or, better, a necessary part of every object relationship.

Having said this, one must add that there is something unique about transference in analytic therapy nevertheless. What is unique about analytic transference is the way it is dealt with. In every other object relationship transference is met with one or another everyday response. A person who makes contact with another may be met with indifference, with interest, with love or hate, with pity, cruelty, civility, rudeness, in brief, in any one of a great variety of ways that are familiar to each of us from everyday experience. Not so if the other person is an analyst in a therapeutic role. In a therapeutic setting transference is analyzed rather than reacted to in any other way. That is what is unique about transference in analytic therapy. Not its appearance, not its nature, not its origin in childhood conflicts, but the response it generates. Transference plays a determinative role in every relationship between people. Only in psychoanalytic therapy does the object of transference limit her or his reaction to analyzing it, that is, to trying to understand its nature and origin and to imparting that understanding to the person who has brought it into the relationship; in this case, to the patient.

There are important practical consequences that follow from what I have just said. Since every manifestation of transference is a compromise formation, it is compounded of wish, unpleasure, defense, and superego manifestations. One can say about transference the same thing that Dr. Boesky said about resistance. Transference is never just defense. Nor is it ever just the expression of a childhood instinctual wish; nor just an expression of anxiety or depressive affect; nor just a means of atonement or of self-punishment. It is always a combination of all these components. Like every other object relationship, it is always a compromise formation. Terms like *defense transference* and *superego transference* are misleading. The defensive aspect of transference may be what is important to interpret to a patient at a particular time. However, if one thinks that is *all* there is to a patient's transference, then one is likely to miss the occasion to interpret to a patient that the very same transference is also a means of self-punishment when *that* is what is important to help the patient to understand. And the same is true for each of the other components of the conflict giving rise to a patient's transference reaction.

Let me give you an illustration of what I am trying to say. The patient was a woman in her midtwenties. A striking feature of her behavior during the second year of her analysis was the frequency with which she argued with me. Even when she resolved she would cooperate at least to the extent of listening to whatever I might say without interrupting me to argue with the first word out of my mouth, her good resolution would evaporate as soon as she came into my office and lay down on the couch. She argued with every breath. She would even argue with me if I repeated what she herself had just said.

When all of this was called to her attention, the patient soon realized that arguing with me was like arguing with her father during her adolescence. Since it happened with me daily for many months and under many different circumstances, its various determinants gradually came to be well understood. For one thing it gratified aggressive and libidinal wishes that she entertained toward me. It was intended to defeat and humiliate me in a particular way and to gratify her wish for sexual intercourse with me as well.

The particular way of defeating me and humiliating me was this: if she could remain relatively calm and goad me into losing my temper and becoming excited and unreasonable, victory would be hers. This idea was one she remembered from her adolescent arguments with her father. If her father lost his temper, if he shouted and swore and was otherwise unreasonable, she would feel triumphant.

That quarreling with me also gratified the sexual wishes she had unconsciously cherished for her father in her adolescence was made clear somewhat later, when she became aware, after yelling at me angrily, rushing out of my office in tears, and locking herself in the lavatory, that she felt like masturbating.

You can see then, that the patient's transference behavior of arguing with me was determined in part by wishes, both libidinal and aggressive, of childhood origin—but only in part. Another meaning of her arguing with me had to do with anxiety and depressive affect, both of which had their origins in early childhood. The depressive affect was connected with her idea in childhood that if only she had been a boy instead of a girl, she would have been her father's undisputed favorite. In her analysis she wanted to be my favorite patient, as one might guess, and the fact that I didn't love and favor her as she wished me to do was something to which she reacted with castration depressive affect; that is, with misery at being a girl and not a boy. At the same time, her vengeful wish to best and, symbolically, to castrate me by outarguing me aroused anxiety related both to castration as retribution and to loss of love.

As for defense, to belittle me by arguing me down defended against her libidinal longings and associated depressive affect and anxiety: depressive affect at being a girl and anxiety that I not love her and turn against her. In addition, her troublesome wishes, her fears, and her misery were all displaced and disguised in their transference manifestation of arguing with me, as they had been in adolescence when she argued with her father. She believed at first that she argued with me not to avoid feeling castrated and inferior, but because it seemed to her that I was always trying to ram down her throat something that was not so and doing it in an arrogant, condescending manner. That is, she attributed to me her own desire to take revenge on me by being arrogant and condescending to me.

Finally, arguing had superego aspects as well. All through childhood the patient was guilty about wanting what she felt was more than her share. To feel that I was provocative, ungiving, contemptuous of her, or otherwise disagreeable represented the punishment and penance she unconsciously felt she deserved and must undergo if she was to be forgiven by mother and other rivals. Thus her bitterest and most cherished reproaches concerned my refusal to advise her how to help the members of her family (mother and siblings) who were the surviving rivals of her childhood.

You can see two things from this brief illustration. The first is that this patient's transference was indeed a compromise formation. It wasn't just wish or unpleasure or defense or superego, it was a mixture of all these components together. The second is that every aspect of the conflicts that gave rise to the patient's transference was important to understand and to interpret at one time or another. To interpret only one aspect of her transference, one aspect of her underlying conflict, wouldn't do, and that is just what is likely to happen if one fails to keep clearly in mind that every transference is a compromise formation. Keeping that knowledge in mind is very helpful in one's day-to-day clinical work.

Is it of practical value in other ways as well? I think so. For instance, the knowledge that transference is part of every object relationship keeps one from worrying about whether a patient is developing a transference or not. It is a mistake to believe that there are patients who never develop a transference or who never develop much of one. To think that way about any patient is to assert the impossible. Transference is ubiquitous. Every object relation expresses the wishes of childhood and the conflicts to which they have given rise. A patient may deny, ignore, or otherwise defend against such thoughts and wishes. A patient may react so negatively, so suspiciously, or with such a need to withdraw from the analyst that analysis becomes impossible. But that doesn't mean that there is no transference, or just a weak one. On the contrary, the indifference, the lack of conscious emotion, the absence of conscious personal interest, the suspiciousness, the antagonism, the withdrawal *are* the manifestations of transference, as Dr. Kafka's and Dr. Willick's cases so clearly illustrate. Such a transference results from the patient's childhood instinctual conflicts just as much as does any other type of transference reaction. Whatever a patient's reaction to the analyst may be, whether it be flamboyantly obvious or silently hidden, it is a compromise formation to be understood and, when indicated, to be interpreted to the patient.

Not that I mean to say that it can always be easily understood and interpreted without difficulty. It is often very obscure, very hard to understand, very hard to interpret in ways a patient can grasp and make her or his own. But it does make a big difference if you know in advance what it is all about. Then as you listen, the bits and pieces that you hear are more apt to fall into place. Incidentally, this is what Freud meant when he wrote about listening with evenly hovering attention. In "An Autobiographical Study" (1924, p. 41) he wrote that an analyst's ability to understand a patient's communications depends on two things. The first is evenly hovering attention. As Freud put it in 1924, an analyst should listen "composedly but without any constrained attention." The second is "a general knowledge of what to expect" based on the analyst's experience. What these authors recommend as "a general knowledge of what to expect" is a thorough understanding of the nature of conflict and compromise formation and of their role in mental life. That is what will be most helpful to analysts in carrying out the treatment of their patients, they say. I concur most heartily.

Chapter 8

Conflict and Compromise: A Discussion

Milton H. Bronstein, M.D.

The first six papers of this book deal with the subject of conflict and compromise from a psychoanalytic, structural model point of view. They differ one from the other depending on the clinical or theoretical emphasis of the particular author.

It should be noted that there are other ways of describing the place of conflict in human psychology. Rangell (1986) and Weiss and Sampson (1986) provide evidence of a decision making function of the ego which is independent of conflict in addition to those dependent on conflict. In this discussion I will limit myself to the frame of reference already presented.

I will begin by turning to a specific aspect of Dr. Arlow's discussion of those who accomplish a great deal in the face of seemingly insurmountable odds. For one individual, a situation may be crippling while the same situation to another may be only a passing insult or at most a temporary inconvenience. My question has to do with those who "succeed" but at a great price to themselves and to those with whom they live. Their compromise formations, which allow success, may include or provoke anger, guilt over anger, or guilt over success, often with denial, disavowal, and isolation of feeling. The price for their success can be formidable. Only with such limitations can some individuals travel a hard-won, reasonably compensated, but very narrow path. For example, J. was an eldest son who had to raise his brothers and sisters because of his mother's disabilities and his father's absences due to work. When he grew up, he became a successful professional man who functioned excellently in his work and enjoyed those things that could be separated from his past. He avoided and would not discuss any event or person associated with his past to the extent that this was possible. He stayed out of those territories, turning to other preoccupations and activities. His professional success was established, but his emotional life was stringently limited. This patient strides an emotional path that has become so narrow that his hard-won balance can barely be maintained.

M. is another example of an accomplished man whose expertise is widely valued. He suffered from a medical condition in his preschool years which required many surgical procedures and left a residual physical defect. The associated psychological difficulty was surmounted by intense, extreme, ongoing, strenuous physical activity throughout his school years, along with equally strenuous academic endeavor. The disability was virtually unacknowledged or, perhaps, disacknowledged. Effective treatment began when the defect was acknowledged and spoken about. Until then, the defect simply did not exist; he could only speak of the environmental difficulties produced by his character trait of driven activity. Success in disavowing the existence of the condition was achieved with ego deforming compromise formations which enabled him to avoid the pain, anger, and depression of acknowledgment. Once the defect was acknowledged, the treatment could proceed and become of great value. Even with massive life inequities it is possible for such individuals to work in analytic interpretive treatment situations.

Regarding Boesky's presentation, it is important to remember that defenses do not disappear after analysis nor do they become "normal." If the work is reasonably successful, defenses become useful in the service of the individual rather than the person being regulated or impaired by them. Defenses may be more or less trouble, they may be more or less useful, but they, like conflict, compromise formation, and resistance, are always there as a part of human existence.

We know also that even after a highly successful analysis, an individual is not transformed into an altogether different person. What is accomplished is a more reasonable arrangement of the attributes of the mind; internally integrated insight allows the patient choices as well as less taxing and less costly compromise formations. Greater productivity and more gratifying personal relationships are possible. The successfully treated patient becomes more the master of his conflicts than vice versa. Modification of the defenses is a useful part of that accomplishment.

Dr. Boesky's story of the boy and his clarinet is an instance of a classic neurotic paradigm. The boy who wants to do as well as the father may or may not transcend the fears and dangers of being hurt or abandoned because of his wishes. It is a universal dilemma that we all encounter one way or another, in our own lives and with our patients whose conflicts and costly compromise formations arise in the wake of similar struggles.

Dr. Tyson traces the development of conflict and suggests that early conflicts can be important throughout our lives. It is important to remind ourselves that the panorama of events in childhood development do not necessarily occur in a straightline fashion; the manifestations of its stages do not disappear with later developments, nor do they necessarily overwhelm or obliterate later stages of the individual's ontogeny. Early conflicts do not necessarily have priority over later ones. What may have been considered a catastrophe in early childhood, with a complicated network of defenses established as a result, may, when viewed at an older age, have resulted in an ego of great adaptive value, one, for example, which is more accessible to analytic treatment.

What is the implication of Dr. Tyson's statement about the teasing mother, and her ambivalently fed child, "Everything that follows will bear the mark of that game." This terminology suggests that the pain and tragedy of the feeding situation will, in one form or another, continue to be felt forever. If that is his meaning, I would disagree; the vicissitudes of ego development may lead to a quite different outcome.

What happens with the patient who shows few, if any, clinical signs until later in life? Is he truly free of the effects of conflict until that time or are such effects simply not seen or observed until the noise of the earlier years quiets down?

What are we to think of the very "good" child who, the parents feel, does not need treatment? Does not this happen from the side of the therapist too? "This is a good child," the therapist might say, "This child does not need treatment." We often see good grades, good deportment, good school relationships, which satisfy not just the parents but therapists as well. Outer behavior becomes the be-all and end-all of "success" with encapsulation and sequestration of unspoken, less visible issues.

Dr. Tyson reminds us of the danger of an "adultomorphic" inaccuracy in reading meaning into an infant's responses. I wonder if there are parallel inaccuracies in doing the reverse, that is, of reading "infantomorphic" meaning into an adult's responses.

Of course, childhood events bear very much on the personality and style of an individual into advanced age. I recall an alert and communicative woman in her eighties who, as a very young child, had to defer to a sibling, to part with a particularly cherished possession, at her mother's request. At the time she seemingly deferred to her sibling without much difficulty. This was to be a pattern in her life; she was asked to give up things, and often did so cheerfully. This general demeanor and character trait led to many positive experiences and not only to exploitation. However, the prohibited, unexpressed resentment was there. As analytically oriented psychotherapy progressed with interpretation of transference and other resistance manifestations, her hidden feelings of anger and guilt, for which she compensated during her entire life, became clear. When she spoke of the childhood incident mentioned, and other similar ones, her face became flushed and she wept as if the event had occurred not many decades ago but the day or week before. She now had the perspective and strength to deal with this previously invisible pain and with the lifelong defenses engendered by it.

Dr. Elizabeth Meyer describes a marital problem clearly and vividly; the therapeutic implications of the wife's conflicts and compromise formations are also demonstrated.

The case contains within it the situation of a friend of the patient who was also a friend of the analyst. This kind of bridge experience, if carefully worked with in the treatment situation, can be of unexpected value to the therapeutic task. Similar issues arise in the analytic training situation where there are many crossovers between patient and therapist, with potential transference and countertransference vulnerabilities.

The word *borderline* often conjures up an image of a condition so regressed and disturbed that avoidance of hospitalization is viewed as a major accomplishment by everyone concerned. Conflicts and developmental catastrophes are so strong and deep that they appear immutable, a deficit of almost constitutional permanency. Dr. Willick shows us how careful and considered work can elicit an understanding of the responsible conflict. The same phenomena are felt by some to warrant measures of an extra-analytic nature. Holding the patient in an open-ended, positive feeling position is not only an analytic artifact but does not necessarily serve the patient. It may serve the needs of the therapist and could lead to a relatively permanent alliance of an almost Svengalian nature.

I am very sympathetic with Willick's decision to be active in eliciting verbalization from his silent, "waiting to be asked" patient and feel, as did he, that otherwise treatment could not take place. At the same time, he never stopped trying to decipher the meaning of this parameter.

I would like to add two examples of different forms of activity on the part of the therapist. The first occurred when I was a resident. A young woman patient sat in the main hallway of the ward leaning against the wall with her head on her knees covered by her folded arms. Each morning as I walked by, I greeted her with "good morning." There was no sign of response, physical or verbal, no movement, no sound, only seeming oblivion. Many months later she greeted me one day and said, "I want to thank you for saying good morning to me each day." Sensitivity to a patient's deeply felt but unarticulated needs is an essential ingredient of therapy of all varieties. The second instance occurred during my early years of analytic training. A patient, who was a supervised case, came in one day and told me that his father, who lived in a faraway city, had a severe depression and was about to undergo electroshock treatment. My patient was extremely upset, anxious, and sad. I felt that I must step outside the analytic relationship and explain to him what his father, whom he deeply loved and resented, was undergoing. I was concerned that my supervisor would not be pleased by this excursion on my part. I did not overlook either my own counter-transferential or other emotional vulnerabilities as I had only recently lost my own father. The supervisor was reassuring and the analysis proceeded in more salutary fashion than before. The episode described was not overlooked in our later analytic endeavors. I mention these clinical events because they are unforgettable and instructive to me.

It would be surprising to me if any experienced clinician, faced with similar situations, would not have acted similarly. Obviously these moments in our careers are not restricted to experiences with those patients whom we call borderline. There are similar exigencies which may occur in any analytic, or psychotherapeutic, treatment.

An added note: borderline characteristics can occur transiently in any of our patients, for a moment or for weeks, during analytic sessions, in an episode of acting out, or in transference storms which may reach almost psychotic proportions. The borderline patient can be analytically approached, but this is not always an easy effort.

Dr. Kafka's contribution to this volume is a clear description of a character disorder, and of a therapist's efforts in eliciting and working with conflicts in such disorders. Because conflict driven behavior in those with character disorders is often ego syntonic, overt signs of unconscious conflict in these patients are carefully sought. Such signs are often not evident in their words.

L., for example, generally spoke in the same way, with serious and restrained expression, with courtesy and consideration, with promptness and careful observation of the requirements of the analytic endeavor. But he would also frequently present situations in which his behavior invited criticism and impatience. As I scanned the analytic situation for signs of conflict, I noted that as he walked into the consultation room he threw his head back as if he expected or, indeed, wished to receive the worst. He had described a relationship to his father which was dominated by episodes of misbehavior, and resultant punishment, which finally became the currency of their love for each other. All this was repeated in the transference as a mode of behavior with me in the hope and expectation that a similar interaction would occur as had occurred with his father. The physical gesture was a reenactment with me of that which occurred as a way of life between him and his father, and was also extended to many other relationships. Analyzing this gesture became a part of our work similar to the more usual analysis of verbal material with other patients.

Dr. Kafka's second patient showed a strong, erotic transference which was manifested by sexual acting out with accompanying anxiety and depression, presumably as a result of his wishes and fears of punishment and guilt. I wondered why an interpretation of the erotic transference was deferred in favor of interpretation of his ways of seeking alienation or punishment and criticism. Could the relief and/or salutary result of the interpretation of the sexual transference have been achieved earlier?

It is true, as Dr. Kafka states, that often those with character disorders do not ask for treatment. Commonly, if ironically, they come for treatment when their alloplastic behavior produces severe difficulty and chaos. Accessibility to treatment is only possible because of this severe disruption of their lives.

To conclude, compromise formations can compensate for emotional and physical pain and, in some instances, survival is dependent on the relief from conflict afforded by them. Chronic and well integrated conflicts may produce seemingly rational decisions which are actually determined by the irrational unconscious mind.

Conflict with its derivative compromise formations can also be painful and crippling in its ultimate result, producing unhappiness and difficulty for the individual, his family, and his associates. Compromise formations may even become lifelong character deformities with incapacitating symptoms and destructive behavior.

Psychoanalytic treatment can expose the nature of both conflict and compromise formation, alleviating emotional burdens with more satisfying compromise formations and permitting a more reasonable existence.

Chapter 9

An Object Relations Approach to Conflict and Compromise Formation

Frederick Vaquer, M.D.

Although I am in basic agreement with the main thrust of each presentation in this book, I do have some minor disagreements with and some major additions to make to the positions taken by the authors. I take a more eclectic approach than they do, and one which affords me what I believe to be a greater number and variety of conceptual tools for application in psychoanalytic theory and practice. I believe it is necessary to supplement and complement the tenets of modern structural theory in order to adequately encompass behaviors exhibited by individuals experiencing disorders far more primitive than those we call neurotic. To achieve this I rely on the work of object relations theorists including Klein (1946), Bion (1957a), Grotstein (1977), Kohut (1977), and Kernberg (1988a,b).

Central to my approach to the understanding and organization of the data of human behavior is the concept of unconscious fantasy. I view unconscious fantasy as starting in earliest infancy when it takes the form of the internal registration of bodily centered events, as protofantasy or coenesthetic sensations (Isaacs,

1952; Opatow, 1989), and only much later develops into the organized representations of reality seen in adults and verbal children (Arlow, 1969a,b). When we speak of an ego and its functions, of id derivatives or of a superego there are definite processes occurring in the individual that we designate by these terms and there are detailed mental representations that are reflective of these processes (Segal, 1964). The who, what, when, where, how, and why of the production and operation of all psychic structure is reflected in the details of currently prevalent, operative, and enduring unconscious fantasy. What we speak of as clinically significant trauma, deficit, conflict, or compromise is represented by a detailed and coherent unconscious fantasy in the analysand. From my perspective the elucidation and understanding of the prevalent unconscious fantasies dominating current behavior in a psychoanalytic situation is the best approach for ordering the data of human behavior in a meaningful, coherent, and consistent fashion.

Unconscious fantasy is the domain of psychic reality. To a great extent it is composed of representations of the interrelationship of varying aspects of the self with internal and external objects. Unconscious fantasy not only alters the perception and interpretation of reality but reality exerts a strong influence on unconscious fantasy. The importance of any environmental factor, whether traumatic or not, or whether impinging on an infant or on an adult, can be correctly evaluated only by understanding the meaning it has for the individual involved. This meaning is inextricably interwoven with the effect the event in question has in terms of activating unconscious fantasies. As Wilfred Bion (1963) notes, unconscious fantasy acts as a preconception which when activated by an appropriate realization, like a lock mating with an appropriate key, yields a conception. The conception in turn can now act as a preconception in cognitive terms or a premonition in the emotional sphere, yielding an ever expanding and increasingly sophisticated internal world of fantasy. The interrelationship with reality is especially important from the point of view of altering the structure of what we call the ego. The structure of the personality can be altered by analyzing the self and object interrelations that encompass the analyst in the form we call transference.

Conflict and compromise are ubiquitous in all human mental behavior. From my perspective, the relevant question is not whether a given bit of behavior involves conflict or is a compromise, but, rather, what sort of conflict is involved, what sorts of processes result in the behavior in question.

I find it useful to view unconscious fantasy as if it were the product of four broadly conceived varieties of personality functioning: normal,[1] neurotic, infantile, and psychotic. I follow, with major amendment, Bion's (1967) usage in that each of these varieties is considered as a mental state, all coexisting in a given individual with one another. At any given time in an analysis an individual will show evidence in behavior of the preponderance of one or another of these mental states which may interpenetrate or contaminate one another. Each state is characterized by different degrees of organization and stability and by the mental mechanisms that form a part of its organization, structure, and modalities of functioning. All dimensions of a given aspect of personality functioning are represented in unconscious fantasy.

I want to emphasize that I am presenting these aspects of personality functioning as neatly separable and easily recognizable independent entities, but this is a heuristic or expositional device. As Boesky points out, we deal not with single compromise formations but with groups of compromise formations which may themselves be in conflict with one another. The states of mind I refer to are compromise formations which are themselves the products of innumerable underlying conflicts and compromises. They are often complexly interrelated, forming patterns that underlie other more easily recognizable and superficially active personality organizations (Grotstein, 1977; Steiner, 1987). They are then described as pathological defense organizations underlying borderline, manic, perverse, schizoid, paranoid, and other varieties of personality disorders.

---

[1] Limitations of space do not permit an explication of the dimension of normal personality functioning. In addition to considerations framed in terms of the real relationship and therapeutic alliance I would include the consideration that any behavior, no matter how seemingly irrational, serves some reasonable goal or end for the patient (Vaquer, 1989).

The Neurotic Aspect of Personality Functioning

This aspect is characterized by unconscious fantasies involving triadic whole object relations that demonstrate object constancy in the face of ambivalence. Themes of rivalry and jealousy predominate, while self and object interrelations are governed by standard neurotic configurations central to which are repressive mechanisms. This is the realm of the normal verbal child struggling with sexual and aggressive impulses and with the accompanying reminders of the danger situations that these stimulate: object loss, loss of the object's love, castration, and punishment by the superego. Transference configurations are the result of displacements from the objects of childhood onto present-day objects. The French remind us that the goals of this oedipal phase of development are predominantly social (Lacan, 1977). This feature, along with the presence of an advanced state of reality testing, results in the fact that when some of these individuals experience a failure in their coping capacities they can effectively be reassured by reality relations, which are used to reinforce failing normal personality functioning. Thus many can be sent off to supportive therapies with good result. Others fail in these efforts and require analytic intervention. It has been repeatedly demonstrated that deep-seated and far-reaching permanent personality change is possible conducting an analysis at this level.

The Infantile Aspect of Personality Functioning

When the infantile aspect of functioning predominates, behavior is characterized by the modalities and features described by Melanie Klein (1946, 1957, 1960, 1963) and her coworkers, and by Otto Kernberg (1988a,b),[2] as encompassing the paranoid–schizoid and depressive positions. These modalities of functioning are reflective of a fantasied internal world populated by various aspects of self interrelating with narcissistic objects and

[2] Kernberg (1988b) states that the predominant organization of psychic structures are neurotic, narcissistic, borderline, or psychotic. My views differ in that aspects of personality functioning are the structures that underlie these pathological as well as normal behaviors. I also consider narcissistic conditions to result from infantile organization while the borderline is an example of the psychotic aspect of functioning.

part objects, or more correctly, by representations of their interrelations. The mechanisms that produce this world and the associated interrelations are splitting, omnipotence, denial, idealization, and projective identification. Each of these terms refers to a process believed to underlie a given concrete fantasy. (For detailed descriptions of these processes and of the fantasies and clinical behavior they result in, see Bion [1956, 1962], Segal [1964], Grotstein [1981], Vaquer [1987].) In any given instance the meaning of the term is no more or less than the specific fantasy referred to. The danger situations extant in this domain are both defended against and produced by the deployment of these omnipotent mechanisms. These danger situations are loss of the self and loss of the object.

If we imagine the domain of this level of personality functioning as extending from a paranoid–schizoid to a depressive pole, the loss of the self is typical of the paranoid–schizoid end of the spectrum. This loss of self is usually experienced as due to an annihilatory attack by a persecuting object or part object in fantasy.[3] It can also be experienced as self-induced. Fear of loss of the object is a depressive anxiety which erupts as concern develops attendant to the experience of the object as a whole person and one that is related to ambivalently by the subject. The person we love and need for our very existence is the same one we hate and wish to destroy because of the pain our experience of them can cause us. Kohut's (1971) idealizing and mirror transferences, in my opinion, are examples of narcissistic object relations produced by the deployment of the mechanisms listed above, as are Kernberg's (1988b) categories of normal and malignant narcissism.

The Psychotic Aspect of Personality Functioning

Sigmund Freud (1937) in "Analysis Terminable and Interminable" states, "Every normal person, in fact, is only normal on the

---

[3] Narcissistic objects and part objects are representational forms beyond the symbolic capacities of infants. What the ultimate nature of fantasy consists of in prerepresentational stages of development is unknown. Any attempt to verbally describe an ineffable experience is unavoidably speculative, adultomorphic, and, to some extent, involves one in the dangers of the genetic fallacy.

average. His ego approximates to that of the psychotic in some part or other and to a greater or lesser extent" (p. 235). Wilfred Bion (1957a) describes patients who exhibit what he calls a psychotic aspect of their personalities: a state of mind or mode of mental functioning which is universal[4] in its occurrence, though often covered over by more normal or neurotic aspects. In the clinically psychotic, either this part is overly developed or the neurotic "cover" fails.[5] Melanie Klein (1946) notes that psychotics, in addition to increased aggression and a failure of primal splitting, display an increase in the frequency and intensity of splitting and projective identification. These quantitative variations interfere with what she calls the normal projective–introjective processes underlying ordinary development (Klein, 1957, 1960). To these quantitative factors Bion (1962b, 1965) adds qualitative considerations and refers to normal as opposed to abnormal splitting and projective identification.

Normal projective identification, Bion (1957b, 1962b) states, is the prototype for all self–object links. What is involved is a fantasy in which the self expels bad aspects into an object for processing and improvement and good aspects for ideal formation (Bion, 1957b, 1962b; Klein, 1963). For the object to accept these projections and improve them through processing into a form that the self can safely introject and use for growth, is within the capacity of a normal mother in a state of reverie (Winnicott, 1956). Bion generalizes from this complex interrelationship to what he calls the container–contained relationship. The normal situation is called symbiotic. The psychotic produces a much different fantasy called parasitic. In a parasitic container–contained interrelationship the fantasied object either refuses to accept projections (Bion, 1957a; Grotstein, 1981) or, on doing so, turns them into something much worse by stripping them of their vitality and

[4] That a psychotic aspect of personality is universal does not imply that we are all psychotic at one time or other. The implication is that all normal personalities exhibit behavior derived from their psychotic aspects. This behavior typically involves fantasied attacks directed against those aspects of the self which govern relations with internal and external reality and are involved with functions such as consciousness, judgment, and sense perception (Grinberg, Sor, & Tabak de Bianchedi, 1975).

[5] It is important to note that evidence of the activity of a psychotic aspect of personality in any given instance does not necessarily indicate the presence of clinical psychosis. A judgment that clinical psychosis exists involves quantitative considerations.

meaning, infusing them with envious sadism, and intrusively returning them in a violent fashion to the self (Bion, 1957a; Vaquer, 1987). Simultaneously the object is felt to be damaged by the projected aspect of self.

The worse case from a developmental point of view is that of a mother who reacts in such a way as to confirm her infant's omnipotent fantasy of a parasitic form of projective identification. Bion considers this type of interrelation to be the chief environmental factor in the production of psychosis. Clinically, a fantasied parasitic interrelationship forms the core of the psychotic transference, which is usually disguised beneath more precipitously formed superficial, thin, though tenaciously maintained, interactions (Bion, 1959, 1962a, 1963, 1965). Projective identification is also used in an attempt to permanently banish aspects of self so that projections into a void or into space are common in psychotics.

Splitting deviates from the normal in the psychotic personality. Ordinary splitting follows certain natural lines of cleavage going along dimensions such as good–bad, top–bottom, front–back, inside–outside. These splits are organized along the lines of certain typical libidinal zonal configurations (Bion, 1965). Psychotics seem to split contrary to these usual rules and produce extremely confusing elements. These elements are expelled through pathways peculiar to psychotics; in that sense organs are often used to externalize and eliminate rather than to take in and register (Bion, 1958). "Things" are preferred as containers rather than objects or part objects, and the resultant products appear bizarre in that they seem the result of agglutination, agglomeration, and compression rather than synthesis and integration of elements (Bion, 1962a). Activity of the psychotic aspect of personality is apt to produce objects which are experienced as extremely bizarre in that they result from splintered, abnormally split, agglutinated, and agglomerated aspects of self and object.

The hatred of reality and of the inevitable dependencies on its objects, along with the occurrence of low frustration tolerance and the preponderance of aggressive impulses characteristic of this aspect of personality functioning, are reflected in the fact that any of the danger situations, neurotic and infantile, are apt to set off those danger situations that are unique to this psychotic realm. These danger situations are nameless dread and catastrophic or psychotic panic. Nameless dread is the experience involved when the self experiences its projections as being stripped of meaning, significance, and vitality by the containing object. Bion believes that this results in the projected aspect of personality being turned into a thing.[6] Catastrophic or psychotic panic results when the self cannot, in fantasy, find an object capable of functioning as a container to contain and transform its projections. Bion describes this as an experience which appears abruptly and violently, arouses feelings of disaster in the participants, and is felt to completely subvert any sense of order in the self or object world. In fantasy, the self is felt to be scattered across the infinite dimensions of psychic space and to be irretrievably lost. Alternatively, the self is experienced as so immense that its contents are scattered and unavailable.[7]

The hatred of reality characteristic of this domain results in fantasized sadistic attacks on any aspect of the self which might have commerce with this reality. Both the self and reality representations are submitted to envious and sadistic attacks. Among those aspects of the ego submitted to attack are the mental representations of sense organs, of verbal and visual thought, and of the apparatus for thinking thought. Links within verbal and visual streams of thought may be severed and sensory organs mutilated in fantasy (Bion, 1959). As verbal and plastic mental representations fail, more primitive thought forms emerge such as ideograms and pictograms (Bion, 1963). These patients often choose or seek out environmental objects which resemble these ideograms and manipulate them in an effort to think, to link these objects integratively and synthetically, but find themselves all too often "agglutinating and agglomerating" instead (Bion, 1958, 1962a).[8] Psychotic aspects of self preferentially target exter-

---

[6] This interreaction is one means of producing autistic objects in fantasy. This can also involve projections into things as well as adhesive identification.

[7] Ogden (1989) describes the anxiety characteristic of what he terms the autistic contiguous position as involving the experience of the impending disintegration of one's sensory surface or of one's rhythm of safety, resulting in the feeling of leaking, dissolving, disappearing, or falling into shapeless unbounded space.

[8] Bizarre objects result from the submission of the representations of the normal, neurotic and infantile domains of personality functioning to abnormal splitting, abnormal projective, and abnormal identificatory processes. The resultant elements are

nal sources of gratification and dependency with fantasied destructive attacks. The psychotic patient's tendency is to refer to these sources in concrete anatomical terms (such as *breast, penis, nipple*), a tendency that often obscures the fact that what is being attacked is a function such as caring, cleaning, and feeding (Bion, 1962a). This psychotic mode of functioning was originally subsumed under the phrase "Transformations in Hallucinosis" (Bion, 1963).

There has been steady development of Dr. Bion's work. Donald Meltzer, J. Bremner, S. Hoxter, D. Weddell, and I. Wittenberg (1975), Francis Tustin (1972, 1986), James Grotstein (1977, 1981, 1987), Sidney Klein (1980), Albert Mason (1981), and Thomas Ogden (1989) have made important contributions to this development in terms of expanding our understanding of psychotic aspects of personality functioning. Together, they have clarified what have been called autistic states of mind with their associated autistic anxieties, mechanisms, and modalities of functioning resulting in a fantasy world of two-dimensional, paper-thin autistic objects related to via the mechanism of adhesive identification (Etchegoyen, 1985). Adhesive identification refers to a defensive surface to surface fusion or adherence to an object in fantasy to overcome a fear of disintegration. It is described as a form of identification that is prior to projective identification in that it does not involve a sense of inner space into which one can project elements of self.[9]

---

further deformed when recombined in that rather than being submitted to synthesis, integration and articulation, those elements are violently impacted, fused and randomly juxtaposed with one another. The components of bizarre objects appear violently compressed, smeared, and randomly heaped on one another. The terms *agglutination* and *agglomeration* refer to these unusual qualities of bizarre objects.

[9] Although I recognize that speculation concerning psychic events in infancy is inevitably adultomorphic, I believe that formulations giving genetic primacy to one form or another of what is basically a fantasy are overly so. It is possible that the infant experiences and registers in memory a sequence involving an internal event such as a gas pain, a self-produced cry, a shift in position, or being held and gently patted on the back followed by a burp and relief. This I would conceptualize might be mentally registered in the form of a fantasy of symbiotic projective identification based primarily on body-centered events. Such fantasies might occur in the absence of concepts of internal, external, self or object. When these concepts are available, they would be used as realizations mating with and transforming body-centered preconceptions into more advanced conceptual forms.

Case Report

A thirty-five-year-old male attorney speaks anxiously of his sexual attraction for a female friend. Whenever he ejaculates he experiences enormous fatigue which he associates to loss of energy. It is tremendously frightening to be unable to function because of fatigue. He recalls a dream. He is in a bar frequented by Hell's Angels and their girl friends; the girls look as tough as their boy friends. Then he's alone with two women, old girl friends who are teasing in a sexually provocative fashion. He becomes annoyed and frightened, he doesn't want to be aroused and flees to a bathroom where, on defecating, he feels tremendous relief. This is suddenly followed by fatigue. He associates to a young psychotic client who experiences loss of control and violent rages and who recently assaulted his mother and sister. He should have arranged for his client to be locked up, my patient states, but it's his job to provide the man with legal representation. He notes that his client is as strong as he is and worries that he might be injured if attacked by him. I comment that in the dream he is expelling via defecation an enraged aspect of himself, felt to be psychotic, because he fears that he will lose control and harm himself or others. He defends himself against guilt at this level. I wonder if he doesn't do something similar on ejaculation and get rid of this violent part of himself, expelling it into his partner, and creating this Hell's Angel in male and female form. As a result, he experiences, in a very concrete way, a loss of strength, vigor, and assertive and aggressive potential. He has gotten rid of a part of him that is as strong as he is and contains all of his strength. In response, the patient reveals a fantasy he often experiences on ejaculation: he sees himself being carried down a raging stream, spinning out of control into a void. It is terrifying. The patient clarifies that this fantasy occurs whether intercourse or masturbation is involved, and I note that he appears to be attempting to rid himself permanently of a part of the self by sending it down into a void. Perhaps he escapes the woman in this way because she is experienced as persecutory, as too much of a Hell's Angel. The patient agrees in such a way as to convey that his agreement is intellectual; there is more to this than can be immediately clarified.

My understanding of the case to this point is that my patient cannot use a woman as a container for his projections. He is immediately inhibited in any attempt to form a neurotic compromise. Such a compromise might occur as follows: In response to a fear of a violent reaction or frustration, a man develops a fantasy, that he deposits an angry part of self in his partner on ejaculation. In his fantasy, gratification results in getting rid of an angry frustrated aspect of self and depositing it into paradise or into a woman's body standing for mother. The dark side of his wish now takes hold and he feels trapped (Mason, 1981). If it goes no further this might result in a persecutory quality adhering to his relations to women but, if he has the capacity for displacement from mother's body onto an aircraft or other enclosure, then a fear of flying or claustrophobia will result. My patient cannot form these neurotic compromises nor can he form a stable persecutory relation. Why not?

In subsequent sessions the patient reveals that he never cuddled with his mother as she reacted stiffly and was uncomfortable with any show of emotion. He cuddled with father who was very affectionate. If the patient is the least bit angry, mother retreats or is unresponsive. He regularly fights with his father and with an older brother, getting into heated arguments with both without creating any lasting problems. As a child, my patient went through a long period of negativism and was reported to have had violent temper tantrums. Mother reacted with indifference. Father would just lock him up in a room or haul him off bodily if he refused to go to school, but never struck him. So it makes some sense that he can't use a woman as a container for his projections. His mother reacts as if she cannot contain any emotional display on his part. But other factors quickly emerge. As Valentine's Day approaches, the patient dreams that he gives a former girl friend a tube of lipstick of his favorite dark red color. As she is applying the lipstick she suddenly starts chewing it and spits out a brownish glop which looks disgusting, like tobacco juice or diarrhea. So we have evidence that not only does mother refuse to accept her son's projections but also that when she does accept them she is experienced as taking in something good and turning it into something bad. Libidinal zonal confusions with oral, anal, and vaginal condensation, agglutination, and agglomeration; distortion of functioning is evidence of abnormal splitting. Another dream provides further clarification:

He goes through a hedge and enters a room. He gets on a couch with a former girl friend. Both are nude. A younger and older man are on couches opposite watching and masturbating. My patient leaves the woman and approaches the male couple because he feels that what is happening with them is much more interesting. He is suddenly horrified and repulsed. He states, "It's bizarre!" The older man has a cigarette instead of a penis, "It's big and covering a hole. It's not a vagina or anus, just a hole." He associates to dreams of innumerable jagged holes in golf courses so that one can't tell where the cup is, to holes in his jacket, and to holes in the acoustical tiles in my office.

He recalls another dream in which a strange automobile appears. Its paint appears "brownish with patches of green and is glopped or heaped on in places." The automobile appears to have been constructed from pieces of other cars some of which have been hammered or slapped onto it. In its rear a tail pipe emerges, stretching out and spewing brownish fumes. We have here a very bizarre object, probably the result of abnormal splitting and condensation, with agglutination and agglomeration producing references to combined parent figures, castration fears, and voids which prevent placing something in a proper container. There are also references to a fecal penis and to fetish formation, elements which can't be reworked by phobic or obsessional mechanisms and transformed into neurotic elements.[10] As these psychotic elements are interpretively sorted out, infantile and neurotic aspects of personality functioning erupt in dreams:

The patient dreams that he is in an apartment and moves a tiny baby boy from the edge of a dining table to its center so that he will be safe from falling. The infant sits on a history or philosophy book which is open to a chapter on Sigmund Freud. He closes the book, smothering the baby, but then opens it to save the child. The child is then described as very active and

[10] The Kleinian position is that it is within the capacity of neurotic and normal aspects of self to transform infantile and psychotic elements into more advanced forms (Segal, 1964).

vigorous. Crawling rapidly across the floor it voraciously chews his carpet with what seem like glinting steel teeth. In another scene he is in his childhood home in Chicago with an old friend that he greets with a hug. The friend is a radical, is tough, appears like a skinhead, and is a member of the Jewish Defense League. Suddenly an animal tries to jump onto his table. It is strange looking, like a mixture of muskrat, possum, and armadillo. Its eyes are red and its colors seem to be gold and blue smeared together. It is frightening. He awakens feeling that he has had a "primitive, crazy experience. It's so unreal and strange, so monstrous and repulsive. I woke up feeling hopeless and suicidal."

From his associations his hatred of hungry, voracious, infantile aspects of the self lead to his wanting to eject them into his history teacher girl friend, his philosopher mother, and into Freud standing for me in the transference. As a result, we are experienced as being as persecutory, voraciously demanding of him, and to be avoided. The infant's steel teeth and vigorous activity form links with the bizarre automobile and animal figures. Putting him in touch with these voraciously demanding desirous aspects result in his dreaming the next day of a large dog that grasps him by the hand and holds him immobilized. He speaks of feeling immobilized by his German girl friend and of his recent fear of dogs. He had never been afraid of dogs but more recently is growing increasingly leery of them. We can see a movement here from infantile, persecutory solutions to phobic means of dealing with his conflicts. With this development he reveals memories of rare instances when mother would become enraged with him and verbally abuse him.

Many neurotic issues were dealt with in this man's analysis but I have demonstrated other, nonneurotic aspects of personality functioning that required at least equal attention.

Two other brief clinical examples will demonstrate my point:

A twenty-four-year-old female musician complained that she was afraid to perform in public. She had many difficulties with her schooling as a result of a lifelong problem with memory. Her symptom was complex. In one instance she imagined that she was playing piano for me and that I was sexually aroused and masturbating. So playing in public was equated with masturbation and her superego response resulted in inhibition of memory, a nice neurotic configuration. There were additional dimensions to her difficulties, however. She reported that there were times when written sheet music was unintelligible to her. It was all jumbled and mixed up or the page appeared blank. This was an extremely serious symptom, a negative hallucination. Some time later I noticed that at times when I spoke, she held her hand up and wiggled it. She revealed that at these times she imagined typing my words onto a sheet of paper. When she disliked what I was saying she typed a jumble and if I persisted she erased the words. Further analysis of this fantasy of omnipotent denial and annihilation of what she disliked resolved her symptom.

A final example demonstrates the relationship of trauma to internal fantasy:

A twenty-two-year-old hospitalized schizophrenic patient is in remission on phenothiazines. When actively psychotic, he hallucinates shooting blue streams of energy from his eyes and fingertips and destroying whatever troubles him. While in remission, he often imagines a similar capacity and easily recognizes that he is imagining. One day while watching television he was disturbed by a commentator and imagined zapping the set. At that instance the set exploded and burst into flames. My patient went berserk, smashing at himself and screaming. He required restraints and continued for a month to be regressed and self-destructive. What I subsequently discovered is that the blue rays represent an evacuation of depression. My patient's mother was emotionally and physically ill all his life. He believed he was at fault. This genetic reality, having an ill mother, confirmed his omnipotent destructive fantasies as a child, a situation symbolically repeated when the set exploded.

I'll close my discussion by addressing myself briefly to the papers that have been presented.

I agree with much of what Dr. Arlow presented but I differ with him on one point. I believe that we do provide patients with something new and essential to change other than interpretation of underlying conflicts. What is provided, and is equally essential, is a consistently understanding object that persists in its stance despite the provocations and attempts at disruption and distortion instituted by the patient. Dr. Willick admirably demonstrates this capacity in his report of his work with what I consider to be a difficult patient. When patients can do this for themselves they have developed what Bion terms the psychoanalytic function of the personality.

Boesky notes that the aggressive and libidinal drives are the wellsprings of human motivation. I don't understand why he limits the aggressive drive derivatives to sadism. What of assertion and defensive activity? I am also not sure that we should limit the drives to two. The Kleinians and Bion have creatively used the concept of an epistomophilic instinct, for instance, as an inborn motive force governing reality relations. Finally, the concept of drives is much too broad to adequately serve as an organizing principle in explaining many aspects of human motivation. I find attempts like those of Dr. Joseph Lichtenberg (1989) to provide us with a theory of structured motivation to have a great deal of merit. There are clearly needs for attachment and affiliation and for the fulfillment of curiosity. Individuals under the influence of psychotic aspects of their personality show particular difficulties in these areas.

I agree with what Dr. Tyson says but I wonder about what he doesn't say or address himself to. How do events in earliest infancy affect the expression and internalization of later developmental conflicts? What are the effects of the internalization of early abnormal infant–caretaker interrelations on the sorts of conflicts he so well documents?

Dr. Mayer's paper is an elegantly presented example of a classically conducted, thoroughly successful psychoanalysis of a neurotic patient. I am also in essential agreement with the points made by Dr. Kafka. In his second clinical illustration, that of the thirty-two-year-old man, I would consider the dehumanization and dreams of being a space explorer as evidence of the activity of a psychotic aspect of personality functioning. Sending curious, exploring, epistomophilic aspects of self into the void of space is an especially ominous dynamic which I suspect represents an attack on essential ego functions. This is followed by homosexual activity, which I would view as an effort to make use of a container to project into and find infantile or neurotic reassurance against the fear of loss of self involved in projection into a void. This same configuration is repeated later when the patient dreams that his brother loses a

finger and this is followed by fantasies of forcing anal intercourse on his analyst. He wants to force an aspect of the self into
his analyst to prevent its permanent loss as well as to control
him as an object. My suspicion is that this configuration is a
complex compromise resulting from the simultaneous activity
of neurotic and psychotic aspects of personality. It results from
the submission of an emotional experience to two different sets
of transformational processes. How one approaches such com-
plexes interpretively is guided first and foremost by the prevalent transference.

Finally, I am in essential agreement with the issues raised by
Dr. Willick. I would be much more active in interpreting what I
believe to be widespread evidence of infantile aspects of personality functioning, including projective identification. In addition, I feel there is some evidence that the patient is, at times,
under the influence of an omnipotent unconscious fantasy, the
sense of which is that she is being held or contained within the
current and past analytic relationship. Specifically, the patient's
wish that Dr. Willick think about her constantly when she is away
from him can be seen as a wish to be contained within his mind
and not ejected as something bad, as she felt her biological
mother had done. I understand her incapacity to recall Dr.
Willick not as a deficit but as an identification with the object in
fantasy who cannot remember her or hold her in mind. These
formulations are meant as additions to and not replacements for
the formulations made by Dr. Willick involving jealousy and
triadic whole object conflicts. Finally, I don't detect enough
evidence in the material he presents to indicate the activity of the
psychotic aspects of personality to consider the patient a borderline. I believe that considering her as an infantile or narcissistic personality type is nearer the mark.

Summary

I have described four aspects of personality functioning that
organize our representation of self and objects in unconscious
fantasy: normal, neurotic, infantile, and psychotic. Following
Bion's (1967) usage, each of these varieties is considered as a

mental state, all simultaneously coexisting in a given individual. At any given time in an analysis an individual will show evidence in behavior of the preponderance of one or another of these mental states which may interpenetrate or contaminate one another. Each state is characterized by different degrees of organization and stability, by the mental mechanisms that form a part of its organization, structure, and modalities of functioning as well as by the anxieties and specific danger situations characteristic of it. All dimensions of a given aspect of personality functioning are represented in unconscious fantasy.

Chapter 10

A Self
Psychological Perspective

Paul H. Ornstein, M.D.

We have been presented with a unique series of six essays on conflict and compromise. This uniqueness resides in the fact that the six authors were selected with the explicit purpose of representing a single point of view within psychoanalysis, although even this single point of view is not monolithic as is clear from some of the variations on the main theme.

I was certain that I could find in these papers the elements common to all psychoanalytic perspectives; those that form natural bridges from one perspective to another and reveal both their similarities and their substantive differences.

A discussant from another theoretical perspective is often a nuisance. He cannot fully approve and affirm the presenters' views if he sets out to consider them entirely from his own differing perspective. He is then rightfully experienced as an external observer, who is unreasonably critical from across that great divide. Moreover, he cannot be heard. He cannot engender a true dialogue. Those on the other side of the divide will not listen to him.

Perhaps the crux of the problem of communication regarding some of the fundamental differences between the various psychoanalytic paradigms hinges on their differing views of what psychoanalysis is; what each considers the psychoanalytic observational method to be; and what basic assumptions (or axioms) inform their respective observational methods. At the heart of each paradigm then is also a different view of neurosogenesis. The differences between the various paradigms and their clinical implications are therefore rightly stressed. But it would be a mistake to emphasize these differences exclusively, without also calling attention to the many points of contact between them. After all, they have a common historical origin and they all deal with the subjective inner world; their subject matter is the same. Freud himself, in his paper "On Narcissism" (Freud, 1914), already formulated the beginnings of an ego psychology, the outlines of an object relations theory, and the rudiments of a self psychology. There must therefore be many connecting links between each of these theories (certainly on the clinical level), no matter how far each claims to have become an encompassing paradigm of its own.

At present there is no generally accepted scientific approach according to which these differing perspectives (or paradigms) in psychoanalysis can be reliably assessed. And there is no established tradition for an open-minded discussion of vastly differing clinical–theoretical approaches. Therefore, to enhance the possibility of a dialogue, I shall first enter, as fully as I can, into the perspectives presented by the authors and reflect on their presentations entirely from within their own theoretical position. I hope thereby to understand and appreciate their work and only raise some questions from the "inside" as it were. I shall then offer an alternative perspective on the central issues that emerged in the six essays.

Views from Within the Authors' Perspective

Some General Remarks—Scanning the Terrain

It is easy to identify the territory that the authors staked out individually and collectively in their contributions because of the lucidity and simplicity with which they presented complex theoretical issues and clinical illustrations. The sequence of the presentations revealed a fine orchestration which made it easier for us to grasp the overall message. Arlow introduced the theory; Boesky elaborated on the details, with special emphasis on compromise formation, and exemplified them; Tyson offered some of the developmental underpinnings for conflict and compromise; while Mayer, Willick, and Kafka, in their own sensitive fashion, illustrated how they thought the theory guided their interventions in a variety of clinical conditions.

Their overall message, as I heard it, went something like this. Modern structural theory has reconceptualized intrapsychic conflict, identified its many sources and components, and placed it at the center of theory and practice. Intrapsychic conflict engenders anxiety, guilt, shame, or depressive affect and thereby demands the formation of compromise solutions. This, in turn, engenders more conflict and more compromise formation, both of which are thus ubiquitous and multilayered. Conflict and compromise is what the mind is made up of in both health and illness. Conflict and compromise is the way the mind works. Thus everywhere we see conflict and compromise, although we are not entirely certain what turns normal conflict and normal compromise into pathological conflict and pathological compromise, certainly a key question in neurosogenesis. What we do know, the authors claim, is that these concepts best account for symptom formation as well as therapeutic change at the present time. How? By identifying the components of intrapsychic conflicts and the components of compromise formations and their interactions with each other.

Insight into these components and their interactions, via focusing on the formation and resolution of resistances, will be accompanied by significant therapeutic change. The clinical illustrations presented all demonstrate, in their authors' view, the usefulness and validity of these assumptions. The patients suffered from diverse clinical conditions yet they could all be approached essentially with the same concepts and theories in mind. There was no need for new concepts or theories; no technical alterations were introduced, except for enabling and maintaining the therapeutic communication where necessary. The concepts and theories of modern structural theory thus clearly apply across all clinical categories; this was their explicit message.

Claims to the contrary, the need for other concepts and theories, such as for instance the concept of "deficit," are therefore in error and have thus far remained scientifically unsubstantiated. By implication the concepts of modern structural theory are considered scientifically sound and well established, even if incomplete and still evolving.

I hope I have grasped and conveyed the central message accurately in this highly condensed resume. But to be sure, and in order to find the specific issues in need of further clarification, let us scan the individual presentations.

Arlow made our swift entry into the frame of reference of the six papers possible with a masterfully comprehensive overview. In it he touched on every single core issue relevant to neurosogenesis, including the current controversies that center around the concepts of trauma and deficit in their relation to conflict. He ended up, not unexpectedly, by putting structural conflict and the ensuing compromise into the very center of his perspective. This led him to redefine trauma as a "special vicissitude of development seen in the context of continuing intrapsychic conflict" (p. 7). He considerably restricted thereby the formerly more significant pathogenetic role of trauma in neurosogenesis. From the perspective of the primacy of structural conflict and compromise formation, Arlow rightly questioned the clinical usefulness and theoretical validity of the concept of deficit; he does not know where to place it, or what to do with it analytically. All of Arlow's views expressed in his presentation are properly embedded in and logically follow from his definition of psychoanalysis "as first and foremost a psychology of conflict" (p. 3), a dynamic and a developmental psychology. These views are inextricably interwoven with his ideas about the nature of the developmental process as this emerges in the psychoanalytic investigative and treatment situation, in which the analyst has a dual role of "observer" and "participant."

Arlow's final challenging questions regarding the pathogenetic role of deficit and its psychoanalytic treatment flow from the consistency of his views. They invite further consideration and I shall take them up in due course.

Boesky put on his theoretical magnifying lens and focused on a detailed explication and demonstration of the specific characteristics and components of compromise formation; and on the nature and components of intrapsychic conflict, detailing their advantages for modern structural theory. He sees these advantages in being able to account for symptom formation as well as therapeutic change. He considers conflict, compromise formation, and resistance as inseparable and the alteration of resistance via interpretation as the vehicle for change. Boesky's microscopic analysis of the key conceptions of modern structural theory is based on what Arlow and Brenner (1964) and Brenner (1982) introduced into psychoanalysis and what Boesky himself synthesized and further elaborated in this paper and on a number of previous occasions (Boesky, 1986, 1988a,b). Glancing at the historical evolution of the concept of intrapsychic conflict and compromise formation, Boesky pointed to the essence of the theory through illustrative clinical vignettes. He chose the concepts of sublimation, acting out, and identification to show us how far and in what specific respects modern structural theory has advanced through a redefinition of these (and many other) concepts by identifying their various components.

It is Boesky's "strong claim" that compromise formation is our best explanation for pathogenesis as well as for accounting for therapeutic change (along with his views on deficit) that invites further consideration.

Tyson set the stage for tracing the development of conflict from the beginning of extrauterine life, by first reminding us, as did Arlow and Boesky earlier, that "conflict exists in all of us" and that "mental health or illness is based, not on particular conflicts, but on the degree of success or failure in resolving the conflicts to which everyone is subject" (p. 31). So far, Tyson maintains, there is complete agreement. He then goes on to say that "this remarkable degree of agreement does not extend to [the question of] how we define conflict, to what its origins are, to what it is that is in conflict, or [to the question of] what to do about it [in the clinical situation]" (p. 31). Tyson believes that the study of conflict in children can shed some light on these questions. In his comprehensive survey he distinguished three different types of conflicts: internal, developmental, and internalized. He pointed to their origin as well as to the timing and context of their emergence, the question of when and how they become built into the mind. He considered the appearance of intrapsychic conflict a developmental achievement, culminating in the well-known conflicts of the oedipal phase. Past that phase, he cautions, "conflicts cannot be understood simply in terms of the time of their origin, but must instead be seen as affecting and affected by all conflicts before and after, and by all the solutions that have been made along the way" (p. 48). He stresses the fact that:

> The child's capacities and preferences for solutions to these [oedipal] problems are dependent in a large measure on what went on before and indeed his burden may be significantly greater if earlier conflicts persist or were dealt with insufficiently. The clinician is often enough faced with a disturbance which has significant oedipal elements but is also pervaded with earlier conflicts which must be addressed as well [p. 47].

No doubt Tyson's perspective is vastly different from Arlow's and Boesky's, but he did not spell out whether or not it still fits under the umbrella of modern structural theory as a variant of it. I wish Tyson had elaborated some more on his last statement and had thereby taken a stand as a child analyst on the question of deficit (in its developmental, clinical, and theoretical dimensions). He could then also have addressed the question of intrapsychic conflicts other than those based on drive derivatives, the only ones Arlow and Boesky appear to have considered of pathogenic significance.

The first two papers I just scanned painted a clear and full portrait of modern structural theory and the third one offered a broadened perspective. They prepared us well for turning our attention to the impact of these concepts and theories on the actual conduct of the treatment process reported in the three clinical presentations.

Mayer skillfully took us all into her consulting room as she reflected on how she happened to choose her patient, Annette, for psychoanalysis, from among other patients with strikingly similar complaints, and then for this particular presentation. She wished to circumscribe or specify the problem area in which she could best illustrate the value of conflict and compromise. Although her patient's complaints were vague and constantly shifting at first, indicating perhaps a more seriously disorganized personality, "a sense of conflict was palpable" underneath it all, and Mayer used this as an indication that she should take this patient into analysis.

The vivid portrayal of the analysis (even as it was highly condensed) includes the description of the patient's feeling about the analyst as "largely characterized by slightly nervous idealization punctuated by brief moments of sadness" (p. 57), a transference constellation which ultimately permitted the reconstruction of its infantile or childhood antecedents. Mayer aptly recognized this as the reemergence in the transference of her patient's negative Oedipus complex. And it is in relation to her recognition of that as the central pathogenetic issue (with which I agree, even if I would interpret its meaning and significance differently), as well as the manner in which she uses the concepts of conflict and compromise that I wish to comment on later.

Willick chose a patient with a borderline condition, whose previous analytic treatment was unsuccessful. He introduced his clinical report by letting us know clearly and succinctly that he was aware of the various clinical and theoretical issues regarding the assumptions of developmental defects or deficits, their supposed origins, and that they were considered by many analysts as unrelated to and/or preceding sexual and aggressive conflicts. Rather than discussing this in the abstract, he embarked on showing us "how one can work with and conceptualize the problem of ego deficit and psychic conflict" (p. 80). It is his way of combining these two concepts, while the theoreticians decry the validity of the concept of deficit and the need for such a combination, that will claim our special attention. In his clinical work, presented straightforwardly with compassion and lucidity, Willick proceeded courageously and with much needed flexibility. My questions relate to two issues: one is that Willick appears to minimize the role of his flexibility and attunement to his patient's needs in the curative process; and the other has to do with his claim that it is not useful to separate ego impairments that are the result of psychic conflict from those that supposedly preceded conflict and have to do with basic structure formation. Why is that not useful and how does he know that it is not?

Kafka chose two clinical vignettes to illustrate how "unconscious conflicts affect all manifestations of behavior" (p. 66), in character disorders as much as in symptomatic disorders. Thus the two are not fundamentally different disturbances, conflict and compromise are central to the understanding and treatment of both. He restricted his focus to illustrating how he engaged his difficult-to-engage patients in an analytic process.

One of the ways in which conflict and compromise manifest themselves in the therapeutic setting is the transference, in the distortions in the patient's experience of the analyst. Kafka's main point in his presentation dealt with how to identify and bring home to the patient his or her transference distortions in order to evoke a more felicitous compromise formation in response to the analyst's confrontations and interpretations. His conduct of the treatment appears to dovetail with Arlow's and Boesky's conceptualizations more than with Mayer's and Willick's. This is what Kafka says: "[U]nconscious conflicts might be more successfully resolved if they could be revealed to the patient and better understood. The task is to discover and help the patient understand his unconscious conflicts and their unwanted, as well as useful, effects. It behooves the therapist to be attuned to signs of unconscious conflict" (pp. 66–67).

Kafka then proceeded to show us how he pursued this effort in his work with two patients. It is in relation to Kafka's interchanges with his patients that I shall examine his message about how to engage patients in a psychoanalytic treatment process.

Having thus scanned all six papers, I shall now examine some of the central themes that emerged in them and I shall do so in the light of the case material presented to us.

A Discussion of Some Key Issues in the Six Presentations

We may identify in the authors' presentations three areas that encompass the key issues: (1) the centrality of conflict and compromise as a basic assumption that informs the observational method and treatment approach of modern structural theory; (2) the question of what is curative in psychoanalysis, including the specific role and function of the analyst as observer and participant in that process; and (3) the controversy about deficit, including the role of trauma and reality in pathogenesis and in the treatment process. All of this should be discussed after a closer look at the clinical contributions.

The basic assumption of the centrality of conflict and compromise already determines our view of the nature of psychoanalysis as an investigative and treatment process; as well as our view of trauma and deficit, since it always makes us search a priori for conflict and compromise. This tight relation of the component concepts of a theoretical system to each other leads to an internal logic that is violated when we arbitrarily lift individual concepts from their native soil for an independent assessment. Each concept makes full sense only in the context in which it was originally developed, unless it is carefully redefined in its new context; but by then it has become a different concept. The careless borrowing of indigenous concepts for use in other contexts is hazardous, because it leads to many misunderstandings. Thus, I believe, the above three issues are inextricably interrelated and cannot be considered independently of one another, a principle that is frequently violated in contemporary psychoanalytic discourse.

What is of more immediate interest for our present purpose, and should serve to organize this part of my discussion, is to consider how far, and in what particular fashion, the concepts and theories enunciated were actually translated into each analyst's attitudes, understandings, and interventions. Are treatment and theory, when looked at from within, truly of one cloth, as the authors portray their work? Or, are there discrepancies, certain experiences within the process, that, in fact, necessitated moving outside of the territory staked out by the theory, while insisting on having essentially remained within the area of conflict and compromise?

The clinical presentations juxtaposed to the theoretical expositions are most instructive in this regard, and I shall take a small "psychological biopsy" of each clinical presentation to shed some light on the preceding questions. For the sake of economy and the cohesiveness of my discussion I should be permitted to regard all six presentations from a broad clinical and theoretical perspective as a single whole, without doing injustice to the individual essays.

I shall begin with Kafka's clinical examples as a baseline for two reasons: (1) he translates his theory into his treatment approach with clarity and consistency, most unambiguously;

and (2) he had chosen both of his patients from the category of neuroses or neurotic character disorders, the traditional, established domain of psychoanalysis. His clinical vignettes have the distinct advantage that we can follow with him, practically step-by-step, the vicissitudes of the patients' irrational reactions to his interventions or other activities, and learn what he does with them. Kafka searches directly for the conflict and pathological compromise both in the transference and outside of it. He confronts his patients with their transference distortions and pathological compromises, in the hope that ultimate insight into the sources of those distortions will modify them. He restricts here his clinical illustrations to a "careful demonstration of the paradoxical and prejudgmental elements revealed through transference manifestations" and considers this "a particularly valuable tool in the treatment of patients with character problems, whose conscious motivation for treatment is not great" (p. 68).

Regarding his immediate goal of engaging his two reluctant patients in analysis, Kafka succeeded. Regarding the hoped for modification of their psychopathology, he acknowledged minimal change in response to his specific interventions in the first instance and a somewhat greater amelioration, over the long run, in the second one. The patients' "transference attitudes" did not yield much to his confrontations. In fact, as Kafka faithfully reports, the first patient objected to many of his interventions and the second one remained "polite, correct, and generally cooperative" for some time, but "seemed emotionally uninvolved" in the face of repeated confrontations and interpretations. We may wonder how the patient could have become more involved emotionally in the face of the specific interventions, each of which questioned the validity of his subjective experiences.

Let us look at a representative sample of interchanges (with each of his patients) to study Kafka's approach and its clinical and theoretical implications.

Patient 1. As the reader will recall, at one point, after an exchange between Kafka and his woman patient regarding the many demands put on her (now by her lover and analyst and earlier in her childhood by her brother), the patient felt criticized by Kafka's remark "that the work situation was evidently yet another setting in which excessive demands were made [on her]" (p. 70). In response, she criticized the treatment and, without having prepared Kafka for it previously, indicated that she would stop treatment right then, rather than pay for her missed appointments during her upcoming vacation.

Kafka expressed his surprise at not having been told about this plan before and questioned the patient's assumption of his unreasonableness and rigidity, which could perhaps best be described as a demonstration, confrontation, and clarification, all in one intervention. Since Kafka demonstrated his flexibility regarding the prearranged vacation by indicating that he would not charge for those missed appointments, his patient decided to stay in treatment.

Kafka then added that many "other examples of mistaken prejudgments" surfaced in the treatment, one of which should be quoted here verbatim:

In one instance, the patient alluded to having received a promotion months after the event, and when I expressed surprise that she had not mentioned this earlier, the patient maintained that I was interested only in problems, not in successes. I replied that her belief that I was only interested in problems might well reflect the fact that she insisted on relating to me according to the view that I am a domineering and demanding person, despite the absence of supporting evidence to that effect [p. 71].

Kafka, true to his theory, challenged his patient's assumptions of his motives as "mistaken" and proceeded to show that they were unfounded. He acted according to his own description of his motives and thus feels justified in pointing out the patient's mistaken notions. I am highlighting these elements in Kafka's approach in order to underline my observation that he, as do all of us, inevitably introduces a variety of other interventions along with his clearly acknowledged demonstrations, clarifications, confrontations, and interpretations, but he does not directly pursue his patient's subjective experiences of him. Perhaps the patient did have some supportive evidence of her own to buttress her assumption; how would we ever find out without asking and without searching in the patient's transference attitudes and enactments for the reflection of such evidence? It is not that Kafka thinks he is always right in his interpretations. But when his patient rejects them; we do not hear him exploring why they failed to make sense to the patient.

Exploration of Kafka's patient's feelings would appear to me to be the only way to get to the transference meaning and ultimate analysis of the distortions, irrespective of whether the source of the patient's observations is internal or external. Instead of subjecting the patient's distortions to such an analysis, Kafka deflects her feelings by directly correcting the distortions which are fueled by those feelings. Such an approach might decrease, rather than increase, the patient's resistances and thus avoid an iatrogenically provoked intensification of them.

These remarks are prompted by the patient's persistent rejections of the analyst's interventions and because in the analyst's own view these have not altered the patient's attitude appreciably. A quick glance at an interchange with the second patient will further sharpen some of these questions and raise some new ones.

Patient 2. A dream of the second patient, a man, should suffice to convey Kafka's line of interpretations with him. "After a party at which a woman seemed attracted to him, the patient dreamed that he was a space explorer, far removed from earth." Kafka says:

> I suggested the interpretation that he seemed to remove himself from human contact in the dream. This was followed by the patient picking up a homosexual partner for a sexual fling, which I again interpreted as an effort to present himself as independent in the sense of not needing others. Perhaps, I ventured, he had never surmounted his disappointment and anger with his mother, who, he might well have thought, had betrayed and abandoned him when he reached adolescence [p. 74].

Kafka then adds that "this line of interpretation seemed to have no effect."

Comments and Questions

We may rightly assume that the analyst had the benefit of the patient's association in addition to a much more extensive knowledge about him than is available to us. We are given the possible precipitant for the dream (the experience of a woman's attraction to him at a party) and then the manifest dream. The interpretation given ("that he seemed to remove himself from human contact in the dream") sounds accurate in a general way, but by-passed the possible specific and immediate transference meaning of the dream. The patient portrayed himself as a "space explorer"—in the analysis. Kafka already told us that the patient was "polite, correct, and generally cooperative, but also tepid" and "emotionally uninvolved." Could the patient himself not have had this same perception of his own experience in the analysis and express it in his dream? Why did Kafka not use his own insight to connect the patient's dream with these feelings in the analysis?

When, in response to Kafka's interpretation, the patient engaged in a fleeting homosexual encounter, Kafka did not explore the patient's transference feelings but quickly moved to a genetic speculation. He did not interpret the motivation of the homosexual fling.

What have we learned from this examination of Kafka's approach? In these instances, his theory translated into a questioning attitude regarding his patients' experiencing of him, while simultaneously he undoubtedly shows great care, concern, and commitment to them. He is rational and logical, bent on exposing, gently and tactfully (as much as such things can be done gently and tactfully), his patients' illogic in their "transference distortions" and "mistaken prejudgments." He expects, as I see it, that his patients should ultimately recognize his attitudes and actions as different from their own immediate, stated assessment of them. And when he points out their attitudes and actions, they should (ultimately) recognize his objectivity. To accomplish this transformation in the long run, he repeatedly demonstrates the evidence he has obtained of their unconscious conflicts. Kafka's theory translates into his understanding of the various manifestations of unconscious conflicts

in their disguises and the pathological compromise they engender. In the instances described, his theory leads to the kind of
interpretations in which he eschews the understanding of the
patients' "distortions" and "prejudgments" from their own subjective perspective as an avenue to their unconscious sources.
Instead, he prefers to correct the patients' distortions directly.

Let us next look at how Mayer translates the conflict and compromise theory into her particular approach to the analysis of
Annette. To begin with she offers us a slightly different perspective on the theory. It is important to examine her language about
conflict carefully to see whether she merely applies the theory less
stringently (or, only less insistently?); or, she simply recognizes
certain needs of her patient and responds accordingly, regardless
of the more exacting demands of the theory as presented in the
three theoretical papers and illustrated by Kafka. Mayer does
speak the conflict-and-compromise-language, but in a different
dialect and with a different accent. While she considers, in agreement with the other authors, that "intrapsychic conflict . . . [is] at
the heart of analytic thinking about psychology," at times this
provides only a "general underpinning [for her] thinking about a
patient" (p. 49), but at other times it makes a "radical difference"
in her approach and treatment choice. When she speaks of mixed
feelings as "conflicted" it is not clear whether Mayer means
pathogenic, intersystemic conflicts, or conflicts in an everyday
sense. This ambiguity is present even where it would seem that
she might mean the former. In discussing Annette's fantasy "that
men are extraneous and women can be completely fulfilling to
each other," she says that Annette:

> [F]inds herself reflecting on the other side, how part of what she
> likes about Joe [her husband] involves his being *different* from her
> mother, and how she does value that difference. She wants what
> he has to offer too. Then she returns to the dream and links her
> mother with the woman who was so gratifying. This back and
> forth, by the way, exemplifies for me the everyday way in which we
> see derivatives of intrapsychic conflict manifest—the expression
> of a wish, the expression of a defense against that wish (often in
> itself representing an opposing wish), then back to the first wish
> [pp. 55–56].

The expression "everyday way" introduces here the ambiguity between pathogenic and ubiquitous, normal conflicts, since the sequence as given could occur in anyone without the presence of a clinical neurosis. This is an ambiguity which I personally find refreshing in that it gives Mayer's presentation its immediate, true-to-life ambience. It is an everyday way of speaking of certain inner experiences. But in the context of this discussion such ambiguity raises questions about the specificity of her language, particularly in view of Tyson's many questions about the sources and nature of conflict and the lack of unanimity about its definitions. This ambiguity persists in Mayer's otherwise felicitous phrase that in Annette's case (in contrast to some of the others she spoke of with similar complaints) "the sense of internal conflict was palpable."

With this phrase Mayer portrays how she decided in favor of an analysis. So far, so good, and aptly described. But, if conflict and compromise are ubiquitous both in health and pathology, should this not, strictly speaking, always be the case? Would we not have to specify more explicitly what we mean by the "palpability" of conflict? Specific or not, as her usage might be, however, and this is most significant, she is certainly not prevented by her conflict-language from hearing other issues in her patient's communications; other issues that she does not immediately reduce to the "basic" elements of conflict and compromise in her interventions. It may even be that it is the very ambiguity with which Mayer talks about conflict that permits her to be more encompassing in what she hears.

An example of the latter is provided in the "episode during which certain shifts in the transference . . . became evident for the first time" (p. 57). Annette's idealization of her analyst was present from early on and was "punctuated by brief moments of sadness." Mayer accepted these idealizations without directly challenging them as defensive distortions and she also accepted (until additional, more compelling, meanings of it emerged) Annette's explanations of her "brief moments of sadness" in the sessions as repetitions of her experiences with her mother. She considered this explanation valid as far as it went, but this insight did not lead to the cessation of these episodes of sadness, whose

precipitants remained unclear and whose identifications by
Annette were "global and vague." It was at this point in the
analytic process, as you may recall, that the analysis of a parapraxis on Annette's part led analyst and patient to the important
discovery of considerable, extra-analytic, hidden gratifications of
her idealizing transference, including certain satisfying enactments. When the opportunities for these ceased and Annette's
vicarious participation in her analyst's admired extracurricular
interests abruptly ended, she became angry with her and sad in a
more sustained fashion. Significantly, Mayer notes: "[Annette]
hated the idea of being angry with me; she didn't want to be" (p.
59). Yet, in her anger she turned intensely critical, and "her tone
was bitter and for the first time her jealousy became apparent" (p.
59). Mayer registers that Annette "was angry because she felt
jealous, because she felt thwarted in her secret helpfulness to me,
and most of all because she was bitterly disappointed at the disruption of what had been our happy and gratifying relationship"
(p. 60). This is a beautiful formulation. It rings true to me and is
well buttressed by the total context in which it is presented. But
where is the intersystemic pathogenic conflict in this language?
Mayer skillfully put all of the above, in retrospect, under the
umbrella of an essentially unresolved "negative oedipal transference," the proper organizing conception in keeping with her
guiding theory. Since Mayer's approach and formulation provide us with those contact points between different paradigms I
spoke of earlier, I shall have more to say about this later in my discussion. Here, I wish to pursue the examination of the preceding
"psychological biopsy" for its clinical–theoretical implications.

Comments and Questions

It appears that Mayer's acceptance of Annette's subjective
experiences, rather than challenging them, allowed for the emergence of her intense "conflicted" longings in the transference
with full force. This also permitted a reconstruction of some
aspects of Annette's relationship to her mother and thus put the
working through process in gear. Could we not tentatively
conclude that, in answer to some of the questions raised in connection with Kafka's approach, the acceptance of Annette's sub-

jective experiences facilitated the emergence of her negative Oedipus complex and the progressive integration of her hitherto unacceptable affects? Mayer's approach certainly did not prevent her and her patient from ultimately discovering the unconscious motives of Annette's transference experiences as well as some of their genetic antecedents. Here we have an ostensible contrast between Kafka's[1] and Mayer's use of the same theory, applied in this instance to a patient with a neurotic personality disorder with notable preoedipal features.

What have we learned from this examination of Mayer's approach? She translates her theory into an attitude of acceptance of the patient's subjective experiences and searches for their unconscious (by definition conflictual) determinants. She thus creates a clinical atmosphere in which the iatrogenic intensification of resistances are minimized and the patient's experiences of the analyst serve as entry points for the understanding of the dynamics and genetics of the patient's psychopathology. Another way to put this is that Mayer used her understanding of Annette's subjective experiences, tentative and incomplete as these were at any particular moment, to have Annette elaborate on them further, in search of their unconscious dynamic and genetic antecedents. Her interpretations appear to flow from what she and Annette had previously jointly understood. This appears to have facilitated their meaningful integration in Annette's adult personality.

Let us finally look at how Willick translates the conflict and compromise theory into his approach to the treatment of Carol. There are many similarities between his therapeutic attitude and the clinical atmosphere he created and those of Mayer. He, too, explicitly described certain components of the treatment situation that indicate a profound influence of the manner in which he treated Carol, aside from his specific verbal interventions. He himself clearly recognized this influence of the relational ele-

---

[1] A word of caution is here in order. It is, of course, impossible to generalize on the basis of Kafka's clinical vignettes presented with the explicit purpose of showing how to engage certain difficult-to-engage-patients in an analysis, to his overall analytic approach. But we only have his specific samples at our disposal for examination. It is conceivable, however, that if Kafka had presented a larger sample and differently focused, there might be a less sharp contrast between his approach and Mayer's.

ments in the treatment process, but failed to take them sufficiently into account theoretically and in his view of the curative
process. His awareness of deficit, even if he assumes that it is
always based on underlying conflicts and he therefore consistently searches for them, seems to have sensitized him to Carol's
archaic needs. This validates Boesky's important point, which I
shall paraphrase: you "see" deficit only, just as you "see" conflict
only, if you think of it as a possible configuration, if such an idea is
available in your repertoire.[2] It would be interesting to hear from
Willick about his views regarding his reluctance to rely on his
own, beautifully garnered and well-described clinical experience
and hear him draw some broader conclusions from them.

Willick's conduct of the treatment and the unfolding of the
therapeutic process, as well as Carol's progress in it, can be
followed in some detail around the two issues Willick felicitously
highlighted: the transference elements of Carol's weekend experiences and the fact that she could not start the sessions on her
own. Willick recognized the complex, rich, and multilayered
issues in both of these behavior patterns and searched for them
patiently (once he realized that confrontations would block,
rather than enhance, therapeutic communication). He describes
the progressive elucidation of previously warded-off, or simply
hitherto unexpressed, inner experiences as he passed many of
Carol's repeated "tests." He was consistently mindful of Carol's
needs and adjusted his approach accordingly, recognizing and
acknowledging the necessity for a modification of his usual
analytic stance and interpretive activity.

Examining a few random samples of these interventions will
reveal the manner in which the conflict and compromise theory
guided Willick in his treatment of Carol. Accepting and explaining Carol's distress over weekends (that he did not exist, if he did
not exist for her, for example) gradually allowed for many other
meanings of this subjective experience to emerge. For quite some
time she had to drive by his house on weekends in order to
diminish her distress. At a later point Willick could say to Carol:

---

[2] None of us actually "sees" conflict or deficit, but choose to use one or the other way
to conceptualize our data of observation; in fact, such conceptualizations are already
influencing our very observations themselves.

"I believe you are angry with me that I do not see you on the weekend and you try to get rid of me and get me out of your life and mind" (p. 84). (He could have added: "And then you desperately search for me by driving by my house.") Later the patient added a new meaning herself: "If you are not with me, I feel I never had you. It's like you never existed for me and with me. I then feel like I made you up and that you are really with someone else" (p. 84). Willick responded: "It sounds as though your feeling now is like a profound feeling of jealousy" (p. 84). "It always was!" responded Carol. Willick adds: "It was only in the fourth year of treatment that she was able to tell me that she really wanted me to sit in the office twenty-four hours a day, waiting for her only and that she did not want me to have other patients or family" (p. 84). These are all expressions of and recognitions of profound needs or affects; where is the intersystemic, drive–defense conflict in this language?

Carol's inability or unwillingness to start the sessions on her own yielded a similar assortment of meanings in response to Willick's step-by-step explorations, and these were equally rich in revealing the genetic sources of her symptomatic behaviors.

It is also noteworthy that after a considerable period of treatment Willick "spent a great deal of time translating the patient's expression 'I can't start the session,' into 'I don't want to start the session' " (p. 88). What emerged in response had to do with Carol's withholding and coerciveness. She knew that if she remained silent, her therapist would speak first, and she wanted to force him to do so for a variety of reasons; in this way she could have a feeling of power over him. All of this now entered the therapeutic dialogue.

Comments and Questions

Taking all of Willick's sample observations and interventions together, the relative absence of a conflict and compromise language in his actual interactions with Carol is impressive. It is as if (just as in Mayer's clinical report) the general, everyday usage of these terms pervades Willick's language and guides his approach, rather than the specific language of drive–defense based, intersystemic conflicts. The fact that Willick was the one who started each session was certainly a modification of the usual analytic approach. His taking over this task from Carol appeared necessary and quite sensible. He seems to have properly responded to her "I can't" but was uneasy about it; prevailing (public) theory called for something else. So he attempted to "translate" this for Carol into an "I don't want to," as if the "I can't" was camouflaging its underlying "I don't want to." Could it be that Willick's behavioral response to the "I can't," along with his interpretive activity, led to a slow transformation and consolidation of Carol's growing capacities in several areas, especially affect tolerance and containment and therefore she could now entertain and express the feeling "I don't want to"? But are we not, as psychoanalytic therapists, ultimately bound to focus interpretively on the experiences expressed in either of these ways, no matter what else we may have to do (in a preliminary fashion) to make meaningful interpretations possible and effective? This is in fact what Willick had done. He appears more theory-bound in his message to us than he is in his actual interactions with Carol; or, more accurately he is there guided by his (private) theory of combining a conflict theory with a deficit theory. (However, the combination does not work smoothly and I shall have more to say about this shortly.) His explanation that he started each session with Carol only in order to enable her to communicate (that is, merely "to facilitate the treatment process"), and not as a therapeutic maneuver per se, is unassailable, but only half the story. The other half is what Carol made of it, how she understood and explained to herself the meaning of Willick's willingness to step in and be available in that fashion, and how she reacted to this as well as what she could enact (because she had to) in the transference as a result of his receptivity and flexibility. Willick's intention was not necessarily what Carol perceived and reacted to. Of course, Willick went along with Carol's behavior not only to be "supportive," or to provide her with a corrective emotional experience, which his approach willy-nilly did provide for Carol,[3] but he patiently continued to explore the varied

---

[3] A proper analytic approach inevitably provides a "corrective emotional experience." Analysis is the most "supportive" of psychotherapies, unless the analyst deliberately refrains from responding at all to the patient's emotional needs as these emerge in the treatment process and insists on insight through interpretations as the

and progressively deeper or more warded-off meanings of her behavior. He did the same with Carol's weekend experiences. In other words, no matter what he did, or said, he essentially remained analytic in his exploratory–interpretive approach. He did everything else in the service of this ultimate task. But nothing could prevent his patient from "extracting" more from the treatment than Willick thought he offered. That applies to all of us, all of the time, and complicates our perception of what the essential curative factors in psychoanalysis are.

Furthermore the patient's ability to extract from the treatment relationship whatever he or she needs, irrespective of what we explicitly offer, also has a bearing on how we do or do not make use of our clinical experiences in formulating or reformulating our theories. Obviously, if we disregard this element, or do not take it seriously as requiring a change in our perspective, it will not play a role in how we view what happens in a treatment process. This brings me back to Willick's main purpose in his presentation: to show us how he combined conflict and deficit in his approach. He responded to deficit while searching for conflict, although he maintained that "it is not helpful to see [Carol's inability to start each session] as a defect" (p. 88). Why not? If this modification was necessary, and not merely a matter of style, should we not try to find the (theoretically explicable) reasons for it? Since Willick ultimately found so many layers of complex affects and conflicts expressed in Carol's behavior (which could be understood and interpreted as well as lead to some reconstructions), he is reluctant to see Carol's symptomatic behavior as based on deficit. This reluctance is understandable, if he restricts his concept to ego deficits. This is a notion few would ascribe to what Carol was suffering from. Apparently, Willick is hesitant to use the deficit concept (although he obviously needs it) because he mistakenly assumes, with the other authors, that the concept would negate the belief that Carol's behavior is motivated, hence meaningful and interpretable. But why could behavior based on developmental deficit not be motivated and ultimately interpretable? Why could such a deficit not be viewed

exclusive analytic tool. But even then relational issues are unavoidably present and those are never negligible.

as leading to secondary conflicts? Based on the conflict and compromise theory presented, Willick is compelled to view deficit as
arising out of conflict. Theory prevents him from conceiving conflict as arising out of a developmental deficit. He dismisses, all
too quickly, the idea of deficit on the basic of failure(s) in "basic
structure formation," without adequate explanation.

Willick's attitude is exquisitely attuned to his patient's needs,
to the point that he does not allow his theory (the one he claims to
adhere to) to interfere with his attitude. He is the only one of the
authors, however, who, when he maintained that he combined
the concepts of conflict and deficit in his work with Carol, offered
an explicit and decisive modification of that theory.

As a result (without describing this as a preliminary, necessary step, but demonstrating it repeatedly in his interventions),
he understood Carol, he grasped the nature and meaning of her
feeling states, and repeatedly communicated his understanding
to her and thereby kept the therapeutic process active. Meanwhile, he consistently searched for dynamic and genetic explanations, and in his interpretations described these essentially in a
deficit language mixed with an everyday conflict language. (The
concept of secondary conflict might well have made his language
more precise.)

On the Range and Limitations of the "Conflict and Compromise Perspective"

What the clinical presentations demonstrated in my view (from
within the authors' own perspective) is that the explanatory
power and therapeutic leverage of the conflict and compromise
theory is at its strongest in uncomplicated neuroses or neurotic
personality disorders. The further we move on the spectrum of
psychopathology toward the narcissistic, then to borderline and
psychotic pathology, the more modification appears to have
been necessary (see Mayer's and especially Willick's presentation). Modifications were indeed introduced but these were
essentially relegated to a mere "technical necessity," in the particular instance, without a correlated attempt at generalization
and change in theory as a result.

What accounts for this reluctance to modify theory in keeping
with observation and practice is too complex to be dealt with here

just in passing, although the fundamental question of what kind of clinical experience warrants a change in theory is an important one for psychoanalysis, and a significant one for the controversy dealt with in this book. In any case, as long as "modern structural theory" assigns a central and primary role to intrapsychic conflict and compromise, it must, by definition, extend the applicability of this idea throughout the entire spectrum of psychopathology. This is logically consistent and on theoretical grounds alone not arguable, once certain basic premises have been accepted. The theory of conflict and compromise is a direct outgrowth of the assumption of the primacy of the drives, or more accurately, of the drive derivatives. The psychoanalytic situation is set up in keeping with the idea that these drive derivatives and the conflicts and compromises they give rise to should emerge in the trans-ference and be interpreted. Insight through interpretation is therefore the key element (or perhaps even the only significant element in this view) of the curative process in psychoanalysis. In this context, drive derivatives, conflicts, and compromises logically preclude the idea of a primary deficit, because deficit (or what might on the surface appear to be deficit) ultimately yields its underlying conflict and compromise structure after painstak-ing confrontations and interpretations. Deficit is thus, in this context, at best of secondary importance. Therefore, as long as deficit is viewed as arising from conflict, its existence is less vigorously disputed (see Willick as compared to Arlow and Boesky). Such deficit does not demand a change in basic concepts (you can take deficit or leave it), thus, it is of no great significance, since it inevitably yields to interpretation. It is then considered by Willick (and to a lesser degree by Mayer) a part of neurosogenesis as articulated by structural theory.[4]

Arlow's description of the analyst as observer and participant is also of relevance here, and without further specification, quite ambiguous. It would make a great deal of difference whether he considered the analyst as an "extrospective" or an "introspec-tive-empathic" observer. It would also make a great deal of

[4] If the reader is concerned that I have portrayed a circularity here, that concern has a basis in the fact that theories and the observations they engender reinforce each other in all of science. The question is only what it is that from time to time widens or reopens this inevitable circle. I shall return to this point later.

difference what he meant by "participant." The term itself (*participant observer*) originated with Sullivan (1956) and is compatible with the external observational stance; it is, in its original context, a social psychological concept and not indigenously psychoanalytic. Arlow did define the analyst's participation broadly as whatever "the analyst says and does." Put this way the definition should be acceptable to all. But what follows narrows the concept drastically. This is what Arlow says: "[The] analyst observes the effects his interventions produce in the stream of the patient's associations and the specific ways in which the analysand responds to the ideas and connections of which the analyst has made him aware" (p. 5). The focus is on how the analysand treats the analyst's interventions, which is in keeping with the analyst's effort to gain insight into the patient's distortions in order to promote insight via interpretations. This may explain why other aspects of the analytic relationship appear to play no significant role in Arlow's definition. But if the impact of reality is also one of the components of conflict and compromise, thus of pathogenesis as a whole, does this statement adequately encompass the analyst's potential impact (other than his verbal interventions) on the treatment process? We have seen in both Mayer's and Willick's clinical reports that such a view does not encompass all of their interventions. The analyst has impact way beyond what he thinks he says and what he thinks he does, unless, of course, Arlow meant to include all of that.

Kafka did not include these elements. Thus Arlow's definition and Kafka's example raise a number of questions. Does modern structural theory define the transference narrowly because it is the only way it can maintain the notion that insight via interpretation alone is the exclusive analytic–therapeutic tool? Does the theory preclude the assumption that the patient's observations contain some truth, the kernel of truth that Freud saw even in paranoid delusions? There appears to be a discrepancy in the clinical presentations regarding the tacit acceptance of the patient's experiences of the analyst as a legitimate starting point for the analysis of the transference experiences in question. This issue can be raised more concretely: could one not begin by wondering where Kafka's patient got the idea that his analyst was only interested in problems? It is a plausible assumption that this could indeed have happened. Why would patients' own ideas about the sources of their assumptions about their analyst not be of overriding interest as an avenue for further analytic exploration of all aspects of the transference? In any case, this issue is very much involved with the controversy about deficit, where the role of the analyst is pictured by the six authors as actively nurturing at the expense of insight via interpretations.

The Authors' Views from a Self Psychological Perspective

Having in the foregoing immersed myself in the perspective of "modern structural theory" as if it were entirely my own, I tried to discern and appreciate the inherent logic of all six authors' clinical and theoretical formulations. I have also tried to identify the discrepancies in the various presentations, as if they represented a single whole. I have underscored why, from their own theoretical vantage point, the authors by and large had to reject any other approach as falling short of their requirements for psychoanalysis as a method, theory, and practice.

The clinical and theoretical problems we all face, however, are not resolved via internal logic alone because there are two "disturbing" outside factors that need to be taken into consideration. The first one (of lesser significance) is, as mentioned earlier, the existence of three different paradigms of psychoanalysis today: ego psychology, object relations theory, and self psychology. Thus, each has to contend with and understand the other two, while we have no generally accepted methods and principles for a comparative psychoanalysis. Yet, with an apparent widespread need and desire for a unified theory of psychoanalysis, we each think that our particular brand of psychoanalysis is already a unified theory. The second one (of overriding importance) is the clinical situation with its demands for an expansion of our horizon beyond the neuroses and the neurotic personality disorders; hence, beyond the central pathogenetic significance of the Oedipus complex. As long as the discourse of modern structural theory does not seriously come to grips with these two outside factors, it can safely maintain its basic, self-imposed insulation against certain aspects of the widening scope of psychoanalysis. I am referring here particularly to Arlow's, Boesky's, and Kafka's contributions. When the discussion moved beyond abstract theory, however, to the developmental (Tyson) and the clinical realms (Mayer and Willick), we see much more clearly the presence of problems that have compelled some analysts to search for modifications in both theory and treatment principles, either as addenda to modern structural theory, or as a part of its comprehensive overhaul, or as an entirely new system.

Of course, it is possible to force unresolved clinical problems into old theoretical and clinical categories, at least linguistically; that is, we can talk about them using the same old language, as if nothing has changed or needed to be changed, and then claim that we were merely flexible when we utilized a different approach and insist on the data not requiring new theories to be adequately encompassed. We may then also acknowledge the need for empathic resonance vis-à-vis certain patients, or certain problems, rather than view this as a basic analytic requirement always, while maintaining the theoretical structure and treatment principles essentially unaltered.

The dominance of conflict and compromise in modern structural theory hinges on its specific views on trauma, reality, and cure, and how these, in turn, buttress the notion of the centrality of conflict and compromise. The circularity I am pointing to is inevitable and characterizes every scientific system. The key questions, then, are these: Where would we find the opening in this circularity? Where and how could new observations enter the system and lead to new theories and new treatment principles? Another way to ask the question is this: What observational data would the authors accept as indicating the need for new theoretical formulations and new treatment principles, if the ones made by Willick and to some extent by Mayer do not count? Did the authors never encounter treatment difficulties and failures that might have been due to our as yet inadequate understanding of the nature of the patient's psychopathology and the correlated treatment approach? And when do treatment failures, stalemates, and threatened dropouts signal the need for different theories and treatment approaches? If we could freely discuss these issues here we would certainly have a fruitful dialogue; one that might take us a few steps beyond the current status of the discourse on comparative psychoanalysis.

It is with these questions as a background that I shall now offer some alternative perspectives on the main themes of the presentations. During the presentation of the first part of my discussion, I was, in fact, also presenting my own fundamental perspective, in my effort to enter into the presenters' clinical and theoretical worlds. For me that is the requirement sine qua non, the first step in the process of trying to understand another analyst's clinical–theoretical perspective. In other words, my message in the first part of my discussion was almost purely a methodologic one, and I expressed it in the manner in which I approached my task. It is the second step that calls for a juxtaposition of conflicting claims, so that I must now (in this second part of my discussion) present a self psychological perspective on the key issues that I outlined at the outset.

The Psychoanalytic Method, Process, and Curative Factors

We often assume that there is a "standard procedure" of psychoanalysis and that all like-minded analysts, those from within the same theoretical perspective, practice it in the same manner. Furthermore, we assume, empirical evidence to the contrary, that we all could easily recognize standard procedure when presented to us and agree on the data it would furnish. Now, there are certain important basic features of an analytic method we could all agree on. But when the standard approach is (inevitably) amalgamated with "what the analyst says and does," the somewhat idiosyncratic nature of the analyst's conduct of treatment seems to overshadow the elements we might consider standard. The problem is compounded by the fact that we often shift our focus all too quickly from procedure to content (or a blurred amalgam of both) and there our consensus often ends with as many views as there are participants in the exercise.

The analyst's participation in the analysis is much more than what he or she says and does, it is what the patient feels and thinks the analyst says and does. The analyst, viewed as a "participant observer" (aside from calling attention to what is going on between patient and analyst, a social psychologic perspective), is a rather pale description of the analyst's analytic role and function, since it does not automatically guide the analyst to the patient's inner experience of him or her. Not focusing primarily on the patient's inner experience will also lead to different ideas about the nature of the analytic process. An entirely different process develops if the focus is on the patient's experience rather than on the patient's "distortions" of the analyst's "actual attitudes, actions, and intentions." This is evident in Mayer's and Willick's clinical reports. How do we know on what level the therapeutic process has to be conducted for optimal results? How does modern structural theory help us find that level? Did Mayer and Willick disregard the rules with their patients? If so, what meaning should we attach to the fact that the rules had to be disregarded? Is it all right to disregard the rules if one goes on to interpret the meaning of the patient's experiences anyway?

All of this is closely tied to the complex problem of what we consider to be curative in psychoanalysis. I only wish to make one comment about this. Arlow and Boesky stressed the exclusive therapeutic function of insight through interpretation. Kafka set out to illustrate this but discounted the relational elements of his approach. Mayer and Willick appeared to me to be closer than Kafka to accepting the fact, at least in their actions, that it is the analyst–patient relationship that is the matrix within which cure takes place and within which insight has a chance to become effective or not, even if they emphasized the central role of interpretation and insight and ascribed to these a more explicit and greater theoretical significance in their exposition than they ascribed to the relational elements. In fact, these relational elements are essential constituents of the transference.

The question arises from my perspective: Are certain layers of archaic psychopathology blocked from emerging in the transference when the exclusive emphasis is on the insight that does not also include equal stress on the relational elements and their interpretations from the patients' perspective? Willick and Mayer seem to be aware of this and I ascribe their successes with their respective patients in large part to this aspect of their work. It is the inevitable combination of the relational and cognitive-emotional aspects of analytic work that encompasses more fully the assumed curative factors. These can no longer be separated from each other in psychoanalysis. Does Mayer's and Willick's inclusion of the relational elements of the treatment process in their work point to the emerging "anomalies" (Kuhn, 1962) of

modern structural theory, which they are attempting to transcend clinically but have not confronted theoretically? The
answers to these questions hinge on (1) the definition of trauma, a
correlated view of the significance of reality, and how these may
affect the way we conceptualize the turning of normal conflict
and normal compromise into pathological forms; (2) what evidential value we assign to what is mobilized and is directly observable in the transference, rather than what is inferred from a
theory-based construction of infantile and childhood experience: "lived experience" as a basis for unconscious fantasy, versus unconscious fantasy as an (innately given) drive-derivative.

I am not suggesting that the findings of modern "baby-
watchers" have an immediate and direct bearing on how to conduct an analysis or how to view the transference. But I am
suggesting that to the degree that we work with developmental
theories that were reconstructed from the working through
process of analysis, we have to correlate and compare our findings with those of infant research, which can now tell us more
about normal development than we may be able to infer from the
pathology we analyze.

What this research can tell us about trauma and reality
dovetails with my criticism of Arlow's views, even while I grant
him the logic of his conceptions from within his own theoretical system.

Trauma, Reality, Pathogenic Conflict, and Compromise

By claiming that trauma is nothing more than a "special vicissitude of development, seen in the context of continuing intrapsychic conflict" (p. 7), Arlow has revised the theory of neurosogenesis. Since drive–defense conflict is built into the mental
apparatus in his view, it is the patient's prior unconscious conflict, rather than what is actually happening to him, that is of
overriding significance. Of course, the prior conflict and the
fantasy that fuels it will often have a decisive impact. But what
we consider primary will affect the analytic climate as well as the
focus of our interpretive interventions. Our interventions will
have one of two effects: we may be able to affirm the validity of
the patients' subjective experiences from their perspective

(rather than as our agreement or disagreement with their validity). Alternatively, our interventions will always question the accuracy and validity of the patients' experiences and thereby inevitably undermine their trust in themselves, preventing the development of the necessary climate of safety that supports the analytic process and creates the prerequisites for structure building and insight.

If trauma, or the effect of reality[5] on the growing psyche is relegated to secondary importance, how do we account for the differences between normal, ubiquitous versus pathogenic conflicts and compromises? Given the particular biogenetic endowment of the individual (the specifics of which we know very little about in any given psychoanalytic situation) we are left with focusing on the patients' inner world and the experiences that might have shaped it (in combination with those unknown constitutional factors). But why do we so consistently and in such minute detail investigate and recount the patient's experiences (with parents, siblings, and other influences) if we do not assign to these a clear-cut, specific pathogenic or neurosogenic role? Why do we disregard in our theory the reality of these experiences in the face of their being relived in the transference (in both Mayer's Annette and Willick's Carol)? I read little of this in the theoretical papers, except for Tyson's; he defined conflict by including some of these reality-influences explicitly and thus had a more encompassing formulation of conflict, without minimizing trauma in pathogenesis. Boesky did list reality as one of the components of conflict as well as compromise, but without explaining how it becomes an etiologically significant part of psychopathology. Do such expectable life-events as the birth or death of a sibling, or loss of a parent no longer count as potentially traumatic? Should these be considered simply as "special vicissitude[s] of development in the context of continuing intrapsychic conflict?" (Arlow, this volume, p. 7).

___

[5] Needless to say, in psychoanalysis we always speak of "psychic reality" which acknowledges that the traumatic impact does not impinge on a tabula rasa in the infant or the child. The question is only how we treat this psychic reality in our clinical interventions: with acceptance, understanding, and explanations regarding its possible genetic sources; or by challenging its validity based on the inevitable distortions we see from the external observer's perspective. Here the idea of preformed unconscious fantasies as against those based on lived experiences will lead to different approaches.

I would agree that we need to know a great deal about such gross events; their timing, the surrounding emotional issues, and how they were responded to by the environment decisively codetermine whether the experience will be "traumatic" or not. It is not the event per se, but the chronic strain in the particular pathogenic relationship that would make the "event" traumatic or, more accurately, would condense and dramatically bring forth the chronic, traumatic influences. I also agree with Arlow that we cannot tell from the external event itself, no matter how extreme the conditions were under which the experience occurred, whether it was actually "traumatic" in the sense of creating psychopathology, or not. That is always a retrospective assessment, unless there are immediate sequelae. Willick and Mayer did seem to take these issues into consideration in their reconstructive interventions, but again without building them into their theoretical perspectives explicitly. These questions are open to empirical study and verification in the transference as well as in independent longitudinal observations of sequelae of what might be conceived of as having been traumatic.

From my own perspective, the pathology-inducing psychic trauma can, indeed, be identified and documented in what is observed in psychoanalysis, and we need not only rely on speculative reconstructions of infancy and early childhood without current, compelling observational data. Arlow is right that we need this sort of analytic evidence, and it is precisely this kind of evidence that validates the trauma concept as well as the deficit concept in self psychology by recognizing the patients' psychic reality in the selfobject transferences, which is always the starting point of our analytic investigation. Both Mayer and Willick provided evidence for the pathogenic impact of some of their patients' childhood experiences, as these were reenacted in the transference. Some of these were actually remembered, others only enacted with the analyst. And these enactments revealed nonremembered, but plausible, actual childhood traumatic experiences.

Thus, the clinical data provided by Willick and Mayer lead me to question Boesky's claim that conflict and compromise are our "best" conceptions to explain pathogenesis as well as change throughout the spectrum of psychopathology. These may be adequate, up to a point, in the neuroses and neurotic personality disorders, but even there something is missing in their usefulness, that "something" relates to (1) what turns normal conflict and normal compromise into pathological forms; and (2) to the fact that the theory relies on insight alone to bring about the desired change. The self psychological perspective on deficit should further expand on these issues.

Deficit—Its Clinical and Theoretical Implications

The concept of deficit is not as alien to psychoanalysis as Arlow and Boesky would have us believe. As we have seen, Willick was compelled to combine his conflict theory with a deficit theory and Mayer entertained that possibility for Annette, but then rejected it in favor of a pure conflict theory. Psychoanalysis has long had a deficit theory, albeit a very different one from what I shall describe here. We have often spoken of ego defects in the psychoses, ego alterations in the neuroses, and ego modifications (ego deformities or distortions) in the personality disorders. But it is understandable, I believe, that these concepts have not been found very useful in clinical work because they have not been developed from the recognition of specific transferences. These concepts had primarily been used "diagnostically" to determine analyzability. The more serious the ego alteration, the less likely that analysis was going to be useful; with ego defects some felt it should not even be undertaken.

Deficit attained a clinically, developmentally, and theoretically significant position in self psychology because its recognition was based on the working through of the selfobject transferences. This offered analysts a therapeutic handle on their patients' clinical problems. Selfobject transferences are mobilized by and reveal patients' thwarted yearnings to grow, to complete development, as Mayer's Annette demonstrated with the reactivation of her needs to idealize her analyst, in order to resolve (i.e., grow beyond) her negative Oedipus complex. I would look at Annette's psychopathology as reflecting a deficit, stemming from the fact that she could not, during her oedipal period or later during her adolescence, complete her developmental task of resolving her negative oedipal relations with her mother. That she had secondary conflicts as a result seemed evident. However, I would not have considered her idealization of her analyst as primarily defensive. I would have viewed it, as did Mayer (and Willick in his patient) to some extent, but a bit hesitantly, as a revival of an unfinished business in her development. The emotional capacities that a phase-appropriate resolution of her negative Oedipus complex would have afforded Annette were "missing" in her psychic makeup. But we would only know this from the details of the working through of her idealizing transference.[6] In Annette's case the working through revealed the

[6] I spoke earlier of contact points between different paradigms. I indicated that Mayer's approach to her patient Annette represented one of those contact points, and I agreed with her formulation that Annette's essential psychopathology derived from her negative oedipal phase (I would call it the negative Oedipus complex, retaining, with Kohut, the term *oedipal phase* to designate normal oedipal experiences), although I shall describe it here in different language. To indicate my reasons for this agreement I shall quote a description of an almost identical situation from the self psychology literature. Anna Ornstein (1983), in her paper "An Idealizing Transference of the Oedipal Phase" had this to say:

> It could be argued that the appearance of idealizing needs that are coupled with sexualization represent the negative Oedipus complex in the transference, a retreat from the infantile sexual longings for the mother and competition and murderous wishes toward the father. The negative Oedipus complex has been viewed traditionally as a pathological constellation when it becomes manifest in the transference. In contrast, in the course of normal development, this phenomenon has been linked to the fate of archaic narcissism. (Blos [1979], says: "The negative oedipal attachment is a narcissistic object tie.") I believe that this contradiction between the interpretation of the meaning of the transference phenomenon in which idealization and erotization are combined can now be understood as an intense (therefore, sexualized) need to be merged with and to be admired by the parent of the same sex. I am suggesting that what has traditionally been described as "the negative Oedipus complex" in the transference, can now be recognized as an effort to resume psychological development at that phase when the child through phase-appropriate mirroring by an idealized homogenital parent acquires pride and pleasure in his own masculine strength or her own feminine beauty and nurturance. Therefore, when, in the transference, the experiential content is either longing for sexual closeness with the homogenital parent or, when the longing appears as "latent homosexuality" in dreams and associations or, when these affects are defended against with an exaggerated emphasis of the positive oedipal affects, the erotization under these circumstances represents the intensity of the longing to be united with and to be mirrored by the idealized homogenital parent [A. Ornstein, 1983].

What is the meaning of this agreement? Does it mean that the different theories that guided these two analysts were of no significance? Of course not. Tersely stated, the atmosphere Mayer created for her patient; the flexibility in the approach she used; the care with which she avoided the relentless conflict and compromise interpretation (although that was her guiding theory) might well have allowed Annette to "use" her analyst in the transference to extract those needed experiences which then permitted

infantile and childhood origins of her traumatic experiences with
her (adoptive) mother, which interfered with her acquisition of a
firmly consolidated feminine self, assuming that hers was essentially an oedipal selfobject transference.

Clinically, then, deficit manifests itself in the development of
one of the selfobject transferences. For example, a patient's silent
and subtle, or more noisy and overt exhibitionistic clamorings
for admiration, affirmation, and validation may ultimately
coalesce into a sustained, fully mobilized mirror transference.
This, too, reveals in the course of its working through process the
infantile and childhood origins of the traumatic experiences that
interfered with the acquisition of a reliable capacity for self-
esteem regulation; and/or for the pursuit of goals; and/or for the
enjoyment of physical and mental activities. It is not the manifest
complaint or symptom, as mistakenly assumed by the extrospective critics, that is decisive, but what the working through of the
transference disruptions and their repair permit us to discover. It
is in these disruptions that we can identify the traumatic influences.
An inadvertently unempathic intervention, an unintended and
often inevitable criticism, such as Kafka's, which led to his
patient's homosexual fling, is traumatic because it repeats in the
transference some prior painful experience which can now be
recalled or reconstructed, and thereby the transference disruption can be interpretively repaired. This is the kind of analytic
experience I had in mind when I said earlier that we now have
observable analytic data for the study of the role of trauma in
pathogenesis, since we repeatedly "traumatize" our patients,
minute as that "trauma" might appear to be in our own eyes.

Developmentally, the word *deficit* in self psychology refers to
two different but related phenomena. One has to do with the
absence, faulty availability, or unavailability of the emotional
nutrients[7] for the maturation and transformation of archaic

---

her to begin to resolve her conflicts. The fact that Annette's feelings of jealousy, rivalry,
anger, and so on, emerged after the slip of the tongue was analyzed does not necessarily
indicate that underneath her deficit there lurked the conflicts and compromises which
caused these feelings to be present. Here is where normal conflicts and compromises
become "pathological" when there is a basic—even if ever so mild—deficit that makes it
difficult if not impossible to resolve normal, developmental conflicts.

[7] It would be a mistake to translate the expression "emotional nutrients" into "oral
supplies" and draw from it far-reaching, but unwarranted, conclusions. This simply
refers to the normal developmental need for mirroring and the availability of idealized
selfobjects for basic structure building in the developmental theory of self psychology.

grandiose-exhibitionism and idealization, which therefore pre-
cludes structure building through transmuting internalization.
The other has to do with the consequences of this absence or
faulty mirroring; or the absence or faulty availability of idealized
selfobjects, leading to faulty or deficient structure building in one
or both poles of the bipolar self. Hence deficit as a developmental
concept refers to the fact that certain basic needs were not met
and resulted in the thwarting or derailment of self development,
leading to a structural weakness or deficiency, proneness to
enfeeblement or fragmentation of self-experience in one or both
poles of the bipolar self.

Dynamically, such structural deficits mobilize the requisite
selfobject transferences and the patients strive to attain belated
maturation and internalization, as both Annette and Carol
demonstrated, by liberating this thwarted need to grow. Patients
with deficits of this type (along with their elaborate defensive
structures that "cover" these deficits or with their compensatory
structures that permit a modicum of adequate functioning in certain areas) are eminently analyzable. The key point is that the
deficits manifest themselves through transferences, which can
ultimately be worked through interpretively in the proper
analytic ambience. The analyst does not address "deficit-
problems" by telling the patient "you have a defect or deficit."
Instead, he or she focuses interpretively on the consequences of
such deficits in the transference and in the patient's life outside of
the transference. The reconstruction of the infantile and childhood antecedents of chronically thwarted developmental needs
lead both to insight and to belated acquisition of those capacities
that were developmentally derailed or arrested. The concept of
deficit, in this context, does not mean that noninterpretive, supportive, or substitutive treatments are required, as some of the
authors of this book have mistakenly assumed. Willick's approach
to Carol, and Mayer's to Annette are good examples of maintaining an interpretive approach while also paying attention to
(and ultimately interpreting) the relational aspects of the treatment experience and also providing what it takes to keep the
process going.

No wonder that modern structural theory did not lead the six
authors to the discovery of developmental deficits underlying
their patients' psychopathology. Such deficits express them-

selves in the selfobject transferences, in the way in which the patient needs and "uses" the analyst as a substitute for "missing psychic structures" (Kohut, 1971, 1977, 1984). The analyst, aside from conceptualizing the transference by including these elements under its umbrella and doing what is necessary to keep the process going, simply applies the two-step approach of understanding and explaining, to deal analytically with deficit-based psychopathology and its secondary conflicts. To state once more, it is the disruption and repair of these transferences that provide us with analytic data about pathogenic traumata and their consequences: analyzable deficits.

I have dealt with the theme of conflict and deficit extensively and more systematically elsewhere (P. H. Ornstein, 1983); here I shall quote from that work, comparing and contrasting our respective fundamental assumptions. (I have spoken there of Freud's and Kohut's hypotheses; modern structural theory may be substituted for the former, to apply it to this discussion.)

1. Freud's hypothesis derives psychic development from the clash of forces of the primary drives with the socializing demands of the parental imagoes as the earliest representatives of the social environment. A psyche that is conceived of as developing out of such a matrix is, by definition, full of primary conflicts. Thus the notion of psychoanalysis as a conflict psychology par excellence is thereby built into our view of human development.

This view has repeatedly been amended, expanded and reformulated by ego psychologists (within the mainstream of psychoanalysis) and by object relations theorists (close to the mainstream). The details of the amendments, expansions and reformulations, however, are not immediately relevant to my argument, because all of them have essentially retained the primacy of the drives in their conceptualizations.

2. Kohut's hypothesis derives psychic development from within the self–selfobject matrix, where the relation between the rudimentary self and its empathic selfobject constitutes the primal unit of psychological experience. Expectably, non-traumatic disruptions of the empathic bond between self and selfobject (optimum frustration) lead to structure building through transmuting internalization. Thus, there is here, by definition, no built-in primary conflict in the psyche. Traumatic disruptions, on the other hand, lead to defects or deficits in structure building, which, in turn, lead to secondary conflicts.

In both of these basic hypotheses psychic structure is built up as a result of optimum frustration. But in Freud's hypothesis optimum frustration involves (basic or primary) drive-related needs and wishes, whereas in Kohut's hypothesis optimum frustration involves nondrive-related, developmental (mirroring and idealizing) needs and wishes. The drives are in this context building blocks or integral components of a cohesive self and appear in isolated, intensified, pathological forms only upon a transient or protracted breakdown of the cohesiveness of the self [pp. 357–358].

There is as yet no scientifically acceptable way to choose one or the other of these basic hypotheses, but that is not where we usually start anyhow. We start with the transferences and their working through. Except that once such a hypothesis about the beginning stages of personality development is introduced as the foundation for the entire edifice of our psychology, the rest follows from it logically. But when new observations cast doubt on the original basic hypothesis, that foundation needs a thorough reexamination.

Conclusion

I should like to close this two-part discussion by further elaborating on the musical metaphor Boesky introduced in order to characterize the advances made by modern structural theory as well as depict some of its limitations. He wrote: "The prior views that sublimation was only a drive derivative, acting out was only a defense, and that identification was the principal if not the exclusive mode for building up the superego was the theoretic equivalent of trying to play a string quartet on just one violin" (p. 25). He identified all the components of that polyphonic fugue (here called conflict and compromise in health and illness) as "drive derivatives, unpleasant affects such as anxiety or depressive affect, defense, superego aspects and reality considerations" and told us that playing that fugue requires the four instruments of the quartet to do justice to the richness of the music, as we now understand it. Well and good. Modern structural theory is in that sense indeed an advance over earlier versions.

But from a current, broader perspective, the theory appears to be restrictive, neither the entire spectrum of health, nor the entire spectrum of psychopathology is adequately encompassed by the concepts of conflict and compromise. Viewed from this angle, we may also wonder: Where is Hartmann's conflict-free sphere of the ego in modern structural theory? Isn't its absence or some other equivalent concept to account for nonconflict based psychic structures and functions a glaring omission? Thus, modern structural theory has no place in its system for certain clinical observations and therefore disregards potentially available, fruitful interpretive interventions.

Picture the string quartet as the patient, playing the appropriate number and kinds of instruments that find expression in a specific polyphonic fugue; the many components of conflict and compromise that add up to the psychopathology. The leader of the quartet (the analyst), leading an observer–listener and participant in this music, has to know what each instrument contributes to bringing that fugue (the psychopathology) alive. He has to know how to help the quartet (the patient) transform individual tunes and tones into a musical experience. That is the skill of the musician–leader, aided by his background knowledge. He identifies the main theme in the score (the patient's central subjective experience) and listens for it; there is always a main theme (one, two or three of them), a leading voice, which should be heard even while the other instruments play. To bring this leading voice out above the other voices is his creative–interpretive skill. This leading voice may be any of the four instruments of the quartet. The voices shift, and it is the conductor's special task to help the musicians create (with the individual instruments and the particular scores prescribed for them) the musical experience of a fugue. If the leader focuses his attention unduly on this or that instrument; if he is caught up with individual scores and the individual tone these instruments are supposed to produce, that is, if he fails to identify the main theme or themes (the primacy of conflict or deficit or the secondary nature of one or the other), the fugue as a whole may never become recreated from the score; the musical experience may never emerge from playing the various instruments. Our focus upon and preoccupation with conflict and compromise, some of the ubiquitous, non-pathological building blocks of human experience, and some of the building blocks of specific forms of psychopathology, may prevent us from grasping the essential quality of the patient's subjective experiences in health or illness.

Furthermore, if everything is conflict and compromise in both health and illness (without a satisfactory explanation as to what turns normal conflict and normal compromise into pathological forms) it is unclear wherein lies any further heuristic value and expanding therapeutic impact of modern structural theory.

Chapter 11

The Authors Respond

Dale Boesky, M.D.

I welcome the opportunity to comment about the discussions by Dr. Vacquer and Dr. Ornstein because they illustrate an important phenomenon that lies at the center of many current and past disagreements about psychoanalytic theory. I refer to the imbalance between theoretic views and the clinical evidence which is adduced to support those views. Before proceeding I wish to explain that space limitations prevent me from commenting on the valuable discussions by Brenner and Bronstein which agree, in essence, with my position. I have chosen instead to focus on the substantive issues of disagreement.

The philosopher Abraham Friedman once commented dryly that it is useful to make some distinctions about the discourse of psychoanalysts. He suggested that we should carefully distinguish between what the psychoanalyst says to his patient, what he says to himself, and what he says to his colleagues. The differences between the three forms of discourse are not a matter of discretion or integrity. They result from the well-known fact that the relation between proclaimed theory and actual practice is notoriously unpredictable. So, when analysts disagree, one of them often implies that the other is fooling himself about what he claims to understand about a patient. The analyst who disagrees usually believes, correctly or not, openly or tacitly, that the other has failed to see the difference between what he actually did or

173

said and what he told himself and his colleagues he did or said. This difference is often implied when one analyst says that another analyst's theory is wrong. He or she will then attempt to show why it is wrong. Gradually, over the years, we have learned a great deal about how to disagree with each other constructively but we still have a long way to go. One of the complex problems in communicating our differences is that we lack a methodology for the clinical validation of evidence. I will attempt in the following remarks to demonstrate how this has affected the present discussion in which we have advocates of two psychoanalytic models, Frederick Vacquer and Paul Ornstein, discussing a third model, the structural model.

Vacquer began with the following statement: "I take a more eclectic approach than they do and one which affords me . . . a greater number . . . of conceptual tools . . . I believe it is necessary to supplement and complement the tenets of modern structural theory in order to adequately encompass behaviors exhibited by individuals experiencing disorders far more primitive than those we call neurotic" (p. 115). In his ensuing summary of Bion's views of the coexistence in all persons of normal, neurotic, infantile, and psychotic mental states, he prepares us to understand what his additional conceptual tools are and why he thinks they are especially useful for the study of infantile and psychotic mental states. As far as I can determine, Vacquer does not claim special advantages offered by his new tools in treating "neurotic states." Their particular advantage is in the treatment of infantile and psychotic states. In these initial statements he prepared us to expect an *illustration* of how his clinical understanding was enhanced by his new conceptual tools in contrast to truth claims or claims of validation. Vacquer then presented three clinical illustrations which, in my opinion, do not clearly illustrate, let alone document, his theoretic assertion.

Case 1
We are told very little about this thirty-five-year-old man other than his dreams and the fact that when he ejaculated he experienced enormous fatigue. Almost the entire illustration consists of a report of his dreams, some of his associations to those dreams,

and what Vacquer thought his dreams meant, together with some of the responses by the patient to Vacquer's interventions.

After the report of the first dream Vacquer tells us that up to this point his patient could not use a woman as a container for his projections. Putting to one side the ambiguities inherent in that statement, we might ask on what data this formulation was based. If it was based on the one dream reported up to that point, I disagree with that explanation of the dream; the dream and available associations are open to other explanations. If on the other hand this "container" formulation is based on other data, we are not told about that data. In the next sentence Vacquer asserts that his patient is "immediately inhibited in any attempt to form a neurotic compromise" (p. 125). The ensuing passage suggests that what Vacquer means is that the patient could not develop a phobic symptom to deal with his conflicts *nor* a "stable persecutory solution." But *both* phobic and persecutory symptoms are compromise formations. Furthermore, one is not on solid ground in saying that a patient is incapable of developing a particular compromise formation. One can only say that up to this point the patient has not done so.

It may be unlikely that a particular patient will develop certain forms of compromise formation but it is difficult to prove that a patient is incapable of doing so. The entire issue is really related to choice of symptom, a highly complex problem. We can say that for any particular patient the compromise formation chosen is the only compromise formation that *this* patient could have chosen at that particular point. In every instance, there are powerful reasons governing the unique and specific compromise formations chosen by any individual patient. Finally, Vacquer seems to ignore the fact that the patient has *already developed* a fascinating compromise formation; his symptom of enormous fatigue after ejaculation. Many analysts would conjecture that, in this man's unconscious fantasy, the woman has drained him.

Vacquer appears to confuse two types of container, one in the patient's fantasy, the other in Bion's theoretic formulation. There is no evidence that the patient is unable or even that he is inhibited in his capacity to form a neurotic compromise formation. Why do we need additional conceptual tools in considering this patient? Presumably to account for his persecutory conflicts and the imputed nonneurotic, infantile, and/or psychotic features. But what is the evidence that the patient manifested infantile and psychotic aspects in *his* personality? All we are told about him derives from the claim that four "states" are present in the mind of all human beings: infantile, normal, neurotic, and psychotic. What we require is some persuasive evidence that this formulation is applicable to this patient in particular. How do his dreams, *taken alone*, illustrate that these new conceptual tools are useful in understanding this man's conflicts? Furthermore the use of dreams for definitive diagnostic or nosologic classification is notoriously unreliable; we must take Vacquer's word for the assertion that the patient was incapable of forming a neurotic compromise formation. Clinical evidence from other patients tell us that dreams can't be used reliably to tell us in which diagnostic category a patient belongs.

If this patient does have neurotic features, how did Vacquer use his different conceptual tools to help him in a manner superior to therapy based on modern structural concepts? Where is the evidence to support any diagnostic assertion at all?

Vacquer next shared a fragment of additional biographical information. The patient recalled perceptions of his mother as an emotionally unresponsive and withdrawn person. In particular she was indifferent to the patient's violent tantrums in contrast to the father who was more helpful. To Vacquer it makes sense to conclude that the patient therefore cannot use a woman as a container for his projections. He then reported another dream in which a former girl friend spits out disgusting brownish glop. Vacquer then makes a remarkable assertion, in view of the fact that we are given no associations to this complex dream. It is puzzling to understand why, in the next sentence, he states: "we have *evidence* that not only does mother refuse to accept her son's projections but also that when she does accept them she is experienced as taking in something good and turning it into something bad" (p. 125; emphasis added). That is a conjecture, not evidence, and it is a conjecture based on a manifest dream together with a fragmentary piece of "historical" information about certain perceptions of the mother. Vacquer next asserted that the dream provides *evidential* documentation for " agglutina-

tion, and agglomeration." And since agglutination and agglomeration are distortions of functioning, Vacquer then claimed
that this was "*evidence* of abnormal splitting"!

You will recall that all of these assertions are based on the
report of a manifest dream. Many analysts would be hesitant to
interpret the *meaning* of a single dream without associations, but
Vacquer is willing not only to interpret the dream but also to use
the dream to propose far-reaching innovations in psychoanalytic
theory which he claims are clinically supported by the evidence
he reports in his vignette. He concluded his vignette with the
assertion that, although many neurotic issues were dealt with in
this case, "I have demonstrated other aspects of personality
functioning that *required* at least equal attention as they involved a
failure of neurotic processing" (p. 127; emphasis added).

That final assertion is not only unsubstantiated but is remarkable for another reason. Vacquer implies that analysts have
arrived at a consensus that, "(when) neurotic processing fails,"
alternate forms of pathogenesis ensue of necessity. There is no
such consensus. The relevant issues of pathogenesis, normal
psychological development, and metapsychology are extremely
complex and unsettled. For example, at what age in this man's
life did his "neurotic processing" fail? Is it true that any patient
who fails to produce a neurotic symptom such as a phobia is dis-
qualified from producing numerous other compromise formations such as neurotic character traits, neurotic relationships,
and the like? Do "infantile" and "psychotic" states when they are
present to an excessive degree imply that the person in question
will always first attempt to "neurotically process" his conflicts
and then turn to another form of processing? These questions
are evoked, rather than answered, by Vacquer's assertions.

Case 2
Vacquer makes an assertion about his second patient which
appears to contradict his prior formulation about the inevitable
consequences when "neurotic processing" fails. He said that his
second patient had "a nice neurotic configuration" (performing
in public had a masturbatory significance for her). But she *also*
required negative hallucinations and omnipotent denial. Why is
it that the "other dimensions" in the first case were forced on the

patient because he was incapable of neurotic processing but in this second case the other dimensions or states were required in the *presence* of a "nice neurotic configuration?"

Drives and Instincts

Vacquer doesn't understand why assertion and defensive activity are not included among the derivatives of aggressive drives in addition to sadism. That is because he evidently has a different view of compromise formation than those which I presented. Sadistic behavior must be distinguished from aggressive or libidinal drive derivatives. Sadistic behavior is not only a drive discharge, it is the consequence of certain conflicts expressed in the form of a compromise formation and also includes, as do all compromise formations, defensive, superego, and affective components. That is also true of assertive or defensive behavior. Just as sadistic behavior is not only sadistic, defensive behavior is not only defensive, it also expresses the influence of drive derivatives. This is also the sense in which Brenner cautioned against the use of the misleading terms *defense transference* and *superego transference*. Complex transference configurations are never solely defensive, or solely "superego" in their dynamic structure.

Finally, Vacquer sees advantages in the concept of some Kleinians and Bionians who refer to an epistemophilic instinct as an inborn motive force. He also prefers the notion of structured motivations which transcend what he feels to be the constraints of drive theory in the structural model. This is a widely prevalent assertion of certain object relations theorists, including Sandler (1983). The notion of an epistemophilic instinct revives the confusion introduced by the instinct psychology of the nineteenth century. If Vacquer has in mind additional evidence about the final disposition of the confusing conflation of instincts and drives, which was settled some forty years ago, he has not said what it is. But staking out claims for new "instincts" requires integration with the substantial literature on the distinction between drives and instincts. As for the claim that there are important "structured conflicts" which are uninfluenced by drives, such a claim requires a new conflict model from which the drives are deleted together with adequate clinical evidence, which is not as yet available in our literature. The unsubstantiated rejection of the drives is an old story in the history of our science and is merely appearing now in new versions. As we shall see, it is an important feature in the discussion by Ornstein.

Ornstein said that there is no established tradition for an open-minded discussion of vastly differing clinical–theoretic approaches. One reason that this is true is that we have not established a consensus for the methodology of clinical validation and disconfirmation. The disagreements which Ornstein expressed in his discussion illustrate some of these problems.

One of the major issues which Ornstein addressed is the difference between his views and those of the six authors in regard to deficits as opposed to conflicts in normal and pathological development. Ornstein said that "No doubt Tyson's perspective is vastly different from . . . Boesky's, but he did not spell out whether it still fits under the umbrella of modern structural theory . . ." (p. 138). I was myself unaware of the vast difference between Tyson's views and my own, but I am left to guess what Ornstein had in mind because he did not say what these differences were and why they were vast. Ornstein wished that Tyson would have expressed his views about intrapsychic conflicts other than those based on drive derivatives so he could thereby have taken a stand as a child analyst on the question of deficit. I am forced to conclude from that statement that for Ornstein it is a proven fact, documented with clinical evidence, that there are important intrapsychic conflicts in children which appear as "deficits" when they grow up and which are "other" than those based on drive derivatives. But that is a spurious assumption. The only way that one could settle Ornstein's claim is to examine individual case material intensively over an adequate length of time with an accepted methodology for evaluating intrapsychic conflict that was "other" than drive related. However, there is no such methodology because the existing methodology for such an evaluation is based on the organizing principles of compromise formation, or at least it has been until the introduction of the claims by self psychologists and certain other adherents of object relations theories that there were important conflicts unrelated to drive derivatives.

I will illustrate the problem in this way. It is quite common and often useful for a small group of veteran analysts to study and discuss a single case with process data. Inevitably disagreements will occur. However, in this illustrative example all the analysts in the group share the conflict model of structural theory. They share the assumption that important meanings are embedded in disguised form in the patient's associations, acting out, dreams, and so on. They share the assumption that the disguised meanings have been disguised in a lawful manner. They can sift and weigh the advantages of one way of organizing the data compared to another with the shared assumption that they are agreed on the nature of the dangers in the mind of the patient that caused him to disguise his hidden meanings in certain ways. The principles of psychic determinism, multiple function, compromise formation, drive–defense–superego configurations, repetitions of themes, contextual shifts, and a variety of other organizing principles well known to experienced analysts and carefully worked out by generations of analysts over the span of almost a century have established this methodology for evaluating clinical evidence. It is certainly imperfect, but it has been gradually refined and is highly useful. In fact study groups of experienced psychoanalysts are often able to reach a high degree of consensual agreement about the evidential claims pertaining to each other's clinical data.

It is well known that not all analysts accept this methodology; comparable dissent occurs in many other scientific enterprises. But if one wishes to use a different model it is necessary to establish a methodology of evidence consistent with that new model. It is not sufficient to make radical modifications in the existing structural model and then attempt to use the methodology of the structural model as evidence one way or another. For example, if one uses a nonconflict model one must find some other way to account for why the patient disguises his meanings. If the alteration of the patient's motives is not due to conflict, why do we need free associations, why do we need the couch, and why do we have to interpret anything? This point is one that has been made already by critics of self psychology (Stein, 1979; Boesky, 1988b).

Throughout his remarks, Ornstein adheres to the view that although the relationship itself is mutative it is still necessary to make some interpretations. But if one finds it necessary to interpret something then one assumes that the patient is hiding something from himself and that implies conflict. If you interpret things to a patient that are assumed to be concealed by the patient himself you are using a conflict model. The patient wants something and yet does not want it all at the same time. Another obvious fact must be considered. For some time we have known that if a different model is used to organize the understanding of the patient's associations, then different kinds of data will be gathered. This difference is profound and begins with the first moment of the first session.

The methodology for validation in the structural model is predicated on the functional and developmental interrelatedness of the drives together with the defenses, the ego capacities, the self-esteem regulatory devices, the pleasure principle, the affects, and the superego. The methodology which has evolved for validation of structural concepts assumes that everything that happens in the mind affects everything else in the mind. One can no more listen to a patient without utilizing assumptions about drives than one can remove defenses, *if one uses the structural model*.

Ornstein disputes Willick's contention that it is not useful to separate ego impairments that result from psychic conflict from those that precede conflict and have to do with "basic structure formation." That is important to Ornstein because of his theoretic commitment to certain assumptions about normal psychological development and pathogenesis. But Ornstein here is ignoring a highly important clarification offered by Anna Freud (1974) about the inseparable developmental interrelatedness of conflicts and deficits.

She prophetically warned against an artificial separation in developmental theories between conflict and deficits, which were in her opinion inseparable and intertwined:

It would be convenient to take the point of view that success or failure on the developmental lines primarily shapes the personalities which secondarily become involved in internal conflict. But any statement of this kind would be a gross falsification once the infant ceases to be an undifferentiated, unstructured being. It would ignore the temporal relations between the two processes which occur simultaneously, not subsequent to each other. Progress on the [developmental] lines is interfered with constantly by conflict, repression, and consequent regression, while the conflicts themselves and quite especially the methods available for their solution are wholly dependent on the shape and the level of personal development which had been reached. However different in origin the two types of psychopathology are, in the clinical picture they are totally intertwined, a fact which accounts for their usually being treated as one [pp. 70–71].

Ornstein wishes us to "untwine" these two forms of pathology. He therefore seems to ignore this problem which Anna Freud pointed out so clearly. When he invites Tyson to examine the problem of "deficits" *outside* of the sphere of conflict, Ornstein seems only to request that Tyson be more open-minded. The issue is not open-mindedness, it is instead an issue of ignoring contradictions. The point is that if Ornstein wishes to deal with mental phenomena that are outside the realm of conflict while still conducting *psychoanalytic* treatment then he should instruct us about how to *articulate* the conflict model with the nonconflict model in childhood development and adult pathogenesis. Then we will need to be told how to examine and understand the communications of our adult patients in such a way that we will have a methodology for distinguishing which of the patient's associations are to be understood as emerging in the framework of conflict and which are entirely free of conflict. We would also wonder what complications would ensue for the patient as the analyst shifted models. It would be ironic indeed if Ornstein were repeating the erroneous idea of Hartmann (1964) that we establish a conflict-free sphere in the human mind within the domain of psychoanalytic methodology. Even more confusing is the fact that Ornstein's model would then be a *non*-autonomous, conflict-free sphere that was pathological rather than adaptive.

A further problem which Ornstein overlooks is that the word *structure* means something very different in the framework of self psychology than it does in the structural model. Within the structural model the term *structural* connotes not only functional continuity, it connotes also a developmental and dynamic interrelatedness predicated on intrapsychic conflict. The developmental structures in the preverbal phase to which Ornstein is alluding represent the primitive psychological substrate and therefore are in a very different frame of reference. Any pathological conflict causes a functional deficit and any deficit of pathological significance is inseparable from a complex pathologic development rooted in conflict (Boesky, 1989). If there are prestructural "deficits" they could not be observed directly by the psychoanalytic method outside of the sphere of conflict because consequences of conflict are all that the psychoanalytic structural model is able to observe and explain. Ornstein says Willick is wrong and other analysts may say Willick is correct. This is a problem that will remain until we establish a consensus on the methodology of evidence.

So, it is evident that there are two ambiguities which Ornstein overlooks. The first is that we cannot settle the disagreement by reviewing the clinical data gathered in the context of one psychoanalytic model by using the methods and theories of another model. Advocates of each model must welcome evidential challenge as none of them have the final truth, but one cannot have an analyst who uses structural theory do an adequate microscopic process evaluation of the data at the end of a lengthy analysis conducted by a Kleinian analyst. All that is likely to happen is that the advocate of structural theory will claim that the Kleinian has missed important issues. The Kleinian may make the same claim. Indeed it is this state of affairs which I believe has led to the schisms of the present time. Ornstein claims implicitly that this is not true in his own case because he has tried very hard to be open minded and to give a fair hearing to the views of the six authors. That is indeed admirable. Each reader will have to decide whether or not and to what extent Ornstein succeeded. But in order to agree or disagree with him we need better evidence from him about exactly what clinical material he disagrees with in the process material of the patient rather than from abstract summaries. If Ornstein were to say that Willick did not give us enough information to prove his claims, Ornstein would have a different kind of disagreement, but that is not his point. What Ornstein actually does is to credit the humanity, empathy, and compassion that Willick drew on to help his patient and discard Willick's views about what Willick did to help his patient. It is as though Ornstein said that the patient was helped in spite of

Willick's theoretic views because Willick was really acting as a self psychologist without knowing it. That might also be so, but where is the evidence?

We also have the problem of how to assess assumptions about the primitive psychologic substrate which precedes structural differentiation. This is the arena of developmental theory that might be called psychoanalytic cosmology. Those who observe babies have published fascinating and ingenious speculations about what they presume to be the intrapsychic events occurring in the infant. They may be absolutely correct. But, in my own point of view, the domain of psychoanalysis is confined to the study of intrapsychic conflict in adults and children past the stage of structural differentiation. Ornstein feels free to mix frames of reference; without hesitation he scrambles the data and methods of nonconflict development and nonconflict pathology with the data and methods of conflict phenomena.

Ornstein wishes to have it both ways. His special use of the notion of deficit does not mean that he abandons the use of interpretation. But you can't "interpret" a deficit that was inflicted on a helpless child. It was not a compromise formation, and there was no motivation, conscious or unconscious, to have the deficit. The relationship with the analyst as a selfobject repairs the deficit. So what does one interpret? One presumably interprets the conflict aspects of the patient's problems. But this assumes that one can do two different kinds of psychoanalysis with the same patient at the same time. What are the criteria used by Ornstein that tell him when to *shift* to interpretations of conflict? If we use two very different maps to navigate the same terrain at the same time, we are going to be in big trouble before we reach our destination. One map is drive and conflict related and the other map is not.

Kafka's Case
Ornstein says: "Kafka, true to his theory, challenged his patient's assumptions of his motives as 'mistaken' and proceeded to show . . . that they were unfounded" (p. 143). Ornstein continues in an ad hominem vein, asserting that Kafka showed no interest in the patient's subjective experience of him. According

to Ornstein, Kafka was true to his theory because he wanted to correct the patient's misperception. That is a quite erroneous description of structural theory. The goal is not to correct the patient but to understand what dangers are avoided by creating and perpetuating a misperception. Indeed, it is often an important part of the working through during the treatment to help the patient to be more tolerant of his misperceptions so that they can be brought into the center of the work. It would seem that Ornstein believes that most of the resistances described by Kafka were iatrogenic. That is indeed a serious challenge. We are left to wonder if the evidence available allows Ornstein to make this assertion without hesitation.

Ornstein has a different view of Mayer's case. He states that it was her ability to "accept" her patient's distortions which facilitated the emergence of important issues, together with a progressive integration of her hitherto unacceptable affects. What Ornstein postulates here is the role of a "corrective emotional experience" with a new object as a mutative factor overlooked by Mayer and Willick in their presentations. Next Ornstein seems to have exactly reversed the true state of affairs. He said: "Here we have an ostensible contrast between Kafka's and Mayer's use of the same theory" (p. 149). There may or may not be a contrast in the actual technical and conceptual aspects of the two patients by Kafka and Mayer, but where is the evidence that these two analysts use the same theory in contrasting and possibly contradictory ways? One might say that we have two analysts who both state that they are using the *same* theory viewed in quite contrasting ways by Ornstein.

Ornstein says that he and I agree that you "see" certain phenomena only if you think of them as a possible configuration. But I said that you see conflict only if you think of its possible influence, with the assumption that the reader would understand that the frame of reference I use is to define the domain of psychoanalysis as finite and limited to the sphere of intrapsychic conflict. If one is using a microscope to observe human tissue and then wishes to visualize the moon, he had best switch to a telescope. We don't attempt to gather data in the same way with these two optical instruments merely because they each use a lens system. Each has its proper use. By analogy, a lens system can be compared to the couch. If two analysts both use a couch but one uses a conflict model and the other does not then those two analysts will observe and then interpret a very different field of observation.

A further word about Ornstein's view of Willick's case. He states that Willick did not allow his use of structural theory to interfere with his good work. Ornstein said: "He is the only one of the authors, however, who, when he maintained that he combined the concepts of conflict and deficit in his work with Carol, offered an explicit and decisive modification of that theory" (p. 154). It will be up to Willick to say whether he has deluded himself in the manner in which Ornstein observes. I think a more economic explanation than the ad hominem view would be to say that Ornstein believes that he has a better way than Willick to explain Willick's patient. According to Ornstein, Willick was flying by the seat of his pants and didn't understand as well as Ornstein understands that the patient improved for reasons which Willick didn't understand. That is different from saying that Willick is falsely claiming to adhere to his theory. It is merely saying that Willick's views are wrong, which indeed they may be. Furthermore Ornstein flatly asserts (p. 153) that Willick responded to deficit while searching for conflict. There is no evidence of that whatsoever. The evidence is that Willick skillfully responded to the emotional needs of his patient, and that Ornstein prefers to equate those emotional needs with deficits for his own reasons. But it is also decidedly incorrect to say that Willick modified structural theory by speaking of deficits and conflicts in the same breadth. That is why I quoted Anna Freud at such length above. It is therefore relevant to ask why Ornstein thinks it would be unacceptable to ask why deficit could not lead to secondary conflicts? Indeed they do, in the sense that Anna Freud described. I think in terms of deficit in my work, but in a very different frame of reference than does Ornstein. His deficit theory describes functional incapacities dating from the preverbal phase that are outside the realm of verbalization, that are outside of the realm of conflict, that are outside of the domain of psychoanalysis as a science of conflict, and which are therefore outside of the sphere of concealed motivations and concealed meanings that can be observed and studied with the structural model.

Ornstein wished that the authors would have said more about how reality becomes etiologically significant in pathogenesis (p. 162). So do I, but that, alas, has been the quest of every psychoanalyst since Freud. It is puzzling that our inability to give the final answer to this question suggests to him that highly important events in the life of the child "no longer count." Another gap in structural theory, according to Ornstein, is the fuzziness about what turns normal conflict into pathological forms. I would prefer to state the question in different terms by saying that the problem is how to better understand the differences and similarities between normal and pathological development, and we are indeed a long way from final answers to this question. But we have also come quite a distance in less than one century.

His second question is more interesting (p. 162). We don't yet have a good-enough understanding of the mode of therapeutic action and the relation between insight and relational factors. My prediction is that as we refine our criteria of evidence and learn more about the interrelation between insight and relational factors we will discover that the sharp distinction between these two categories masks the complexity of the manner in which they are interrelated. For example, Freud insisted on the importance of relational matters when he quarantined the unobjectionable positive transference to protect it from being analyzed away too soon. Furthermore, many discussions of the new object and the analyst as container muddle the difference between means and ends. It is not enough for the analyst to be continuously reliable, but the sicker the patient the more the analyst must be especially attentive to the relationship. In my opinion the profound importance of the interaction between the patient and analyst is indisputable. Instead of repeatedly insisting on the already obvious importance of the relationship, we will do better to become more observant about which specific aspects of the relationship are important and in what way and for what reasons with which specific patients, and we will have to forge a methodology for confirming or disproving the conjectures formed along the way.

Another word is in order about Hartmann's concept of the conflict-free sphere. My own explanation for this is that Hartmann shared Freud's hope of establishing psychoanalysis as a general psychology, and in that I think he failed. As a consequence I think we have a deeper respect for the boundaries of psychoanalysis as a scientific domain bordered by the phenomena of conflict. In his concluding remarks Ornstein wonders what the future of the structural theory will be if everything is conflict. An extension of his remarks is that this overemphasis on compromise formation leaves us with a homogenized field of view in which everything is just a compromise formation, and there are no longer individual boundaries to distinguish one thing from another in the mind. That is a confusion between the method of understanding and the subject matter. The subject matter of psychoanalysis is the enormously diverse realm of conflict. The use of compromise formation as an organizing principle is a powerful inducement to always try to account for all of the components of conflict instead of giving only a one dimensional view. To say that the genetic code consists of endless variations and recombinations of DNA and RNA molecules is not to say that zebras are indistinguishable from butterflies. In fact the discovery of the universal isomorphism of the genetic code affords a better understanding of phenotypic diversity. So it is with the use of compromise formation as a conceptual tool. The recognition of the isomorphic structure of normal and pathologic conflict may help us to better distinguish the crucial differences in their manifest expression.

I do agree with Ornstein that the structural model has had little to offer about the interaction of the analyst and patient. Our literature to date too often reports only the interpretations of the analyst and not the manner in which the analyst arrived at those interpretations. I believe that one of the contributions of the various object relation theorists has been their useful and correct insistence on better theoretic accounting for the role of the relationship with the analyst. But, thus far, their questions have been far more valuable than their answers.

Near the end of his discussion of Willick's case Ornstein illustrates the problem I described at the beginning of these remarks. He stated, after citing instances of affective intensity by the patient: "These are all expressions of and recognitions of profound needs or affects—where is the intersystemic, drive-defense conflict in this language?" (p. 151).

It is just such a profound misunderstanding of each other's

views which sometimes make me wonder if our expectations for clear communication between different schools of thought may represent a triumph of hope over experience. I feel that it will serve us all well to rethink the possibility that we may in our certainty about the correctness of our views be doing just what Ornstein does with that last question. If we learn as a result to check our evidence again, he will have placed all of us in his debt.

Robert L. Tyson, M.D.

Dr. Brenner's frame of reference views conflicts as derived from childhood instinctual conflicts. The conference was not focused on this issue, but something should be said about it. The complexities of development as we understand them today make it imperative to reexamine the tempting simplicity of the view that all conflicts are ultimately instinctual conflicts. To give just one example within the framework referred to, an instinctual conflict means not that instincts are in conflict, although in a wider view of the mind that is possible, but that there is a conflict between a wish for instinctual gratification and a superego prohibition. Theoretically, therefore, conflict does not exist before the superego is in operation, and since within this framework the superego is the product of oedipal resolution, conflict does not exist before this period of development.

Observation demonstrates differently and calls for a reassessment of the timetable of superego formation (Tyson and Tyson, 1990) as well as a reevaluation of the nature of infantile gratifications. Again within this framework, the superego prohibitions, when they occur, are taken as prima facie evidence that the wish is of instinctual origin. This assumption is based on the notion, an early one in the history of psychoanalytic thought, that all wishes are of instinctual origin and therefore anything that opposes them is evidence for such wishes. However, aside from the tautology involved, the superego functions involved in identifying wishes deemed necessary to be opposed are not concerned with their ultimate origin. Rather, they are focused on an implied threat to internal standards, such as those embodied along the course of development in the ego ideal, a constituent of the superego. While some of these standards refer to instinctual gratification, not all of them do, nor do all of them derive from instinctual beginnings. In addition, there may be a misidentification by the superego of a wish as instinctual, or even a failure to identify an instinctual wish correctly. To state that when the superego opposes a wish it means the wish is of instinctual origin, therefore, is an oversimplification of the superego function, of superego development, and of the nature and origin of wishes.

I want to address Dr. Brenner's comment, made in the course of restating some of my remarks, that preoedipal conflicts "have become not just intertwined with the wishes and conflicts of the oedipal period but truly part of them" (p. 99). This is a hopeful view of an optimal developmental result more honored in the breach than in the accomplishment. There is no magical transformation that guarantees the melding of all conflicts from one stage into those of another. Rather, the achievement of reasonably successful resolution of earlier conflicts is necessary to permit balanced forward development. One consequence of this balance is the opportunity to rework earlier conflicts in terms of the later ones, something which is a part of normal development. I suggested this by saying that past the point of the Oedipus complex, all conflicts cannot be understood simply in terms of the time of their origin. This means that, first, conflicts that are colored by an earlier origin will also carry indications of the contemporary level of development; and second, that conflicts that appear for the first time in a later stage are affected by the nature of earlier conflicts and their resolutions. Thus the clinician sees that some earlier conflicts have truly become part of later ones, others remain "intertwined," as it were, and others persist relatively unaltered. The clinical import of these distinctions is a caveat that interpretive work is best based on an understanding of which of these developmental pathways are most relevant to the material at hand.

While transference matters are not the primary focus of this conference, Dr. Brenner's comments about them involve the developmental issues just referred to. For example, he states that, "Such a transference results from the patient's childhood instinctual conflicts just as much as does any other type of transference reaction (p. 105). In view of the expanded framework of development to which I have been referring, transference manifestations may be based on conflicts other than instinctual ones, and derive from other developmental levels than those of childhood. Consequently the therapist must work harder to distinguish among the sources of conflicts rather than to assume all are instinctual and to determine what developmental level is involved rather than to assume it is always "just childhood." My own clinical experience suggests that transference interpretations that are informed by such a differentiated developmental view are likely to be more accurate than interpretations that are not so informed and also likely to be more effective therapeutically.

Dr. Bronstein has raised an interesting question about what I mean by the lasting effects of early experience. He is concerned that I mean that the pain and tragedy of infantile traumata will continue to be felt forever (I do not), and he wonders whether I see development as taking place in a "straight-line fashion" (I do not). He agrees with the notion that an adultomorphic bias can distort our scientific understanding of infant responses (though he does not comment on my assertion that "such a tendency may well be necessary for optimal growth and development," [p. 32]). However, he points out another possible avenue of distortion in the reverse direction, and that is the infantomorphic application of early developmental meaning to adult responses and behavior. To summarize, while Dr. Brenner assumes my meaning to be that all conflicts prior to the Oedipus complex disappear into the maelstrom of that later turmoil, Dr. Bronstein implies that I believe that all early catastrophic or traumatic experience is preserved in observable symptoms or behavior. I can only conclude that I did not make my position sufficiently clear so as to preclude these conclusions, though I have done so extensively elsewhere (Tyson, 1986; Tyson and Tyson, 1990). I welcome the opportunity for a brief clarification here.

    With respect to the effect of early traumatic experience, there is no question but that ego plasticity and resources can often creatively and advantageously shift the individual from the position of helpless victim to that of mastery and control. This in itself makes my point that our lives bear the marks of early experience, since without that experience there would be no necessity for the degree of mastery and control observed in such persons. The example of "the good child" offered by Dr. Bronstein is also excellent and to the point. As a child and adolescent analyst, I have seen the unfortunate consequences of adults taking for granted that "the good child" is not in "bad trouble" or else he or she would be "bad." As an analyst of adults, I have seen examples of such "good children" being the only ones to know they were in "bad trouble" until they were old enough to do something about it themselves. The marks are there, and some price is paid for them. They may or may not be visible as psychopathology or as useful capacities. If not visible, the price may be small, or latent, or only become manifest given some environmental stress later in life (Freud, 1937).

As for straight-line development, the schematic progression of conflicts I described may be misleading as a consequence of the heuristic device of sequencing. But a sequence of events is not straight-line development but one aspect of a larger complex. "The process of development can be conceptualized as the evolution of a number of functions that come to be linked and associated with other functions forming a system. Many systems evolve in this way, and the developmental trajectory of each intertwines with that of the others. These various systems eventually coalesce to form the relatively stable organizing structural units of id, ego, and superego, which maintain a dynamic equilibrium with each other and with the external world" (Tyson and Tyson, 1990, p. 32). "The metaphor [of developmental lines] remains useful, however, only to the extent that [it] is understood to refer to the sequential changes in any one of the many personality systems and represents a cyclical and spiraling pathway, one that is not linear in nature" (p. 36).

Dr. Vaquer provides an articulate exposition of a particular object relations point of view in which "what we speak of as clinically significant . . . conflict . . . is represented by a detailed and coherent unconscious fantasy in the analysand" (p. 116). There is a difficulty in specifying exactly when in the course of development a fantasy can be said to be present in an infant's mind. In Dr. Vaquer's theoretical framework there is no such difficulty, and he states clearly that, in his opinion, the infant has the capacity for unconscious fantasy from earliest days, a Kleinian axiom currently under renewed and vigorous debate. It is probably for this reason that Dr. Vaquer wonders about what I do not consider; for example, how events in earliest infancy affect the expression and internalization of later developmental conflicts. I believe he is referring to the Kleinian conviction that early fantasies that are supposed to exist in the infant's mind influence and structure the course of the mother–infant relationship, and that it is the content and sequence of these fantasies that is alleged to determine the nature of the infant's conflicts and the degree to which normality or pathology results. It is precisely those assumptions of the existence of early unconscious fantasy and of the accompanying mental structures that come into question when one examines the emergence and development in the infant of the elements of conflict according to the best definition yet available.

There is another possibility to consider here, even though I have the impression it differs from what Dr. Vaquer had in mind. This other possibility refers to the impact of a grossly pathological environment first and best studied by Spitz (1945, 1946a). Spitz demonstrated that when there is insufficient stimulation during the first year of life, there are dramatic and devastating effects on early development including the beginnings of object relationships. The infants he studied were left alone for long periods of time, and sucking and other pleasures in the context of affective interaction with a steady caregiver were largely absent. The result was a syndrome he termed *hospitalism*, part of which included a profound developmental retardation in all spheres. This would qualify as a response to Dr. Vaquer's other query about "the effects of the internalization of early abnormal infant–caretaker interrelations on . . . conflicts" (p. 129) and of course a great deal more could be said about abnormalities. However, I restricted the focus of my presentation to the "normal" or "average expectable" development. It is important to clarify early developmental events that are *not* pathological because our understanding of this area has been clouded by our preoccupation with psychopathology. Consequently we have often identified and labeled expectable developmental phenomena in infancy with pathological terms from adult illness (this is the adultomorphic error, e.g., manic defenses, paranoid and depressive positions).

Dr. Ornstein's essay has greatly broadened the scope of the discussion beyond the original charge, an inevitable result of the fact that his assumptions, those of self psychology, differ substantially from the assumptions of the authors and the other discussants. Therefore, when he refers to the *gaping divide* between the authors' views and the views of others, the differences are the consequence of his being asked to discuss the presentations from another perspective. Also, he does not address the differences between the authors' respective theoretical positions but for the purposes of his argument assumes they are all the same. In addition, I believe he excessively polarizes these positions, for example by stating, incorrectly, that modern structural theory has dispensed with Hartmann's conflict-free sphere and that consequently everything is conflict and compromise in both health and illness (p. 170).

Another point with which I disagree is Dr. Ornstein's conclusion that the authors "had to reject any other approaches falling short of their requirements for psychoanalysis as a method, theory, and practice" (p. 157). Dr. Ornstein's conclusion cannot be based on the material the authors presented, since they have not attempted to make such comparisons between approaches but only to offer their own. Therefore his conclusion regarding rejection must derive from other considerations outside the range of the assigned topic. I will limit my response to points he makes that are relevant to issues of development and conflict.

Dr. Ornstein puts his position clearly in several places, for example, at the beginning by saying that he will examine the authors' views from their own perspectives and then he will go on to reexamine them from a self psychological perspective. But later on, he declares that: "Each concept makes full sense only in the context in which it was originally developed, unless it is carefully redefined in its new context; but by then it has become a different concept" (p. 141). However, he does not address the difficulties he creates for his own endeavor by this acknowledgment that the self psychology context is sufficiently different from those of the authors and other discussants that all such comparisons are essentially invalid without a careful examination of the meanings of all the terms used, an examination that makes no initial assumptions about terminological or definitional equivalences. In brief, given one set of assumptions or another—the self psychological as represented by Dr. Ornstein or another as represented by one of the authors—his clear implication is that different internally coherent conceptual systems result and they cannot be compared without doing serious injustice to their meanings. I certainly agree with this.

Undeterred by these difficulties and in an effort to demonstrate the advantages of his preferred assumptions over those of the others, Dr. Ornstein examines each presentation in what he believes to be its own perspective in order to delineate what appear to him to be inconsistencies and restrictions in the underlying theory. In spite of his own disclaimer that a concept viewed in a different context becomes a different concept, he asserts that he finds theoretical deficiencies and associated clinical consequences that he believes to be best accounted for and remedied by the theories of self psychology. As mentioned earlier, I shall restrict my response to those aspects of his discussion that are relevant to matters of development, especially as they relate to the concept of conflict.

To begin with, Dr. Ornstein appears initially to assume that all conflict is pathogenic, since that is the only aspect of conflict to which he refers at the start. For example, he says among the issues on which he will focus will be "trauma, reality and its relation to pathogenic conflict and compromise" (p. 136). However, by thus neglecting the evolving rich tapestry of interdigitating conflict and adaptation throughout the course of development (a complex psychic process which includes defense, compromise, and symptom formation) in favor of the pathological, he polarizes the discussion in preparation for his effort to show the superiority of self psychological theory. An example of this polarization is in his declaration that modern structural theory has no need for the concept of deficit (p. 136), a point to which I will return. This position is puzzling especially in view of his acknowledgment (p. 139) that Dr. Willick takes account of the presence of ego deficits in presenting his work with a borderline patient, and that Dr. Willick proposed that it is not clinically useful to distinguish between ego impairments that result from psychic conflict in contrast to those that may have preceded conflict and have to do with basic structure formation. It is as if Dr. Ornstein is convinced that the notion of psychological deficit is evidence of defection from adherence to structural theory, whereas in fact there is nothing in early or contemporary structural theory which is incompatible with the concept of deficit.

A bit later, in discussing Dr. Mayer's clinical presentation, Dr. Ornstein acknowledges what he calls an "ambiguity between pathogenic and ubiquitous, normal conflicts" (p. 147), adding to the ambiguity by introducing the term *normal conflict* without indicating the perspective from which this term should be viewed. He then proceeds to utilize this ambiguity by delineating the clinical advantages of understanding the patient's subjective experiences rather than her conflicts. Only much later does he go back to consider normal conflict and finally (n. 6, p. 165) he explains his view that a conflict is pathological when it is not resolved, perhaps particularly when the reason for the lack of resolution is a "basic deficit." Dr. Ornstein's view differs from what I understand to be "Freud's findings that mental health or illness is based, not on the content of particular conflicts, but on the degree of success or failure in resolving the conflicts to which everyone is subject" (p. 31). According to this latter position, therefore, there is no such thing as a pathological conflict, but only pathological resolutions. In addition, Dr. Ornstein unfortunately does not make a distinction between a basic and a non-basic deficit, nor does he consider what it is that is deficient when there is a deficit. The confusion is made greater by his statement that "normal conflicts . . . become 'pathological' when there is a basic . . . deficit that makes it . . . impossible to resolve normal, developmental conflicts." As I have described in my presentation, a developmental conflict is not an intrapsychic conflict but a conflict between the developmentally appropriate wishes of the infant and the wishes of the mother. It precedes the appearance of an internalized conflict which is derived from it. There is nothing in this formulation that makes the distinction that Dr. Ornstein seems to be making, that developmental conflicts are normal, and that other kinds are not. Furthermore, I know of no observations from the field of infant and child development, or from child and adult analysis, to support this notion. I suspect that these confusions follow from the fact that Dr. Ornstein's definitions of conflict and of deficit are not derived from the context of the structural theory but from self psychology where they carry very different implications.

It isn't at all clear to me what place Dr. Ornstein believes these different conflicts—developmental, normal, pathological—have in the developmental process, whatever definitions may be used. It also is not clear why Dr. Ornstein believes that understanding Dr. Mayer's patient's subjective experience can be achieved without understanding her conflicts as well, or even why it would be desirable to make such a distinction. Something of his intention does become clear, however, when he states that he sees nothing pertaining to conflict in Dr. Mayer's description of her patient's bitter disappointment "at the disruption of what had been our happy and gratifying relationship" (p. 60).

One way to see conflict in Dr. Mayer's description would be to understand that her patient is exploiting the transference relationship in a reenactment of earlier, perhaps childhood, solutions to earlier conflicts; Dr. Ornstein's implication seems to be that the patient's affect is the expression of a frustrated need which secondarily could lead to the generation of conflicts. In spite of an apparent recognition of the links between affects and conflict, he seems to see them as separate and independent mental events. Indeed, he goes on to suggest that the crucial thing for this patient was not the resolution of conflict, but "the progressive integration of her hitherto unacceptable affects" (p. 149); thus he introduces a new term, presumably from the different context of self psychology, and one that therefore requires, but here lacks, a careful definition of what is meant by "integration," by "unacceptable," and by "affects" (e.g., integration into what and by what; unacceptable according to what criteria which are effective as judged how; and implemented by what means; affects with or without ideational components, as parts of mental representations, or as emotive concomitants of physiological states?).

In addition, Dr. Ornstein seems to expect the nature of the conflict to be stated at each point, and when instead the presenter describes something about the patient's affect, he infers that structural theory is inadequate to the occasion, much as he does in his discussion of Dr. Willick's use of the term *ego deficit*. He repeats this approach later when he sees only "expressions of and recognitions of profound needs or affects" but nothing of conflict in Dr. Willick's description of the treatment of his patient, Carol (p. 151). In discussing this point with respect to Dr. Mayer's patient, I have already shown how the analyst may conceptualize the conflicts which underlie both the verbalized and the enacted expressions of the patient's feelings and needs. This kind of conceptualization permits the analyst to make interpretations beyond surface manifestations; such interpretations allow the patient insight into and afford better resolutions for those inadequately resolved conflicts that persist from childhood and adolescence, conflicts for the relief of which the patient previously has had only endlessly repetitive emotional experiences that are only transiently "corrective" but permanently disappointing.

Finally, Dr. Ornstein is uncertain whether my presentation is consonant with modern structural theory, and he wishes I would take " a stand as a child analyst on the question of deficit (in its developmental, clinical and theoretical dimensions)" (p. 138).

With regard to the question of deficit, this is another one of those terms that carry significantly different connotations in psychoanalysis in general than in self psychology. Perhaps it would be worthwhile sometime to spell out these differences, but for the moment I want to point out that child analysts, and in particular those who find themselves in harmony with the work of Anna Freud, have been confronted with questions of psychological deficit and have addressed them developmentally, clinically, and theoretically. Deficits affecting defense formation, drive intensity, and ego and superego structuralization, as well as the impact of these deficits on the requirements of clinical technique are all well known. These issues are addressed throughout Anna Freud's writings and by many workers who have trained at or been affiliated with the Hampstead Clinic, now The Anna Freud Centre. It should be pointed out that the usual context in which these issues are discussed is not one dealing with deficit alone, but one is which manifestations of deficit are considered together with the whole spectrum of clinical phenomena, including manifes-

tations of drive, defense, object relations, and development—
whether achieved, aborted, arrested, and detained—all this in
the framework of the structural theory.

To be sure, there is no one set of axioms, premises, and
statements to which every analyst who considers himself to be a
"structuralist" would give unqualified agreement. And as Dr.
Ornstein demonstrates, analysts who do not subscribe to the
structural theory can hold views of that theory that differ considerably from the views of analysts who do find it useful.

I perceive my position to be within modern structural theory,
and it has been spelled out in detail elsewhere (Tyson and Tyson,
1990). The basis for Dr. Ornstein's uncertainty is unclear to me.
Perhaps it is related to a developmental perspective with which he
is unfamiliar, a perspective based on the concept of developmental lines as referred to in my presentation. This might explain his
request that I address the question of intrapsychic conflicts other
than those of drive derivatives, when in fact the notion of internal
conflict that I did describe does not in itself require drive
derivatives to be in conflict. However, the question of what it is
that is in conflict, as I pointed out in the beginning of my presentation, is not settled or agreed upon even by all those analysts who
consider their thought to be within the framework of the structural theory. The view that all intrapsychic conflict is between
drive derivatives is not a necessary hypothesis of the structural
theory, nor does the structural theory require that all such conflict be understood in those terms. In my mind, there is more to
be said on the topic of what it is that is in conflict, a question not
settled by this present work, but then it was not meant to focus on
that issue. It is to be hoped that the subject can be pursued
elsewhere.

Elizabeth Lloyd Mayer, Ph.D.

Dr. Brenner, I think, concisely described the agenda of all four
discussants in his introduction: how do we know what to do when
we set out to treat any given patient? The theory of conflict and
compromise, he tells us, has practical value because it helps us
answer that question. It helps us decide what to do as well as
when to do it, and how. Certainly, that is how I use the theory of

conflict and compromise in my daily work. It is a kind of background which organizes what I actually see and feel and experience with my patients into a series of constellations that may be ultimately analyzable.

But I want to emphasize that it is a *theory* which guides how I think about what I observe and experience with my patients. Structural conflict and compromise formation are not what I actually observe. I don't "see" conflict or compromise. I see what I take to be evidence that conflict and compromise are useful inferences to make about what is fueling a patient's perception or affect or idea at any particular moment. Such inferences have, for me, been validated many times by the increased freedom and self-understanding that a patient experiences when I help him or her understand a particular experience as expressive of conflict or compromise. That is why I stick to the theory. It has been useful. That is also why I see no problem posed by what Dr. Ornstein has called my everyday use of language (including use of the word *conflict*) to describe what I experienced with Annette on the level of what I was actually able to observe in our sessions, such that inferences about structural conflict were always secondary phenomena, emerging from the context of everyday language and immediate experience. It seems to me that the two levels of meaning are different but always need to be closely linked.

So that is the background against which I want to take up several other points raised by Dr. Ornstein. But first (and this will lead naturally into my discussion of Dr. Ornstein's points), I do want to describe what is at least a difference in emphasis between me and Dr. Brenner, if not an actual disagreement. He suggests that "In a therapeutic setting, transference is analyzed *rather than* reacted to in any other way. That is what is unique about transference in analytic therapy. Only in psychoanalytic therapy does the object of transference *limit* her or his reaction to analyzing it, that is, to trying to understand its nature and origin and to imparting that understanding. . ." (p. 102; emphasis added). Now I would alter those sentences slightly. For me, psychoanalytic therapy is not precisely defined by the fact that the analyst/therapist *limits* his or her engagement with transference to analyzing it. Partly, I don't actually find that such limitation turns out to be possible, even with the most stringent attention to how I interact with my patients and the most careful efforts to maintain "analyzing" as my top priority with patients. But more to the point, I hear it as a misemphasis in *defining* what for me makes therapeutic work analytic. I would alter Dr. Brenner's definition to say that the thing that makes a therapy psychoanalytic is the extent to which analyzing and understanding constitute the primary or ultimate *goals* of the therapeutic engagement, not the extent to which the analyst restricts his involvement to nothing but those activities. I do believe that plenty goes on in the analytic encounter *besides* analyzing, and that doesn't detract from the fact that psychoanalysis is possible. Indeed, it is often all those other things which set the stage for analytic work to take place, and provide for the substance of the analysis. I should add that I'm talking here about more than how the analyst helps create a therapeutic or working alliance with a patient: I am talking really about the fact that the analyst engages, even *enacts* with his or her patient and with that patient's transferences in myriad ways all the time. What defines the therapeutic work as analytic is the fact that neither patient nor analyst sticks with engagement and enactment as goals of the treatment. They subject all those engagements to analytic scrutiny as much as they can, and *that is* what sets analytic work apart from many other varieties of therapy; it's not set apart, in my view, by the fact that the analyst restricts his engagement simply to analyzing.

This brings me back to Dr. Ornstein. My guess is that he will find what I've been describing to be compatible with the ideas he has put forth. Indeed, I would guess he will find what I've been saying so compatible that I anticipate his reaction will be not unlike his reaction to my work with Annette. Since *that* reaction left me with the vague feeling that I was being congratulated for no longer beating my wife, I'll address what I believe to be our basic difference in perspective. I remain delighted at his enthusiastic response to my approach, but I don't find myself accepting his premise that its success rested on my having, in practice if not in principle, abandoned the particular conflict and compromise theory which most of us have enunciated in these papers.

Dr. Ornstein asks, both of me and of Dr. Willick, whether

there were aspects of what we did with our patients that derived from things besides the ways in which we understood conflict and compromise to motivate our patients. He takes it further: Were there *discrepancies* between what we did and what our theory of conflict and compromise would suggest we should have done? Specifically, was "the clinical atmosphere" within which we worked, our "attitude of acceptance of a patient's subjective experience," our preference for "interpretations which flowed from what patient and analyst had previously understood," our "emphasis on the relational elements of the transference and interpreting from the patient's perspective," and finally, our "acceptance of the patient's experience of the analyst as a legitimate starting point for the analysis of transference experiences"— were those features of our work really an outcome of our conflict model? Or did they represent our less-than-stringent application of that model (best case) or (worst case) did they represent a triumph of our underlying good-heartedness over our willingness to do what our theory would suggest we should be doing?

I hope my initial remarks with reference to Dr. Brenner's discussion may start to answer these questions.

I will start with the issue of how I understand the theory of conflict and compromise formation in relation to the question of technique. The theory of structural conflict orients my inferences as I try to understand what motivates a particular remark or behavior or affect in my patient. It is a theory entirely consistent with the way I establish what Dr. Ornstein calls the clinical atmosphere within which I work with a patient. In fact, it helps me understand vicissitudes of that atmosphere as they occur over time. It also is crucial in helping me understand how to make interactions to a patient in such a way that the patient can hear and utilize them, indeed, feel understood by them. In fact, I find that interpreting resistances based on my understanding of structural conflict makes patients by and large feel *understood* and thereby creates just the clinical atmosphere which Dr. Ornstein feels is so important to therapeutic work. (This is not to say that there aren't times when patients feel challenged and *mis*understood by resistance interpretations, but even then I find the conflict–compromise model is useful in helping me know how to help patients learn to understand how they have felt misunderstood.)

So, in one sense I can answer Dr. Ornstein simply: since I see the way I worked with Annette (and the way I try in general to work) to be entirely consistent with my theory of conflict and compromise, Dr. Ornstein's remarks are essentially irrelevant. "Acceptance of a patient's subjective experience," "interpreting from the point of view of the patient," and so on, are in no way exclusive of a conflict model. From that standpoint, the real problem which Dr. Ornstein enunciates has to do with the fact that the implications for technique which *he* draws from the conflict model have, in my view, the quality of straw men and would, I agree, lead patients to feel misunderstood, beleaguered, and even attacked in ways which sound antitherapeutic to me, as well as to Dr. Ornstein.

Having said all that, I do also believe that Dr. Ornstein is reaching for something very significant in his discussion which I shall try to specify in terms that make sense to me. On the one hand, I think it is important to recognize that what I have called a straw man in Dr. Ornstein's critique has not been as absent from interpretations of formal theory and therefore clinical practice as we might like to think. To that extent, while I don't see Dr. Ornstein making a valid critique of the conflict–compromise model per se, I do think he is making a valid critique of some of the ways it has been interpreted. Pointedly, he asks us about therapeutic failures and stalemates. Might it be that there have been problems in how the conflict–compromise model has been applied such that an emphasis on interpreting conflict has sometimes overridden concerns with whether those interpretations are being presented in ways that a patient can actually hear and use? I think probably so, and I think Dr. Ornstein does us a service when he highlights the problem.

Another way to put this is to see Dr. Ornstein as usefully addressing the issue I raised earlier with reference to Dr. Brenner's definition of what makes a therapy analytic. I think Dr. Ornstein is suggesting that it is necessary and useful to do many things with our patients besides what we might categorize as the pure analysis of conflict and compromise. As I have tried to point out, I agree with Dr. Ornstein here. And I agree with (and admire) what I see as his honesty in saying that we should examine what we *really* do with the patients and see if it includes anything besides what we would strictly call analyzing conflict. If it does, we need to expand our theory of technique to include those other things. Here I think Dr. Ornstein is suggesting that many things which analysts have subsumed under vague terms like *tact* and *timing* should not remain so vague or so extraneous to our formal theory of technique. They belong as much to technique as do principles by which we interpret underlying conflict.

If Dr. Ornstein will allow me to interpret him this way, I should like to say that I think he is right, that I think our theory of technique has given short shrift to these aspects of the analytic engagement as well as to how complex they are. They are not just necessary conditions for analysis, assumed as necessary by any good analyst. They *are* analysis, just as much as conflict interpretations are. Where I disagree with Dr. Ornstein is when he says we need a new theory to cover these matters because they are not compatible with our conflict and compromise model. The question of deficit versus conflict is not the relevant one for me: the question is whether we need to expand our theory of technique within the conflict model so that we can understand more of what we actually do with our patients in *all* phases of our engagements with them. I see no reason why that expansion should not occur under the overall rubric of conflict and compromise as overarching principles by which the mind operates. That is a separate matter from the question of whether developmental deficits constitute aspects of our patients' problems with which we try to help them. Deficits are a reality, just as are constitutional givens. But both become dynamically embroiled in the human psyche, in what we call structural conflict, from very early on. I believe it is as we understand the nature of that embroilment that we become able to use the conflict model to analyze the many aspects of what goes into makinig each patient's psychology unique.

Ernest Kafka, M.D.

Drs. Brenner, Bronstein, and Vaquer have followed a traditional method that allowed them to take advantage of their years of clinical experience and show their thinking about how best to make generalizations related to it. They have provided clinical illustrations which add to our own experiences derived from working with patients. In addition, they have shown convincing reasoning in relating their illustrations to generalizations about psychological functioning.

Such generalizations help us to integrate our thinking about the complex data of psychologic functioning. We should be aware that no generalization can encompass all the data that is available, and that, therefore, the preferences we have in using theories reflect the influence of the data at hand, as well as our own personal, stylistic preferences.

These three discussants, and the authors, have emphasized factors that we all seem to agree play a part in influencing behavior. Generations of therapists and patients have reached similar general clinically close conclusions. These resemble the broader generalizations, the paradigms that are useful for organizing thoughts, that are more related to personal preference in organizing ideas, and that are discussable as to their advantages and disadvantages. To me they differ from these too: to my mind, they are less theoretical and closer to clinical descriptions. In a moment, I would like to mention some of these less theoretical generalizations, my "facts."

Dr. Ornstein, by contrast, claimed that he represented a fundamentally different paradigm. He organized his argument first by making assertions about what structural theory is, and about what those who employ such terms as *conflict* and *compromise* think. Second, he interpreted clinical examples given by others to try to show that treatment he claims is imposed on patients by structural theory therapists is harmful to those patients. Third, he also endeavored to explain his "paradigm" and to distinguish it from what he claimed was the structural "paradigm."

I think that his view differs in language and emphasis but is not a fundamentally different paradigm. Dr. Ornstein set up a straw opponent, an invented version of structural theory. He also erred in second guessing what were no more than case illustrations of the snapshot kind, at least in his lengthy comments about my case examples. I think he was quite wrong in his assertions about what theoretical generalizations I prefer to use.

I will not have time to describe my views about Dr. Ornstein's "paradigm," but I must disagree that I have much in common with his straw structural analyst who, I think, serves as a foil for polemical and unfounded assertions. Further, I will take the opportunity to make some comment about Dr. Ornstein's discussion of the case examples I gave.

Now, I will return, briefly, to a statement of what I think of as facts. I know that the following is only a sketch, and I hope it will be received as such. These facts include: (1) that individuals are motivated to pursue personal aims which become more complex and undergo modification during the course of development and maturation; (2) that individuals possess capacities that also evolve during the course of development; (3) that evolution and change occur throughout life; and (4) that the influence of the individual's context, and especially of the interrelationship with objects, the influence of experience, is profound.

The human mind organizes and gratifies, suppresses, delays, and harmonizes many divergent and convergent aims, conscious and unconscious, to the extent possible, given the specific situation and mind concerned. For convenience, we can describe these aims as libidinal, aggressive, defensive, and moral. Other terms are, and have been used by authors who find them more helpful. All these aims and the manner of their modulation are influenced by experiences. Experiences are felt and understood consciously and unconsciously and these understandings are influenced by how experiences are interpreted. The interpretation of experiences, in turn, is influenced by personal history, by past interpretations of experiences in the context of past mental states, including the maturational state and the wishful state of mind at the time. Such interpretations, in large part unconscious (unconscious fantasies), influence expectations. The more or less successful modulation and harmonization of forces, we term *compromise formation*.

My technical approach to patients is a consequence of a conviction that what I have just stated is accurate. This approach is to help the patient discover and consider how his development occurred, how the interrelations of the internal context of mental conditions and the external context of his relationship to his world over the course of his history influenced his theories about himself and about reality, and his modes of dealing with his inner aims, of finding gratification, security, and self satisfaction in his adaptation.

Dr. Ornstein proposes a different view. That is, that it is important to focus "primarily on the patient's inner experience." Clearly, to me, attention to inner experience is only one part, albeit an important part, of the therapeutic work. In order to set himself apart from me, to show he had something fundamentally new and better to offer, Dr. Ornstein made certain claims.

He claimed that I "acknowledged minimal change in response to . . . interventions in the first instance" (p. 142). The second patient remained emotionally uninvolved "in the face of repeated confrontations and interpretations" (p. 142). He thought it a thing we might wonder at, "how the patient could have become more involved emotionally in the face of specific interventions, each of which questioned the validity of his subjective experiences." I "eschewed" "the understanding of the patients' 'distortions' and 'prejudgments' from their own subjective perspective" (p. 146). I was "oblivious" to the "fact" that I "discounted" the "relational elements of [my] approach." I made an "inadvertently unempathic intervention, an unintended and . . . inevitable criticism . . . which led to the patient's homosexual fling," an intervention whose effect was "traumatic because it repeated some prior painful experience. . ." (p. 166). I should have "focused" "primarily on the patient's inner experience." I failed to "directly pursue" the patient's subjective experiences of me. My "theory translates into an attitude of disbelief and skepticism" regarding my patient's experience of me and this resulted in "an iatrogenically provoked intensification" of one patient's resistances (p. 144).

I fully agree with Dr. Ornstein's opinion, that one must listen to one's patient. In responding to my contribution, however, I think that Dr. Ornstein failed to follow his own advice. He did not listen to what I said.

My paper was entitled "Technical Considerations in Treating Patients with Character Disorders." I was concerned with describing one way of dealing with a particular problem presented by some patients in the opening phase of treatment. Those patients were people who had little understanding that they had psychological problems, and little interest in talking about themselves.

I suggested that sometimes one can show such people that therapy might make sense for them. Sometimes, I proposed, one can do this by demonstrating that an aloof, frightened, or suspicious attitude directed toward the therapist before any experience with him could account for it, an attitude that predated any contact with the therapist, might merit investigation. A small sample of my relation with a patient who wanted to break off treatment because she assumed I intended to charge for missed appointments when she took a vacation she had planned before beginning was one illustration of the point.

I pointed out to her that her assumption, which, if she acted on it, would make it impossible for her to benefit by treatment, was incorrect. The result was that she continued her treatment. I wrote:

> In both cases, the material is disguised to preserve confidentiality, and selected, and abstracted for the sake of focusing on the point to be illustrated, that is to say, that careful demonstration of the paradoxical and prejudgmental elements revealed through transference manifestations is a particularly valuable tool in the treatment of patients with character problems, whose conscious motivation for treatment is not great" (pp. 67–68).

Why does Dr. Ornstein laud me for describing unsuccessful cases? I cannot accept this praise. The patients cited and I were quite satisfied wiht the therapeutic results. How does Dr. Ornstein know, from a selected, disguised description of part of what took place in the early months of a treatment, used to illustrate a particular point, that the treatment was unsuccessful?

Why does Dr. Ornstein claim I questioned the "validity" of "each of" the patient's experiences with me? I questioned the appropriateness to the specific situation of certain beliefs of the patient, on a particular occasion, not the validity of each of her experiences of me.

Where does Dr. Ornstein find evidence of my skepticism and disbelief about the patient's experience of me? What makes him think I disbelieved that she feared me?

And what is the evidence that I iatrogenically strengthened the other patient's resistance? How can he presume to know I made "an advertently unempathic intervention, an . . . unintended criticism" which led to "my patient's homosexual fling," which was "traumatic?" How can he draw such broad and unfortunate conclusions from such a modicum of evidence?

Where did I "eschew" or "discount?" Did I do this by keeping to my subject? I merely wanted to show that in some patients, this was "a particularly useful" approach. I never implied it was the only potentially useful approach, nor that it was all that happened in the treatment.

I want to reassure Dr. Ornstein that he need have no fear that I failed the man who took refuge in a homosexual adventure, by neglecting to discuss with him the many reasons he had for doing so. Among the reasons were a need to deny his affection for me, and to limit his fear of a variety of anticipated consequences his love and desire might have if he allowed it to flourish and be expressed. Even if I had wished to, I could not have written everything that took place.

It is certainly true that my comments indicated that I thought it likely, at that point, to be worthwhile for the patients to pursue a particular line of thought rather than some other. All comments are selective, and imply a suggestion of directions to follow, and others to put aside, at least for the time. Had I done what Dr. Ornstein recommends, to "directly pursue the patient's experience" of me, that would have had a similar result.

The patient might then have turned away from a consideration of how her experiences related to her relationship with me, and what historical factors, what unconscious transference elements, what previous experience might have influenced it. Actually, my impression at the time was, that my intervention was the best way to help the patient stay in treatment.

If Dr. Ornstein "immersed" himself in the six papers, I would suggest a reimmersion, at least in mine. I also find little evidence that he showed an understanding of my views in what he wrote in his section "entirely from within" my theoretical position.

Again, in the following, I can only indicate the outlines of my views. I do so hesitantly, and only to describe some of the ways in which I think Dr. Ornstein's representations in speaking for me are mistaken.

I did not illustrate how I thought "the theory guided my interventions in a variety of clinical conditions." I illustrated a point of technique in a particular situation with two particular patients.

I did not present, nor do I have an "overall message" that places intrapsychic conflict "at the center of theory and practice." Conflict is important, but so are, among other things, opportunities for gratification, defense, and learning in inter-relationships with institutions and objects, including analysis and the analyst, and collaborations among, as contrasted with con-flicts between, varying aims. Also worthy of examination and dis-cussion in analyses are the integrative capacities and integrative experience involving insights, adaptation, history, and context.

Dr. Ornstein says that I think "conflict engenders anxiety, guilt, shame, or depressive affect and thereby demands the for-mation of compromise formation." I do not. I think that people have conflict and anxiety, guilt and shame, and depressive affect, and pleasure, achievement, and invention as well, because they achieve partial success harmonizing their incompletely under-stood and only partly satisfiable needs and desires in a context that they also incompletely understand, and which is often threatening and frustrating.

I do not think the concept of deficit is erroneous. I have a con-cept of deficit, and once wrote about cognitive problems and their influence in a patient's development and on his analysis (Kafka, 1984).

Deficit, disability, disease, talents, and developmental influ-ences all contribute to psychological adaptational organization. Deciphering what is what is difficult. Sometimes, what looks like a deficit isn't one. Like the famous cigar, which might be a cigar, the manifest appearance of what looks like a deficit might well be a manifest appearance, capable of being examined and shown to be an adaptive arrangement reflecting a modicum of deficit perhaps, but also, ability and competence.

On the other hand, what looks like a mainly developmentally influenced condition can turn out not to be. There is an overlap between deficit, disability, and disease on the one hand and mainly developmentally, adaptationally influenced difficulties on the other. In the past, some authors' overenthusiasm led them to propose that psychological, developmental factors were the main causes of such conditions as autism, forms of psychosis, and psychosomatic diseases. Such claims have had to be severely modified. No one now would propose treating a patient with peptic ulcer using psychoanalysis alone. Caution in drawing general conclusions seems advisable and further investigation needs to be done.

I don't think "insight through interpretations as the exclusive analytic tool" (fn. 3, pp. 152–153). I think insight in the analytic sense is an experiential part of a satisfying, useful reorganization of mental contents, a reorganization that revises understanding of the past and expectations of the future. It can occur in the very special context of a situation entered into by two people who relate to each other in a very particular way for very particular ends, that is in an analysis, and can be a very good thing. It can occur in other situations as well, and other things than insight occur in analyses.

I don't think I "preclude the assumption that the patient's observations contain some truth." I don't "disregard the reality" of the patient's experiences relived in the transference. Rather hesitantly, I included a genetic construction in one of my case examples, despite the fact that it did not illustrate the main point I wanted to make. I would have thought this might have pleased Dr. Ornstein, since he favors the idea that transference experiences can be useful because they make it possible that "prior experiences can now be recalled, or reconstructed and thereby the transference disruption can be interpretively repaired."

However, Dr. Ornstein did not hesitate to criticize me for this construction, too, on the grounds that I "did not explore the patient's transference feelings and quickly moved to a genetic speculation" (p. 145). He cannot logically have it both ways.

Finally, in answer to Dr. Ornstein's question, "Where is Hartmann's conflict-free sphere of the ego in modern structural theory? Isn't its absence or some equivalent concept to account for nonconflict based psychic structures and functions a glaring omission?" (p. 170). I would like to suggest that he look at Volume 4, 1989, of the *Psychoanalytic Quarterly* devoted to Hartmann's contributions to contemporary analytic thinking. In "The Contribution of Hartmann's Adaptation Theory" (Kafka, 1989), I discussed Hartmann's concept of change of function. I showed how the acquisition of the power to actualize wishes, and to understand more about the consequences of such actualizing, influences morality and character development in adolescence. I elaborated similar ideas in "The Uses of Moral Ideas in the Mastery of Trauma and in Adaptation" (Kafka, 1990). I think Dr. Ornstein will find the concept of conflict-free ego functions is alive and well and useful to me.

I think Dr. Ornstein has not done well in falling into the temptation to second guess a colleague, particularly in the absence of even the data of a detailed case presentation. He has also erred in trying to lump too much into the basket of the "them" as opposed to the "us," those presenters of a putatively remarkable, new, fundamentally different paradigm among whom Dr. Ornstein numbers himself. As Dr. Ornstein recommends, if you wish to know what someone thinks, sometimes you have to ask and then, it pays to listen.

Above all, we should all bear in mind that individual human behavior is idiosyncratic, is formed over time, has many interwoven determinants and purposes, and occurs in living animals with immanent constitutional characteristics. Understanding of it can only be incomplete. Enthusiasm is not an alternative to careful study.

There are kernels of truth in Dr. Ornstein's discussion. As he says, it is worthwhile to hear a variety of views about how we can organize psychoanalytic data, as well as to hear a variety of data. I include among these, views and data derived from investigation of society, of education of child and adult development, of neurophysiology, of medical conditions, and from many other approaches.

Martin S. Willick, M.D.

Dr. Brenner, in his usual masterly way, gives us a clear and concise summary of the centrality of the concept of compromise formation in the understanding of pathology and as a guiding principle in the conducting of an analysis or psychoanalytically oriented psychotherapy.

Dr. Bronstein agrees with the importance and relevance of the authors' points of view and also reminds us to be aware of and account for certain processes of healthy adaptation that arise out of conflict and trauma.

Dr. Vaquer presents a clear review of Bion's concepts and illustrates them with his own cases. Dr. Vaquer states that he is in essential agreement with me, but that, in addition:

> [T]here is some evidence that the patient is, at times, under the influence of an omnipotent unconscious fantasy, the essence of which is that she is being held or contained. . . . Specifically the patient's wish that Dr. Willick think about her constantly when she is away from him can be seen as a wish to be contained within his mind and not ejected as something bad, as she felt her biological mother had done" [p. 130].

He adds that this is in addition to my formulations of "triadic whole object conflicts."

I have no problem with including preoedipal conflicts in the patient's pathogenesis since such conflicts influence and become intertwined with later, oedipal ones. However, when Dr. Vaquer says that my patient is being "held or contained" by me he is most likely using these terms in a different way from the way in which I would use them. I believe that he sees such holding and containment as being functions provided by the mother during the first year of life in accord with the formulations of Bion and Winnicott. My view is that such holding and containment takes place throughout childhood. The two-year-old as well as the five-year-old wants to be constantly thought of when the mother or the father is away. This wish might be especially acute when a sibling is born and is not necessarily primarily derived from experiences in the first year of life when such fantasies may not really be present. In addition, a child's wish that a parent accept its hostile and murderous wishes without reacting with extreme rage need not be conceptualized as a "holding or containing" function which is at work primarily during the earliest months of the infant's life. Such a function is an ongoing aspect of an adequate caretaker's response to his or her child's frustration and hostility throughout childhood and adolescence.

Now to turn to Dr. Ornstein's comprehensive discussion. It is not possible to enter into a full review of the differences between self psychological concepts and those of structural ego psychology. I will instead use Dr. Ornstein's comments about my case presentation to highlight the principal areas of agreement, disagreement, and misunderstanding between us.

First, I wish to make it clear that I do not believe that every manifestation of every mental illness can be satisfactorily explained as a compromise formation resulting from conflicts between the drives and the ego with its defenses and superego functions. As I mentioned in my paper, and have tried to show elsewhere (Willick, 1990), many of the symptoms and abnormalities of the major adult psychoses are the result of primary biological abnormalities in brain functioning. This is not to say that people suffering from schizophrenia and bipolar illness do not have the usual conflicts of mental life with resulting compromise formations. However, the major etiological components are often biological impairments and ego defects with which the ego has to deal. Therefore, I believe that in mental illness there are ego defects and functionally important ego deficits. (In this regard it is unfortunate that the Kleinian and Bionian formulations often do not make any distinctions among the various types of adult psychoses and treat them as though they have common etiological roots in impairments of psychic structure due to environmental causes.)

However, as I said in my presentation, we are, in discussing the origins of ego deficits in severe personality disorders, whether they be narcissistic or borderline or some other types, primarily talking about deficits that are caused by developmental failures arising from impaired nurturing early in life, not from acquired or inherited biological abnormalities. We are essentially trying to address impairments in the building up of psychic structure. The latter can only be defined by an examination of the ego and its functions which include, of course, the nature of object relations.

In discussing my paper, Dr. Ornstein raises some very important and relevant questions. He writes that I "appear to minimize the role of (my) flexibility and attunement to the patient's needs in the curative process" (p. 139). More important, he believes that I fail to realize that what I did intuitively in order to conduct the treatment should have led me to the conclusion that the patient did have the very deficits that I am reluctant to attribute to her. In other words, although he compliments me on my therapeutic technique, he feels that I am unwilling to draw the correct conclusions from my understanding of the need for that technique. Dr. Ornstein concludes that the patient used me as a selfobject and was suffering from a failure to develop a cohesive sense of self. He believes that it would be useful to me and to my patients if I used self psychological formulations that explain how it came to pass that she was left with deficits in her psychic structure that compelled her to need me and others as selfobjects.

My first response is that I did not minimize the role that my therapeutic stance played in the curative process, nor do I argue against the importance of a "corrective emotional experience." I wish that I could have learned more about the meaning to my patient of my supportive interventions, but, as I tried to show, this patient did not freely communicate her thoughts to me. She has now stopped treatment after seven years and, unless she returns, I will not be able to add a great deal to that understanding. What I can say about Carol is that there is no clear evidence that my helpful supportive technique indicates the presence of the types of ego deficits that Dr. Ornstein is referring to. He feels that it is sufficient to use the quality of the transference to deduce the nature of the patient's internal deficits just as we use the nature of the transference (as well as other aspects of the patient's functioning) to deduce conclusions about drive-related conflicts and compromise formations. I am much more reluctant to do so; I find it very difficult to verify failures in structure formation from work with adult patients.

One of the most serious misunderstandings that some self psychologists have about those of us who are characterized as "classical ego psychologists" is that they conceive of our concept of drive-related conflicts and compromise formation in a much too restricted way. For example, Dr. Ornstein describes my successive interpretations about my patient's experience that I "did not exist" for her on the weekends. He then quotes me as follows: "It was only in the fourth year of treatment that she was able to tell me that she really wanted me to sit in the office twenty-four hours a day, waiting for her only; she did not want me to have other patients or family" (p. 84).

Dr. Ornstein then writes, "These are all expressions of and

recognitions of profound needs or affects, where is the intersystemic, drive–defense conflict in this language?" (p. 170). I cannot believe that he thinks that analysts like myself do not recognize, in our theories, that patients have "profound needs and affects." There surely is nothing about that recognition that distinguishes self psychology, object relations theory, or ego psychological theory. His question, "where is the intersystemic, drive–defense conflict in this language?" is indicative of an important misunderstanding.

My use of the concepts of sexual and aggressive drives is much broader than Dr. Ornstein seems to believe. I include under the heading of the sexual drives all those longings to be loved, to be loved exclusively with no rival, to be special, and to be on the mind of the loved object incessantly. I also include wishes to be admired, praised, adored, respected, and understood. All of these "sexual wishes" that Carol had—the mental representations of the sexual drives—are just as important as and become intertwined with the more explicit sexual wishes to be attractive to her father, to have sex with him, and to have his baby.

Therefore, the "intersystemic, drive defense conflict in this language" is as follows: Carol had all of those sexual wishes described above, although the more explicitly sexual ones were most intensely defended against and only emerged to a certain degree in the year of treatment that followed the presentation of this paper. These wishes, many of which were not conscious to her, were warded off by defense mechanisms of repression, displacement, and protective, narcissistic withdrawal, to mention only a few. These wishes aroused anxiety not only because she feared she would be rejected and hurt, but also because she feared that she would be punished for their fulfillment.

In order to answer Dr. Ornstein's question more completely, I would have to describe all of the aspects of her aggressive drive as well, those feelings of rage, envy, murderous intent, rivalry, and competitiveness which, like the sexual wishes, are derived from both the preoedipal and oedipal phases. An examination of defenses against and superego condemnations for her anger and hateful thoughts—the mental representations of the aggressive drive—would delineate the "conflict." In addition, I would include in any such discussion of these conflicts the narcissistic wounds engendered by them and the methods of coping with narcissistic injury.

In other words, I find nothing in the language that I used to describe Carol's thoughts and behavior that cannot be explained by or incorporated within the drive-defense, compromise formation model, provided that that model includes the sexual and aggressive drive derivatives in their broadest sense. In addition, that broad sense includes all the aspects of narcissistic vulnerabilities, narcissistic defenses, and narcissistic fantasies which accompany the development of object relations throughout childhood and adolescence. I am less persuaded than Dr. Ornstein is that we have to conceptualize a separate developmental line for the vicissitudes of narcissism.

Finally, Dr. Ornstein asks why do I not find it helpful to think of Carol's problems as involving a defect in structure formation that is primary while the conflicts that I described are secondary to this basic defect. I have answered that I dealt with her conflicts in the best way that I could without using the concept of a primary defect, and that my supportive techniques do not, in themselves, demonstrate the presence of either defect or deficit. More important, I have said that the danger in thinking of Carol's problems as indicating a primary defect is that an analyst might neglect those very aspects of conflict that I found to be so helpful to her in understanding herself.

References

Abend, S., & Porder, M. (1986), Identification in the neuroses. *Internat. J. Psycho-Anal.*, 67:201–208.

Adler, G. (1985), *Borderline Psychopathology and Its Treatment*. New York: Jason Aronson.

American Psychiatric Association (1980), *Diagnostic and Statistical Manual of Mental Disorders* (DSM-III), 3rd ed. Washington, DC: American Psychiatric Press.

Arlow, J. (1960), Fantasy systems in twins. *Psychoanal. Quart.*, 29:175–199.

—— (1969a), Unconscious fantasy and disturbances of conscious experience. *Psychoanal. Quart.*, 38:1–27.

—— (1969b), Fantasy, memory and reality testing. *Psychoanal. Quart.*, 38:28–51.

—— (1976), Character and communication: A clinical study of a man raised by deaf-mute parents. *The Psychoanalytic Study of the Child*, 31:139–163. New Haven, CT: Yale University Press.

—— (1980), The revenge motive in the primal scene. *J. Amer. Psychoanal. Assn.*, 28:519–541.

—— (1981), Theories of pathogenesis. *Psychoanal. Quart.*, 50:488–514.

—— (1986), The relation of theories of pathogenesis to psychoanalytic therapy. In: *Psychoanalysis: The Science of Mental Conflict*, ed. A. Richards & M. Willick. Hillsdale, NJ: Analytic Press, pp. 49–64.

—— (1987), The dynamics of interpretation. *Psychoanal. Quart.*, 56:68–87.

—— Brenner, C. (1964), *Psychoanalytic Concepts and Structural Theory*. New York: International Universities Press.

Balint, M. (1958), The three areas of the mind: Theoretical considerations. *Internat. J. Psycho-Anal.*, 39:328–340.

Bene, A. (1977), The influence of deaf and dumb parents on a child's development. *The Psychoanalytic Study of the Child,* 32:175–194.

Bion, W. (1956), Development of schizophrenic thought. In: *Second Thoughts.* London: Pitman Press, pp. 36–42.

—— (1957a), Differentiation of the psychotic from the non-psychotic personality. In: *Second Thoughts.* London: Pitman Press, pp. 43–64.

—— (1957b), On arrogance. In: *Second Thoughts.* London: Pitman Press, pp. 86–92.

—— (1958), On hallucination. In: *Second Thoughts.* London: Pitman Press, pp. 65–85.

—— (1959), Attacks on linking. In: *Second Thoughts.* London: Pitman Press, pp. 93–109.

—— (1962a), A theory of thinking. In: *Second Thoughts.* London: Pitman Press, pp. 110–119.

—— (1962b), *Learning from Experience.* London: Heinemann.

—— (1963), *Elements of Psychoanalysis.* London: Heinemann.

—— (1965), *Transformations.* London: Heinemann.

—— (1967), *Second Thoughts.* London: Heinemann.

—— (1970), *Attention and Interpretation.* London: Tavistock.

Blos, P. (1985), *Son and Father, Before and Beyond the Oedipus Complex.* New York: The Free Press.

Blum, H. (1979), On the concept and consequences of the primal scene. *Psychoanal. Quart.,* 48:27–47.

Boesky, D. (1982), Acting out: A reconsideration of the concept. *Internat. J. Psycho-Anal.,* 63:39–56.

—— (1986), Questions about sublimation. In: *Psychoanalysis: The Science of Mental Conflict,* ed. A. D. Richards & M. S. Willick. Hillsdale, NJ: Analytic Press, pp. 153–176.

—— (1988a), The concept of psychic structure. *J. Amer. Psychoanal. Assn.,* 36 (Suppl.):113–136.

—— (1988b), Comments on the structural theory of technique. *Internat. J. Psycho-Anal.,* 69:303–316.

Brenner, C. (1974a), On the nature and development of affects: A unified theory. *Psychoanal. Quart.,* 43:532–556.

—— (1974b), Depression, anxiety, and affect theory. *Internat. J. Psycho-Anal.,* 55:25–32.

—— (1975), Affects and psychic conflict. *Psychoanal. Quart.,* 44:5–28.

—— (1979), The components of psychic conflict and its consequences in mental life. *Psychoanal. Quart.,* 48:547–567.

—— (1982), *The Mind in Conflict.* New York: International Universities Press.

—— (1986), Discussion. In: *The Reconstruction of Trauma,* ed. A. Rothstein. Madison, CT: International Universities Press, pp. 195–204.

Breuer, J., & Freud, S. (1895), Studies on Hysteria. *Standard Edition,* 2. London: Hogarth Press, 1955.

Brody, S. (1956), *Patterns of Mothering: Maternal Influence During Infancy.* New York: International Universities Press.

Bronstein, M. H. (1991), Review. *How Does Treatment Help?* ed. A. Rothstein, M.D. (1988). *Psychoanal. Quart.,* 1:117–120.

Call, J. D. (1964), Newborn approach behaviour and early ego development. *Internat. J. Psycho-Anal.,* 45:286–294.

Emde, R. N., & Sorce, J. F. (1983), The rewards of infancy: Emotional availability and maternal referencing. In: *Frontiers of Infant Psychiatry,* ed. J. D. Call, E. Galenson, & R. L. Tyson. New York: Basic Books, pp. 17–30.

Esman, A. (1973), The primal scene: A review and a reconsideration. *The Psychoanalytic Study of the Child,* 28:49–81. New Haven, CT: Yale University Press.

Etchegoyen, R. (1985), Identification and its vicissitudes. *Internat. J. Psycho-Anal.,* 66:3–18.

Fenichel, O. (1945), *The Psychoanalytic Theory of Neurosis.* New York: W. W. Norton.

Fraiberg, S. (1982), Pathological defenses in infancy. *Psychoanal. Quart.,* 51:612–635.

Freud, A. (1962), Assessment of childhood disturbances. *The Psychoanalytic Study of the Child,* 17:149–158. New York: International Universities Press.

—— (1963), The concept of developmental lines. *The Psychoanalytic Study of the Child,* 18:245–265. New York: International Universities Press.

—— (1965), *Normality and Pathology in Childhood: Assessments of Development.* In: *Writings,* Vol. 6. New York: International Universities Press.

—— (1966), Foreword. In: H. Nagera, *Early Childhood Disturbances, the Infantile Neurosis, and the Adulthood Disturbances.* New York:

International Universities Press, pp. 9–10.

———— (1974), A psychoanalytic view of developmental psychopathology. In: *Writings,* Vol. 8. New York: International Universities Press, 1981, pp. 57–74.

Freud, S. (1912), The dynamics of transference. *Standard Edition,* 12:97–108. London: Hogarth Press, 1958.

———— (1914), On narcissism: An introduction. *Standard Edition,* 14:69–102. London: Hogarth Press, 1957.

———— (1923), The ego and the id. *Standard Edition,* 19:1–66. London: Hogarth Press, 1961.

———— (1924), An autobiographical study. *Standard Edition,* 20:3–74. London: Hogarth Press, 1959.

———— (1926), Inhibitions, Symptoms, and Anxiety. *Standard Edition,* 20. London: Hogarth Press, 1959.

———— (1937), Analysis terminable and interminable. *Standard Edition,* 23:211–253. London: Hogarth Press, 1964.

Freud, W. E. (1968), Some general reflections on the metapsychological profile. *Internat. J. Psycho-Anal.,* 49:498–501.

Grinberg, L., Sor, D., & Tabak de Bianchedi, E. (1975), *Introduction to the Work of Bion.* London: Karnac Books.

Grotstein, J. (1977), The psychoanalytic concept of schizophrenia. I. The dilemma II. Reconciliation. *Internat. J. Psycho-Anal.,* 58:403–452.

———— (1981), *Splitting and Projective Identification.* New York: Jason Aronson.

———— (1987), The borderline as a disorder of self regulation. In: *The Borderline Patient,* ed. J. S. Grotstein, M. F. Solomon, & J. A. Lang. Hillsdale, NJ: Analytic Press.

Hartmann, H. (1939), *Ego Psychology and the Problem of Adaptation.* New York: International Universities Press, 1958.

———— (1964), *Essays on Ego Psychology.* New York: International Universities Press.

———— Lowenstein, R. (1962), Notes on the superego. *The Psychoanalytic Study of the Child,* 17:42–81. New York: International Universities Press.

Hochschild, A. (1989), *The Second Shift: Working Parents and the Revolution at Home.* New York: Viking, Penguin, Inc.

Isaacs, S. (1952), The nature and function of phantasy. In: *Developments in Psychoanalysis,* ed. J. Riviere. London: Hogarth Press, pp. 67–121.

Jacobson, E. (1953), The affects and their pleasure–unpleasure qualities in relation to the psychic discharge processes. In: *Drives, Affects, Behavior,* ed. R. Loewenstein. New York: International Universities Press, pp. 38–66.

——— (1964), *The Self and the Object World.* New York: International Universities Press.

Jones, E. (1929), Fear, guilt and hate. *Internat. J. Psycho-Anal.,* 10:383–397.

Kafka, E. (1984),Cognitive difficulties in psychoanalysis. *Psychoanal. Quart.,* 53:533–550.

——— (1989), The contribution of Hartmann's adaptation theory with special reference to regression and symptom formation. *Psychoanal. Quart.,* 58:571–591.

——— (1990), The uses of moral ideas in the mastery of trauma and in adaptation. *Psychoanal. Quart.,* 59:249–269.

Kernberg, O. (1988a), Psychic structure and structural change: An ego-psychology–object relations theory viewpoint. *J. Amer. Psychoanal. Assn.,* 36:315–338.

——— (1988b), Object relations theory in clinical practice. *Psychoanal. Quart.,* 57:481–504.

Khan, M. (1963), The concept of cumulative trauma. *The Psychoanalytic Study of the Child,* 18:286–306. New York: International Universities Press.

Killingmo, B. (1989), Conflict and deficit. Implications for technique. *Internat. J. Psycho-Anal.,* 70:65–81.

Klein, M. (1946), Notes on some schizoid mechanisms. In: *Envy and Gratitude and Other Works, 1946–1963.* London: Hogarth Press, 1975, pp. 1–24.

——— (1957), Envy and gratitude. In: *Envy and Gratitude and Other Works, 1946–1963.* London: Hogarth Press, 1975, pp. 176–235.

——— (1960), A note on depression in the schizophrenic. In: *Envy and Gratitude and Other Works, 1946–1963.* London: Hogarth Press, 1975, pp. 264–267.

——— (1963), On the sense of loneliness. In: *Envy and Gratitude and Other Works, 1946–1963.* London: Hogarth Press, 1975, pp. 300–312.

Klein, S. (1980), Autistic phenomena in autistic patients. *Internat. J. Psycho-Anal.,* 61:395–402.

Kohut, H. (1971), *The Analysis of the Self.* New York: International Universities Press.

—— (1977), *The Restoration of the Self*. New York: International Universities Press.

—— (1984), *How Does Analysis Cure?* Chicago: University of Chicago Press.

Kris, E. (1950), On preconscious mental processes. *Psychoanal. Quart.,* 19:540–560.

—— (1956), The recovery of childhood memories in psychoanalysis. *The Psychoanalytic Study of the Child*, 11:54–88. New York: International Universities Press.

Kuhn, T. (1962), *The Structure of Scientific Revolutions*, 2nd ed. Chicago: University of Chicago Press, 1970.

Lacan, J. (1977), *Écrits: A Selection,* trans. A. Sheridan. New York: W. W. Norton.

Lichtenberg, J. (1989), *Psychoanalysis and Motivation*. London: Analytic Press.

Loewald, H. (1960), On the therapeutic action of psychoanalysis. *Internat. J. Psycho-Anal.,* 41:16–33.

Mahler, M. (1975), On the current status of the infantile neurosis. *J. Amer. Psychoanal. Assn.,* 23:327–333.

Mason, A. (1981), The suffocating super-ego: Psychotic break and claustrophobia. In: *Do I Dare Disturb the Universe?,* ed. J. Grotstein. Beverly Hills, CA: Caesura Press, pp. 139–166.

Meers, D. (1966), A diagnostic profile of psychopathology in a latency child. *The Psychoanalytic Study of the Child,* 21:483–526. New York: International Universities Press.

Meissner, W. W. (1978), Theoretical assumptions of concepts of the borderline personality. *J. Amer. Psychoanal. Assn.,* 26:559–598.

Meltzer, D., Bremner, J., Hoxter, S., Weddell, D., & Wittenberg, I. (1975), *Explorations in Autism*. Perthshire: Clunie Press.

Modell, A. (1976), "The holding environment" and the therapeutic action of psychoanalysis. *J. Amer. Psychoanal. Assn.,* 24:285–308.

Nagera, H. (1963), The developmental profile: Practical considerations concerning its use. *The Psychoanalytic Study of the Child,* 18:511–540. New York: International Universities Press.

—— (1966), *Early Childhood Disturbances, the Infantile Neurosis and the Adulthood Disturbances*. New York: International Universities Press.

Ogden, T. (1989), On the concept of the autistic contiguous position. *Internat. J. Psycho-Anal.,* 70:127–140.

Opatow, B. (1989), Drive theory and the metapsychology of experience. *Internat. J. Psycho-Anal.,* 70:627–644.

Ornstein, A. (1974), The dread to repeat and the new beginning: A contribution to the psychoanalysis of narcissistic personality disorders. *Annual of Psychoanalysis,* 2:231–248. New York: International Universities Press.

––––––– (1983), An idealizing transference of the oedipal phase. In: *Reflections on Self Psychology,* ed. J. D. Lichtenberg & S. Kaplan. Hillsdale, NJ: Analytic Press, pp. 135–148.

––––––– (1986), The holocaust: Reconstruction and the establishment of psychic continuity. In: *The Reconstruction of Trauma,* ed. A. Rothstein. Madison, CT: International Universities Press, pp. 171–194.

Ornstein, P. (1974), On narcissism: Beyond the introduction. Highlights of Heinz Kohut's contributions to the psychoanalytic treatment of narcissistic personality disorders. *Annual of Psychoanalysis,* 2:127–149. New York: International Universities Press.

––––––– (1983), Discussino of papers by Drs. Goldberg, Stolorow and Wallerstein. In: *Reflections in Self Psychology,* ed. J. Lichtenberg & S. Kaplan. Hillsdale, NJ: Analytic Press, pp. 339–384.

Rangell, L. (1986), The executive functions of the ego. *The Psychoanalytic Study of the Child,* 41:1–37. New Haven, CT: Yale University Press.

Rapaport, D. (1953), On the psycho-analytic theory of affect. *Internat. J. Psycho-Anal.,* 34:177–198.

Richards, A., & Willick, M. (1986), *Psychoanalysis: The Science of Mental Conflict.* Hillsdale, NJ: Analytic Press.

Ritvo, S. (1981), Anxiety, symptom formation and ego autonomy. *The Psychoanalytic Study of the Child,* 36:339–364.

Roth, S. (1988), A woman's homosexual transference with a male analyst. *Psychoanal. Quart.,* 55:28–55.

Sandler, J. (1974), Psychological conflict and the structural model: Some clinical and theoretical implications. *Internat. J. Psycho-Anal.,* 59:413–425.

––––––– (1976), Actualization and object relationships. *J. Phila. Assn. Psychoanal.,* 3:59–70.

––––––– (1983), Reflections on some relations between psychoanalytic concepts and psychoanalytic practice. *Internat. J. Psycho-Anal.,* 64:35–46.

Segal, H. (1964), *Introduction to the Work of Melanie Klein*. New York: Basic Books

Settlage, C. F., Curtis, Z., Lozoff, M., Silberschatz, G., & Simburg, E. (1988), Conceptualizing adult development. *J. Amer. Psychoanal. Assn.,* 36:347–369.

Sorce, J., Emde, R., & Klinnert, M. (1981), Maternal emotional signaling: Its effect on the visual-cliff behavior of one-year-olds. Presented at The Society for Research in Child Development Meeting, Boston, Massachusetts.

Spitz, R. A. (1945), Hospitalism: An inquiry into the genesis of psychiatric conditions in early childhood. *The Psychoanalytic Study of the Child,* 1:53–72. New York: International Universities Press.

———— (1946a), Anaclitic depression: An inquiry into the genesis of psychiatric conditions in early childhood. *The Psychoanalytic Study of the Child,* 2:313–342. New York: International Universities Press.

———— (1946b), Hospitalism: A follow-up report. *The Psychoanalytic Study of the Child,* 2:113–117. New York: International Universities Press.

———— (1957), *No and Yes: On the Genesis of Human Communication.* New York: International Universities Press.

Stein, M. (1979), Review of *The Restoration of the Self,* by H. Kohut. *J. Amer. Psychoanal. Assn.,* 27:665–680.

Steiner, J. (1987), The interplay between pathological organizations and the paranoid schizoid and depressive positions. *Internat. J. Psycho-Anal.,* 68:69–80.

Stolorow, R., Brandchaft, B., & Atwood, G. (1987), *Psychoanalytic Treatment an Intersubjective Approach.* Hillsdale, NJ: Analytic Press.

Strachey, J. (1934), The nature of the therapeutic action of psychoanalysis. *Internat. J. Psycho-Anal.,* 15:127–159.

Sullivan, H. A. (1956), *The Collected Works of Harry Stack Sullivan,* Vol. 2. New York: W. W. Norton.

Tolpin, M. (1971), On the beginnings of a cohesive self: An application of the concept of transmuting internalization to the study of the transitional object and signal anxiety. *The Psychoanalytic Study of the Child,* 26:316–352. Chicago: Quadrangle.

Tustin, F. (1972), *Autism and Childhood Psychosis.* Science House.

———— (1986), *Autistic Barriers in Neurotic Patients.* London: Karnac Books.

Tyson, P., & Tyson, R. L. (1984), Narcissism and superego development. *J. Amer. Psychoanal. Assn.,* 32:75–98.
——— ——— (1990), *Psychoanalytic Theories of Development: An
Integration.* New Haven, CT: Yale University Press.
Tyson, R. L. (1986), The roots of psychopathology and our theories
of development. *J. Amer. Acad. Child Psychiat.,* 25:12–22.
Vaquer, F. (1987), Bion's concept of the psychotic aspect of personality. *J. M. Klein Soc.,* 52:86–100.
——— (1989), A note on envy. *Melanie Klein and Object Relations,*
7:4–10.
Waelder, R. (1936), The principle of multiple function. *Psychoanal.
Quart.,* 5:45–62.
Wallerstein, R. (1983), Self psychology and "classical" psy-
choanalytic psychology—The nature of their relationship: A
review and overview. In: *Reflections on Self Psychology,* ed. J. D.
Lichtenberg & S. Kaplan. Hillsdale, NJ: Analytic Press, pp.
313–337.
Weiss, J., & Sampson, H. (1986), *The Psychoanalytic Process.* New York:
Guilford Press.
Willick, M. S. (1990), Psychoanalytic concepts of the etiology of
severe mental illness. *J. Amer. Psychoanal. Assn.,* 38:1049–1081.
Winnicott, D. W. (1956), Primary maternal pre-occupation. In:
Collected Papers. London: Tavistock, 1958, pp. 300–305.
——— (1963), *The Maturational Processes and the Facilitating Environ-
ment.* New York: International Universities Press.

Name Index

Abend, S., 25
Adler, G., 83
Arlow, J., ix, 5-7, 11-13, 26, 99,
    100, 107-108, 116, 128,
    135-138, 140, 155, 156, 158,
    160-164

Balint, M., 8
Bene, A., 9, 11
Bermner, J., 123
Bion, W., 115, 116, 117, 120-123,
    129-131, 213
Blos, P., 165n
Blum, H., 6
Boesky, D., ix, 8-9, 24-25, 99-101,
    102-103, 108-109, 117, 129,
    136-138, 140, 150, 155, 158,
    160, 162-164, 169, 172-189
Brenner, C., ix-x, 6-7, 16, 18-19,
    26, 33, 45, 137, 173,
    189-191, 199-205, 212
Breuer, J., ix, 7
Brody, S., 40
Bronstein, M. H., x, 173, 191-192,
    204-205, 212-213

Call, J. D., 34
Curtis, Z., 39

Emde, R., 45
Esman, A., 6
Etchegoyen, R., 123

Fenichel, O., 6
Fraiberg, S., 34
Freidman, A., 173
Freud, A., 8, 35-36, 41, 47-48,
    181-182, 186, 198
Freud, S., ix, 3-4, 7, 17, 26,
    100-102, 106, 119-120, 126,
    134, 168-169, 187, 192
Freud, W. E., 41

Grinberg, L., 120n
Grotstein, J., 115, 117, 119-120,
    123

Hartmann, H., 32, 43, 170, 182,
    187-188, 211-212
Hochschild, A., 50
Hoxter, S., 123

Subject Index